Revoluti
Tunbridg(

The remarkable role of Tunbridge Wells
in the development of revolutionary politics in Britain
1884 - 1920

Dedicated to the socialists of the Southern Counties:
Past, Present and Future.

Julian Wilson

Royal Tunbridge Wells Civic Society
Local History Group Monograph No.14
November 2018

**Published in Great Britain in November 2018 by the
Local History Group of the Royal Tunbridge Wells Civic Society,
in association with the Tunbridge Wells Labour Party.**

ISBN 978-1-9997462-1-6
The text is set in Bookman Old Style 10 pt.
and the covers in Bookman Old Style 11 – 28 pt.

The Royal Tunbridge Wells Civic Society is a non-party-political
organisation representing the interests of all those who live and work in
Tunbridge Wells. It has published some 19 books on the local history of
Tunbridge Wells. This latest book reveals aspects of local history previously
unknown or unappreciated. Its publication coincides with the Centenary of
the foundation in November 1918 of the Labour Party in Tunbridge Wells
and many other constituencies.

A full list of the Society's publications will be found at the end of this book.

Printed and bound by DPI Print & Production Ltd, Tonbridge TN9 1BH
Barcode generated with TEC-IT Barcode Software

CONTENTS

Tunbridge Wells 1909 North Ward

Tunbridge Wells 1909 East Ward

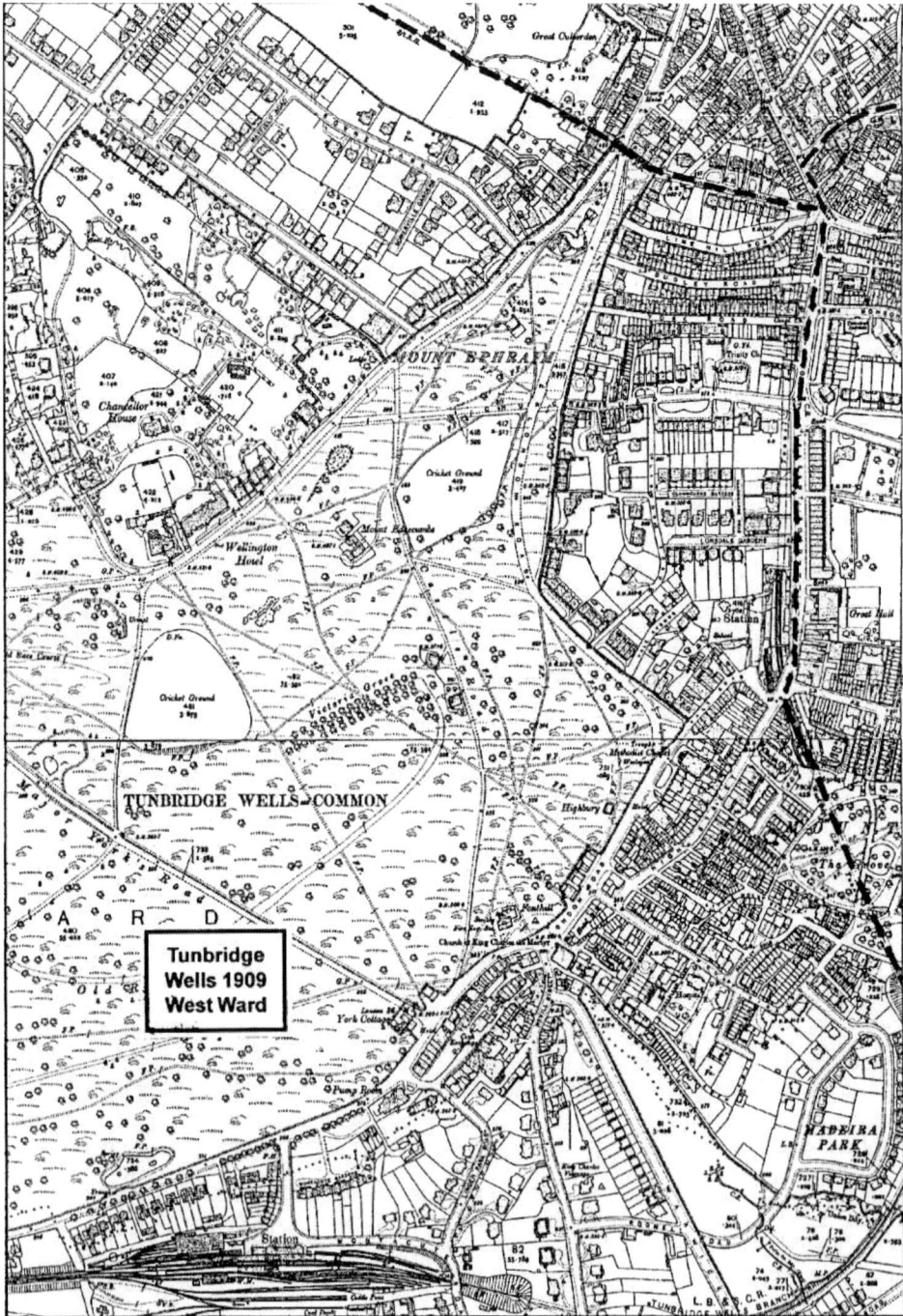

Tunbridge Wells 1909 West Ward

Tunbridge Wells 1909 South Ward

Abbreviations

BSP	British Socialist Party
CPGB	Communist Party of Great Britain
ILP	Independent Labour Party
LRC	Labour Representation Committee
NDL	National Democratic League
NCCL	National Council for Civil Liberties
NSS	National Secular Society
NUWSS	National Union of Women's Suffrage Societies
PLP	Parliamentary Labour Party
SECFSS	South Eastern Counties Federation of Socialist Societies
SDF	Social-Democratic Federation
SDP	Social Democratic Party
SPGB	Socialist Party of Great Britain
SLP	Socialist Labour Party
TWT&LC	Tunbridge Wells Trades & Labour Council
TWWWEC	Tunbridge Wells War Workers' Emergency Committee
WCG	Women's Cooperative Guild
WFL	Women's Freedom League
WSPU	Women's Social and Political Union

INTRODUCTION

The Social-Democratic Federation and the town of Tunbridge Wells make surprising bedfellows. The political party, the first and largest of the organisations which revived socialism in Britain during the 1880s, and the earliest to systematically put Marxist ideas before the public, championed the rights of the unemployed, opposed colonialism and war, criticised what it regarded as hypocrisy dressed up as organised religion, and proudly saw itself as part of an international revolutionary movement. It was certainly significantly to the left of most modern European labour or social-democratic parties.

Tunbridge Wells, on the other hand, has a rather different reputation. One of E. M. Forster's characters slated it as a town of very limited horizons which was hopelessly behind the times. Somewhat later, the historian Richard Cobb's memoirs of his Tunbridge Wells childhood only reinforced the impression of a community refusing to acknowledge that they lived in a changing world. Both men came from middle-class backgrounds. Cobb, by then a noted writer of 'history from below', acknowledged that in his youth he knew little of the working-class districts of the town stretching from the War Memorial to High Brooms. Even though Forster later became a socialist and Cobb specialised in the history of the French Revolution, neither appears to have been aware of any left-wing tradition in the town.

One would expect Nigel Cawthorne's recent and entertaining collection of letters taken from the pages of the *Tunbridge Wells Advertiser, Outraged of Tunbridge Wells* to confirm the stereotype of an ageing colonel angry about minor failures of etiquette. The book though contains a surprising number of letters from socialists, as well as those who clearly feared the labour movement. Both sets of letters might, for different reasons, be best described as having been written by those disgusted *with,* rather than *of,* Tunbridge Wells.[1]

Perhaps against the odds, the Social-Democratic Federation had won itself a place in Tunbridge Wells by the late summer of 1886. Its branch lasted, though under the names Social Democratic Party and British Socialist Party, until at least 1919. The growth of the

---

[1] *See Cobb, R., Still Life (London: Chatto and Windus, 1983); Forster, E.M. A Room with a View (first published 1908).*

trade union movement, and, from 1918, of the Labour Party at Tunbridge Wells and in the Tonbridge Parliamentary Division, of which Tunbridge Wells was the principal town, stemmed largely from its pioneering work. George Dutch, who joined about 1910 and recorded his memories for posterity in the 1960s and 1970s described the first members of the branch as 'magnificent specimens of the independent intellectual craftsman whose unrewarded efforts built up, or at least laid the foundations for the Labour, Trade Union and Cooperative Movement'.[2]

The SDF achieved a level of success in Tunbridge Wells which activists in other places might have hoped to emulate. In 1898 one radical newspaper ranked the local movement as equivalent to those in West Ham, Glasgow, Bradford and Manchester and claimed that it left Birmingham, Sheffield, Leeds and Liverpool in the shade. It had three councillors on Tunbridge Wells Borough Council by 1900, part of a socialist block of seven. In 1903 – before the Labour Party had even been formed - the Conservative *Courier* admitted that municipal elections were being fought 'on socialistic lines'.[3]

There are reasons then for considering that the history of the branch is of more than merely local interest.

In particular it casts light on two questions about both the SDF and the wider labour movement which have been a matter of debate amongst historians and lead to controversy in the modern movement to this day.

The first is the question of racism, and in particular anti-Semitism. There is no excuse for some of the ideas expressed by some within the movement. Henry Mayers Hyndman, the party's long-standing leader, seemed unable to decide between socialist internationalism and a residual nationalism. His default response was to blame 'Jewish influences' for the outbreak of the Boer War. The party's grassroots rejected such attitudes in 1900 by passing a resolution condemning him and forcing him to step down temporarily from his position. I have found no instances of anti-Semitic or other racist views among the members in Tunbridge Wells. Indeed, having invited a Jewish party member to address meetings on Tunbridge Wells Common in the aftermath of a series of pogroms in Russia

---

[2] *George Dutch's personal statement (full version) Imperial War Museum (Document 7651).*
[3] *Article from New Age reproduced in the Tunbridge Wells Advertiser 4th November 1898.*

which followed the Revolution of 1905, the branch even collected money to arm the survivors.

The other issue relates to the role of women within the movement. Misogynistic views were not uncommon amongst British socialists (though they were far from universal). The party's in-house philosopher, Ernest Belfort Bax, for example, had some extremely odd ideas about whether women should engage in public life. These must have severely limited the party's appeal to the female half of the population. Yet once again the Tunbridge Wells branch seems to have been more enlightened. In an era in which many believed that men and women should occupy separate spheres, a woman ran the Marxist economic classes while some of the men looked after the children in the Socialist Sunday School. Although full equality was not achieved, women did take leading roles in the branch throughout its existence and a remarkably high proportion of the national party's leading female activists spent time in the branch.

The Social-Democrats of Tunbridge Wells can also be credited with taking decisions that shaped the evolution of the socialist movement nationally. In November 1888 they persuaded the party's Executive to expel Henry Hyde Champion, then one of its most prominent members. Although it is a convoluted tale, the repercussions of this act have been seen as paving the way to the formation of the Independent Labour Party and later establishing the groundwork for the alliance between trade unions and socialists which led to the formation of the Labour Party in the 20th century.

Almost twenty years later the branch successfully defended the idea of working in a cross-party alliance with members of other socialist organisations, emerging in rather better shape than the leading opponent of such alliances, Ramsay MacDonald, later Britain's first Labour Prime Minister.

In 1916 the socialists of Tunbridge Wells made perhaps their most significant intervention of all. Infused with a fervent internationalist and anti-militarist spirit, it proposed a motion to the party's annual conference which triggered the withdrawal of the party's pro-war minority, including Hyndman. The party thereafter unequivocally opposed the continuation of the conflict.

The Tunbridge Wells Social-Democrats embraced one of the great traditions of skilled working-class life in late-Victorian England – that of intellectual self-improvement. Becoming a socialist, then perhaps even more than now, had much in common with religious conversion, though one based on an analytical approach to economics, history and philosophy rather than a belief in the supernatural. Joining the SDF involved far more than signing a piece of paper, paying regular subscriptions, and buying *Justice*, the party's newspaper. Many members became serious students of foreign relations, history and economics. Some learned French and German to read works by leading Marxists, while others studied non-socialist thinkers including Adam Smith and John Stuart Mill, or pursued their personal interests in fields from the sciences to literature.

George Dutch summed this spirit up beautifully in front of a tribunal which refused his claim to be recognised as a conscientious objector. He had been a socialist 'ever since he had been able to think'. This conversion experience, strengthened by the spirit of fellowship in the branch and the wider movement, changed lives forever and, in the case of Dutch and two comrades, William George Veals and Edward Collison, prepared them for three years of incarceration in a mixture of military barracks and civil prisons.

Socialist ideas set the imaginations of many young men and women alight in Tunbridge Wells from the early 1880s and continued to do so for the lifetime of the branch. Radical ideas, such as secularism, common ownership of land, trade unionism and universal suffrage already circulated in the town. Pamphlets such as Marx's *Wage Labour and Capital* and *The Communist Manifesto*, written jointly with Engels, widened the terms of political debate away from ideas such as individual self-reliance – and the class relations which they disguised - which were predominant in mid-Victorian Britain.

Personally I find all this easy to understand, as imbibing such ideas allowed me, as someone born under Margaret Thatcher to understand that growing inequality, vindictive anti-trade-union legislation, the official promotion of reactionary social attitudes and the privatisation and marginalisation of public services were not the result of some natural law, but instead resulted from conscious decisions, or, in a nutshell, that there is *always* an alternative

Did these women and men leave any lasting impression on Tunbridge Wells and beyond? The book will demonstrate that the branch played a very significant part in spreading socialist ideas throughout the counties of Kent and Sussex. This is particularly true in the case of Maidstone, Hastings and Sevenoaks. After 1906 this work was placed on a more systematic footing by the South-Eastern Counties Federation of Socialist Societies, an organisation in which Tunbridge Wells activists played an important part. Thus the development of the Labour Party across the south-east region owed much to the branch's pioneering efforts.

In Tunbridge Wells itself, the town's Cooperative Society, which soon became the district's largest retailer, owed much to the efforts of the Social-Democrats, not least to William Willis-Harris, whose premises the society took over. The SDF also took leading positions on the town's Trades and Labour Council, which represented the interests of trade unionists and fought for working class representation. The roots which these organisations, both of which long outlived the branch, built in the town, in particular the working class districts of the East and North Wards, together with its methods of organisation, set the stage for the Labour Party's later presence in the district

Yet the SDF always remained a minority in Tunbridge Wells. Throughout its history it was only the third largest political organisation in the town, some way behind the Conservatives and Liberals. It had perhaps about 150 members in the late 1880s, falling to a mere handful in the early 1890s and then recovering to claim about fifty members in 1896 and two hundred in 1908.

For half of its lifespan it had no club or meeting house. The Conservatives, in contrast, had two Constitutional Clubs, a Conservative Association, a branch of the Primrose League and a Conservative Working Men's Association, as well as any number of sympathetic aristocrats and retired industrialists willing to allow their estates to be used for fetes and rallies.

Yet hard work made up for limited numbers and resources. The branch sometimes met four or five times a week. Letters about socialism – for or against – appeared in virtually every edition of the town's papers for over three decades.

Although the Social-Democrats of Tunbridge Wells would not have subscribed to the anarchist idea of 'propaganda by deed' – though this did not prevent their enemies accusing them of arson attacks in the 1880s – they used a range of methods of direct action to advance its agenda. In 1917 they even briefly embraced the Russian idea of the Workmen's and Soldiers' Council. One of their youngest members, Alf Killick, was a leading participant in the mutiny at Etaples in 1919, the largest in modern British history.

This book, published to commemorate the centenary of the founding of the Tunbridge Wells Labour Party on 12th November 1918, will hopefully raise awareness of the left-wing traditions found within our community.

A note on Sources

Soon after embarking on this project it became clear that all branch minutes and other formal records have either been lost or destroyed. However careful reading of the socialist press – in particular *Justice*, the *Clarion* and *Labour Leader* – together with West Kent's Liberal and Conservative papers such as *the Tunbridge Wells Advertiser* and *The Kent and Sussex Courier* has filled in many of the gaps.

Martin Crick's excellent *History of the Social-Democratic Federation* remains the standard work on the subject; Karen Hunt's *Equivocal Feminists: The Social-Democratic Federation and the women question 1884-1911* is particularly interesting in view of the significant number of leading female activists associated with the branch.

Edward Royle's work on the National Secular Society and David Howell's *British Workers and the Independent Labour Party* both assist in placing the Tunbridge Wells branch of the SDF in the wider context of late nineteenth century radicalism and labour. Cyril Pearce's work on the anti-war movement in Huddersfield, *Comrades in Conscience: The Story of an English Community's Opposition to the Great War*, also crystallised my thinking about its Tunbridge Wells equivalent.

A number of autobiographical or semi-autobiographical works were among the more unexpected discoveries.

A founding member of the branch, Constance Howell, wrote a novel *cum* memoir *A More Excellent Way*, in 1888. This, in thinly fictionalised form, traces her political progression from a childhood in India, to membership of the NSS as a young adult and ultimately, to the establishment of the SDF's Tunbridge Wells branch (she calls the town 'Heathborough'). In this last section, she brings to life milestones reported rather dryly in the town's newspapers, such as the earliest meetings on the Common and the opening of a Socialist Hall.

The novel has a lot to say about the class system and often does so with a great sense of humour: the ignorance of the 'educated' middle class ladies who are unaware of the differences between secularism, Irish Nationalism and devil worship; the prejudices of a struggling Tunbridge Wells boarding house keeper desperately trying to keep up appearances and whose real reason for despising the working class is that she is little better off than they are; and the contradictory attitudes of a 'Conservative working man', all stand exposed. There are clear similarities to Robert Tressell's classic socialist novel *The Ragged Trousered Philanthropists*.

The other memoirs deal with the later years of the branch's existence.

George Dutch, who died in 1980, wrote detailed memoirs of his time in the Social-Democratic Party, the BSP and the No-Conscription Fellowship, as well as the mixture of brutal punishment and occasional kindness shown to him during his period of incarceration.

Alf Killick, of similar age to Dutch, discussed the influences his family and friends had on his decision to become a socialist, a childhood in which his political views solidified and his decision to join the army, though in a non-combatant role. They all contributed to his impressive acts of insubordination while serving in northern France. The Militant Tendency, a Trotskyist group within the Labour Party, published this memoir in about 1968. A series of memorial lectures about radical history commemorated his later role as a pioneer of the socialist movement in Southend.[4]

A sad 'near-miss' came with David Geer. In October 1949, a month before his ninetieth birthday, the Secretary of the Labour Party's Luton Branch wrote to Morgan Phillips, then the party's General Secretary, to ask them to contact Geer to obtain his story, as he had 'been one of the very earliest of Socialist councillors in Tunbridge Wells' and 'had played a very large part in the formation of the Movement in that area.' Phillips confirmed that Geer would be invited, health permitting, to the fiftieth anniversary of the foundation of the Labour Party. Both men hoped that the Tunbridge

---

[4] *An Alf Killick Educational Trust was set up which ran a series of lectures. The British Library holds a pamphlet called Chartism and other antecedents of the Labour movement in Essex: the sixth Alfred Killick memorial lecture held at the Central Library Southend-on-Sea on 28th November, 1986, by Arthur Stanley Newens ; chairman: Alex Pendle.*

7

Wells branch would meet with him to record his role for posterity, though I can find no record of this having happened. By this time Geer must have been one of the last surviving of those who had been active in the socialist revival of the 1880s, and had already helped the author of a biography of Tom Mann by providing a copy of a letter from 1886. He died a year later.[5]

I would also like to thank:

- The staff of the public libraries at Tunbridge Wells, Tonbridge, Sevenoaks, Maidstone, Hastings and Brighton, as well as the British Library and the collections at Senate House (London), the Universities of Reading and Sussex, the Bishopsgate Institute, the Imperial War Museum, the Working Class Movement Library at Salford and elsewhere, for the assistance I have received.
- Trevor Hopper who very helpfully made his doctoral thesis on the growth of the movement in the South-East, especially Hastings, Brighton and Portsmouth, available to me. I would also like to thank Dan Huckfield, Peter Ryley and David Killingray, all of whom have focussed my thinking and shared their own research with me.
- Pat Wilson, without whom this book might never have been published. He showed my manuscript to John Cunningham, the Chairman of the Local History Group of the Royal Tunbridge Wells Civic Society, who thought that it revealed aspects of Tunbridge Wells local history (as well as national history) previously unknown or unappreciated and which deserved wider recognition; and so offered to publish it as part of the Society's library of local history.
- As a result, Chris Jones, Mary Arigho, John Cunningham and Pat Wilson have all helped to turn my prose into something rather more reader-friendly.
- My family, friends and colleagues who must by now be fed up with hearing about the socialist movement of a century or more ago.

Any errors or omissions are, of course, my own.

---

[5] *Labour Party Archives GS/JUB/84 & GS/JUB/85.*

*Victorian Tunbridge Wells as it may have wished to see itself.
The event and date are not recorded, but the photograph clearly shows an
important civic event outside the South-Eastern (latterly Central) Station,
attended by men and women of all backgrounds.*

COPY of VERSES

ON THE

Threatened Lock-out

OF THE

KENT AND SUSSEX LABORERS.

Tune :—We don't want to Fight.

The farmers of Old England,
  Are at their tricks again,
To cut the labourers wages down
  They're trying might and main ;
Down in Kent and Sussex too,
  A lock out they'll engage,
Fifteen thousand men they want,
  To rob them of their wage.

They don't want to strike,
  But by jingo if they do,
The Kent and Sussex labourers
  Will make the farmers rue ;
Tho' fat and full of pride,
  And rich as jews beside, [England.
They shall not starve the labourers of Old

I need not tell you all,
  Labourers wages are but small,
For a drop of eighteen pence a week,
  The masters now do call.
The farmer drinks his wine,
  Their wives and daughters shine,
The men that earns the wealth for them,
  In poverty must pine.

A man must have a tidy cheek,
  To want his men to work,
For eight or nine shillings a week,
  Slaving like a Turk ;
That is all there's left you know,
  When rent and schooling's paid,
That is how the working men,
  By farmers are betrayed.

Farming men are worse paid
  Than any I am sure,
They have no chance to rise in life,
  Because they're kept so poor.
Some call this merry England,
  And so it is for them,
Who live upon the flesh and blood,
  Of honest labouring men.

If the weather should be wet
  They cannot work at all,
Their wages then on Saturdays,
  Are brought down very small.
Down in Kent and Sussex too,
  Deny it if you can,
The farmers pigs are better fed,
  Than many a labouring man.

Thousands in this country,
  Scarcely would believe,
The cruel starving wages
  That poor men do receive.
They work themselves to skin and bone,
  While they are alive,
To the Union, and a pauper's grave,
  The worn out man they drive.

Gentlemen to take the air,
  From London often go,
They say the country's beautiful,
  And so it is we know ;
But if they had to plough and sow,
  And keep a family too,
They'd say why this is slavery,
  And I'm sure that would be true.

A broadsheet, dating from the lock-out of members of the Kent and Sussex Labourers Union in 1878, which was probably printed at Maidstone. This adapted a rather jingoistic popular song of the same year and these attitudes are reflected in the unfortunate references to 'Slaving like a Turk' and 'rich as Jews beside'.
The Union had a branch at Tunbridge Wells throughout its existence.

CHAPTER 1   SPARKS IN THE WIND

The activists who set up the Tunbridge Wells branch of the Social-Democratic Federation did not enter the world with their political ideas already formed. Their attitudes and values were coloured by their experiences of living and working in the town, through the church or chapel, in the schoolroom, discussions with friends or in political associations or trade unions.

Older relatives and colleagues also influenced their outlook. Alf Killick later recalled his grandmother 'who used to regale me with stories of the privations endured by the workers in the "hungry forties". She was a child at the time, attending the old village school. Many were the times when she had to go to school without breakfast.' Killick's apprenticeship to a socialist shoemaker in the town confirmed his political leanings. Killick joined the socialist movement toward the end of the period. Earlier members may well have heard stories from the first decades of the nineteenth century.[6]

It is worth looking briefly at Tunbridge Wells and the political traditions within it to see whether these can help explain how socialism took root there so strongly.

It is tempting to push the timeline back as far as possible. Some of the key events which shaped English history took place in Kent and Sussex, from the Roman invasions to the Battle of Britain. Left-wingers have drawn inspiration from the fact that many of the events of the Peasant's Revolt of 1381 and Jack Cade's rebellion of 1450 took place in the two counties. Many socialists of the 1880s, such as Hyndman and William Morris, considered these uprisings to have been led by proto-socialists. Their interpretations of these events, such as Morris' *Dream of John Ball*, tied in with the mid-Victorian interest in all things medieval, something equally seen in the architecture and furniture of the period. One of the region's leading activists cited the work of Ball, Cade and Wat Tyler in his address to the 'Reds of the South-East' as late as 1907.[7]

---

[6] *Killick, A., Mutiny! An account of the Calais Soldiers' mutiny in 1918 written by a leading participant (London: Militant Pamphlets c1978) p3.*
[7] *Coxall, B. nd Griggs, C, George Meek, Labouring Man; Protégé of H.G. Wells (London: New Millennium 1996) p128. See Salmon, N, A Reassessment of A Dream of John Ball (William Morris Society Spring 2001)*
http://www.morrissociety.org/JWMS/14.2Spring2001/SP01.14.2.SalmonBall.pdf.

But these events pre-date Tunbridge Wells by centuries. Even at the start of the Seventeenth Century it did not exist in any meaningful sense. The founding of the modern town, conventionally dated to the chance discovery of a chalybeate spring in 1606, should be considered the real starting point for this survey. It is of significance that the political and religious divisions of the Seventeenth Century are still so strongly embedded in the geography of the town. Margaret Barton's early history, and local tradition, suggest that some Presbyterians and Anabaptists left the nearby villages of Rusthall and Speldhurst to settle there, perhaps under the protection of soldiers loyal to Cromwell. These families gave the biblical names of Mount Ephraim and Mount Sion to the areas to which they moved. Those loyal to the monarchy dedicated the Chapel of Ease to Charles I in 1676, sixteen years after its restoration.[8]

The Restoration marked the start of the great period of prosperity for Tunbridge Wells as a spa. The geographical setting was one of the main attractions, something which remained true for several centuries. It had little grand architecture. At its heart lay Tunbridge Wells and Rusthall Common, a sandy heath with grazing livestock, picturesque clumps of rocks, pine trees, ferns and ponds. The oldest part of the town, around the Pantiles and Chapel Place, stood at the southern edge with groups of lodging houses and shops on Mount Ephraim (to the North) and Mount Sion (to the East) retaining their separate village-like identities. The first turnpike to be built in Kent connected the town to Sevenoaks by way of Pembury and Tonbridge in 1709. Others to Maidstone, Tenterden, Lewes and Rye soon followed. The permanent population grew slowly, reaching about 1,200 in 1800, still smaller than Tonbridge or Sevenoaks, let alone Maidstone or Hastings.[9]

---

[8] Barton, M., Tunbridge Wells (London: Faber and Faber 1937) pp105-106.
[9] For the improvement to transport see Lawson, T., and Killingray,. D., (eds) An Historical Atlas of Kent (Chichester; Phillimore & Co. 2004) pp 59 -60.

From about 1800 the town changed, with the focus moving away from visitors to more permanent residents. There were other changes too. After 1789 the French Revolutionary and Napoleonic Wars dominated many aspects of life in Britain. Politics polarised: some saw in the French Revolution a vision for a better future, while to others the threat of invasion triggered a nationalistic and reactionary response. Tunbridge Wells, at least at first, turned on those who sympathised with the revolution. Local landowners had little difficulty raising a militia to repel the possibility of a French invasion. In 1792 a cart carried an effigy of Tom Paine (author of 'The Rights of Man', and a supporter of both American and French revolutions) through the town to the Common where it was first whipped and then burned.[10]

Four years later John Gale Jones, a London radical, travelled from London to Rochester, Chatham, Gravesend and Maidstone to establish a network of corresponding societies and perhaps attempt to establish a British republic on the lines of France. It is unlikely that he ever considered making the trip south to Tunbridge Wells, which had neither the population nor the military significance of the Medway Towns or Maidstone, and it is hard to know what sort of reception would have greeted him had he done so. Yet he would have found some friends in the district.

Research by Roger Wells has shown that a corresponding society was formed in the town in 1797 and that it survived until 1801. Samuel Waddington, who lived at Southborough, then a small village two miles from Tunbridge Wells on the Tonbridge road, became the most high-profile agitator. Many contemporaries regarded his jailing in 1800 under an Act of Parliament which had long fallen into disuse to be an act of revenge by the state. A celebratory dinner in Tunbridge Wells followed his release, after which teams of men hauled his carriage in triumph from there to Maidstone, the county town.[11]

Peace finally came in 1815. For a few years, Tunbridge Wells, like the rest of Kent and Sussex, seemed more placid than other parts of the country. Displaced workers in the Midlands and Lancashire

---

[10] See O'Gorman, F., 'The Paine Burnings of 1792-3' in Past and Present 2006, Vol. 193, pp111-155.
[11] Wells, R., 'English society and revolutionary politics in the 1790s: the case for insurrection' in Philp, M. The French Revolution and British Popular Politics (Cambridge University Press 1991) p240; Hay, D., 'The State and the market in 1800: Lord Kenyon and Mr Waddington' in Past & Present 1994 pp114-147.

vented their anger on the machinery which had destroyed their jobs, while in Manchester the authorities violently dispersed a peaceful reform protest at St Peter's Fields with the loss of at least eleven lives and hundreds of injuries. The most radical action in Tunbridge Wells seems to have been in November 1820 when Richard Delves, a prosperous local farmer and leading townsman, supplied meat and drink for a public gathering on the Common to celebrate the failure of Parliament to convict Queen Caroline of adultery. The action reflected a mood of deep hostility towards the monarchy but seems tame by comparison.[12]

Yet, like many of the cities which had seen flashes of rebellion, the town experienced extremely rapid population growth. Tunbridge Wells grew more than six-fold in just four decades, reaching 8,000 in 1841. A lot of people turned to charities for coal for fuel. Hundreds of people settled in closely-packed districts such as Crown Fields (now the Royal Victoria Place shopping mall), Windmill Fields (near St Peters Church) the Lew (opposite Skinners School) and Hervey's Town or Harveytown (now the area occupied by the Crescent Road car-park), while at the other end of the income scale the Calverley Estate – virtually a self-contained new town – provided an elegant crescent of houses, several large villas and a market, inn and shops.[13]

Socialism can be said to have arrived in Tunbridge Wells in 1829, when supporters of the British Association for Promoting Cooperative Knowledge, a national organisation based in London's Hatton Garden, formed a local branch. They opened a shop in Harveytown and wrote their own pamphlets and leaflets, as well as distributing those of the national society and the *Co-Operator*, a journal produced by Brighton's Dr. William King.

Although they drew inspiration from pioneering socialists such as Robert Owen, they recruited primarily from the working class, who were to be the agents of their own destiny, rather than rely on the goodwill of philanthropists or enlightened industrialists. The organisation's pamphlets and leaflets described how growing poverty for the majority seemed to coincide with a handful becoming extremely wealthy. It publicised an early version of the labour theory of value, later to be developed by Marx, together with

[12] Chalklin, C, *Tunbridge Wells, A History* (Chichester: Phillimore & Co Ltd 2008) p52.
[13] See the chapter by Lionel Anderson in *400 Years of the Wells: A History of Tunbridge Wells* , Cunningham, J., (ed) (Tunbridge Wells 2005), pp 80-96.

analyses of rent and interest. Redistribution of land, to be worked collectively, and the use of manual labour, rather than machinery, formed the remedy.[14]

The response to the new group foreshadowed the reaction to the SDF half a century later. Its activities offended Reverend Pope, then the most prominent of the town's Anglican clergy, who declared Cooperative principles to be 'infidel' and the elimination of poverty to be contrary to the teachings of the Gospel.

Others wrote hostile letters to a Brighton newspaper, some of which were reproduced and then challenged by Dr. King in his journal. One attacked the 'judicious management of several young and old ladies' involved in the scheme – one of whom was Lady Noel Byron (former wife of the poet) – and its support for encouraging 'independence, freethinking and all the admirable schemes of Cobbett, Owen, Thompson, Flaron and the various enlightened reformers of the day'. The business also sold mottled soap and bad tea. A second writer made serious allegations that the shop's scales defrauded customers. The premises 'resembled a chandler's shop of the worst description'.[15]

The letters contain some interesting details. The society had fifty to one hundred members. The second correspondent was particularly offended by books 'of that description' being sold at a shop which pretended 'to be for the good of the poor'. The 'respectable' part of the community should protest against it. Very similar letters were penned in opposition to the Social-Democrats in the 1880s, while the belittling of the efforts of female activists and the hostility of the Church also resurfaced in near-identical terms.

---

[14] See the Maidstone Journal and Kentish Advertiser, December 1 1829.
[15] Mercer, T. W., Cooperation's Prophet and the Cooperator (Manchester: Cooperative Union 1947) pp11-12, p35.

A contemporary cartoon from Punch showing how poverty tempted rural labourers to commit arson

The period of apparent tranquillity ended a year later. The Swing Riots broke out in the summer of 1830, with arson attacks around Sevenoaks and machine-breaking in the east of the county. These tactics converged and the riots spread rapidly into Sussex and then across much of the country, reaching as far north as Cumbria. Over the next nine months, hundreds of arson attacks took place in West Kent and East Sussex alone.

Letters threatening that their property would be destroyed were sent to farmers, clergy and other figures of wealth or authority. Firearms were occasionally deployed, especially in the Sevenoaks area. The Government stationed troops at Tunbridge Wells to quell the unrest, and this explains why large bands of protestors did not enter the town itself, although they came as close as Groombridge and Tonbridge, both under five miles away. Despite these precautions, there were a few arson attacks in Tunbridge Wells. Fires broke out on two consecutive evenings in Tunbridge Wells in early November and a spate of threatening letters followed. An arsonist also targeted a stack adjacent to the workhouse on Rusthall Common towards the end of the month.[16]

The Swing Riots, together with other serious disturbances across Great Britain and Ireland, most dramatically those at Bristol and Nottingham, shook the confidence of the political elite and again raised the spectre of revolution. Several of the sources suggest that

---

[16] *For the Swing Riots see Griffin, C., The Rural War: Captain Swing and the Politics of Protest (Manchester University Press 2012); Hammond, J.L. and Hammond, B, The Village Labourer 1760-1832 (London: Longmans, Green and Co. 1920); Kent County Council, The Swing Riots in Kent, Extracted from sources at the Centre for Kentish Studies (Kent County Council 2003) p42; Reay, B., The Last Rising of the Agricultural Labourers: rural life and social protest in nineteenth century England (Oxford: Clarendon 1990); Hobsbawm, E.J., and Rudé, F.E., Captain Swing (London: Lawrence & Wishart 1969).*

for a time the Government effectively lost control of the entire district between Maidstone, Brighton and Hythe. Bands of rural labourers forced unpopular Poor Law overseers or clergy to leave their communities. Groves credits these workers with forcing farmers to grant significant wage rises and later seeding rural trade unionism. Carl Griffin's more recent account shows that any gains were short-lived, though he credits Swing with precipitating the formation of rural political associations in Sussex and Kent, some of which collectively demanded higher pay.[17]

The Tories had already begun to reform the British state by allowing Dissenters and Catholics to vote. Parliamentary reform, championed by the new Whig Government, followed in 1832. This doubled the number of County Members of Parliament representing the parts of Kent (such as Tunbridge Wells, Tonbridge and Sevenoaks) which were neither ancient boroughs nor large enough to justify the creation of new urban seats. The Poor Law Amendment Act two years later had an immediate impact on working class families, reducing access to outdoor relief and forcing those who could not support themselves into the workhouse. Spartan conditions and segregation by age and gender soon drew comparison with prisons. The Tunbridge Union established its workhouse at Pembury, just outside Tunbridge Wells.

This spirit of reform encouraged Tunbridge Wells to establish proper self-government for the first time in 1835. Few places were in greater need of change. Here, on top of the fast-growing population, the town had historically been split between two counties and three ancient parishes.

Only owners and occupiers of property worth £50 a year had the right to join the new Improvement Commission, thereby denying the vote to most tradesmen and all artisans. Women similarly had no right to vote. Reform followed in 1860 with the property qualification reduced to £30 a year, though plural voting made this system perhaps even less democratic than its predecessor. As late as December 1882 one observer noted some men had as many as nine votes each while the poor had none. However, on the positive side, significant public works took place during these decades to provide the town with reliable and clean sources of water, light the streets and deal with sources of disease. Compared to neighbouring

---

[17] Groves, R., *Sharpen the Sickle! The History of the Farm Workers' Union* (London: The Porcupine Press 1948) p16; Griffin, *Rural War*, pp308-325.

Tonbridge, which remained under the control of the Parish Vestry until 1870, when it appointed its own Improvement Commission, its record is relatively impressive. Tunbridge Wells experienced one outbreak of cholera, in 1853, while the populations of Tonbridge and Maidstone each suffered from the disease in 1832, 1849, 1851-4 and 1866.[18]

The other major reform from above, strange as it may appear today, concerned religion. The anti-clericalism of the French Revolution and the turbulent politics of many growing towns led those in authority to conclude that a programme of church-building and the reconfiguration of parishes could help provide social stability. In August 1824 a public meeting recognised that many in Tunbridge Wells had 'no place of worship on the Establishment' and some hundreds of the poorer classes never have the opportunity, and in fact never do enter a place of worship. Only the original Chapel of Ease, built for the town as it existed in the Seventeenth Century, together with several Methodist and Baptist chapels, served the community. Holy Trinity followed in 1829 and Christ Church, on the High Street, opened in 1835.

In 1833 the town became a separate parish. By the middle of the century church-building was booming. The 1851 Census, which revealed relatively low levels of church attendance, particularly amongst working class men and women, again focused attention on places where the population had risen. At Tunbridge Wells, as with many other towns in southern England, an influx of moneyed new residents wishing to establish themselves socially led to ample funds being made available. As a result, new places of worship sprouted across the landscape. Some of the indoctrination lacked subtlety – a now rarely-sung verse of a well-known hymn first published in the revolutionary year of 1848 taught generations of Sunday-school children that inequality was divinely ordained:

> 'The rich man in his castle, The poor man at his gate,
> God made them high or lowly, And ordered their estate.'

God, according to this view, undoubtedly voted Tory. Many clerics did all they could to retain social control of the town for decades to come: the Vicar of St Peter's from 1895 to 1912 had his family sit at the back of the church to observe who had attended. Only

[18] See the chapter by Lionel Anderson in 400 Years of the Wells pp 80-96; The Tunbridge Wells Advertiser December 15th 1882; An Historical Atlas of Kent, p161.

tradesmen who worshipped at the Church could provide services to the vicarage and, if they missed a service they had to explain themselves. Such factors later led socialists such as Constance Howell and Tom Jarvis to describe Tunbridge Wells as 'pious, if not to say bigoted', and to condemn the amount spent on 'pseudo-Christianity' while so many local children went hungry.[19]

Although less well documented, the 1830s also accelerated the growth of political movements at the grassroots. This is particularly true with trade unionism. Partial legalisation of trade unions in the mid-1820s gave working class people the right to openly combine to demand increases in pay, shorter hours and better conditions. Legalisation had the side effect of increasing the distinction between friendly societies, which provided insurance against illness or other misfortune and often had members working in many different parts of the local economy, and trade unions, which organised those working in particular industries. By the mid-1830s the building trades in Tunbridge Wells and Maidstone seem to have become strongly unionised and their strikes received coverage in the regional press. Activists in the two towns worked closely with one another.[20]

Individual, as well as collective, methods of protest continued. Arson attacks similar to those of the Swing Riots remained fairly common in the Weald, although explaining the motivation for them can be difficult. Some resulted from wage disputes or political grievances; others may have been the result of children playing with matches or the carelessness of inebriated labourers.

Occasionally they made the national press. The *Champion*, a radical paper, noted that the Tunbridge Wells area had long been inhabited by a lot of 'idle and depraved characters' who had committed large numbers of rural crimes. On 19th October 1836 a well-known poacher and a livery servant were indicted on the capital charge of burning down a barn at Frant. The *Morning Post* in December that year reported the destruction of a barn and lodge at a farm near Langton Green, just to the west of Tunbridge Wells. Three other arson attacks had taken place in the neighbourhood very lately. Such fires often proved spectacular. Witnesses in Tunbridge Wells thought that they could see the northern lights on the evening of

---

[19] *Chalklin, Royal Tunbridge Wells p54; Howell, C, A More Excellent Way (London: 1888) p173.*
[20] *Maidstone Journal and Kentish Advertiser 10 March 1834; See Postgate, R., The Builders' History (London: Garland 1984) p57.*

11th January 1841; the next day they discovered that a barn and adjacent buildings belonging to a Mr Baden Powell at Ashurst, several miles away, had been set alight. A spate of arson attacks the year before in Rusthall and Speldhurst had also targeted the property of Baden Powell, as well as being responsible for destroying two barns near the same workhouse which had been targeted in 1830.[21]

Disappointment amongst working class working men and women that the reforms of the 1830s had done little for them, and certainly had not given them the vote, lay behind the growth of Chartism. Those who have looked closely at it have noted its relative weakness in southern England, though it certainly gained some support in Tunbridge Wells, Tonbridge and surrounding villages in the late 1830s and 1840s. Collections for national campaigns are recorded in 1839. It had more of a base in the Medway Towns and, of course, in the big cities such as London and Manchester.

Some sources suggest that it might have won a bit more support in West Kent than is generally recognised. Robert Gammage, a Chartist speaker, wrote about a visit to Tunbridge Wells in 1842. Here he met Mr Lawner, a basket-maker, and Mr Curtis, a coach-trimmer. They attended a meeting together and it is significant that Gammage described Curtis as more of a Socialist than a Chartist. A few years later, supporters of Feargus O'Connor's Land Company, which aimed to set up rural communes, established a branch in Tunbridge Wells in the 1840s. In 1848, a year of revival for the Chartist movement, Tunbridge Wells' radicals held a dinner to celebrate the revolution in France that year. Chartism's hold on radical working people faded slowly: George Dutch even wrote that the SDF's branch in Tunbridge Wells had been founded in the 'late Chartist 80s', though the movement had vanished some decades before then.[22]

---

[21] *The Morning Post December 2nd 1836; The Champion November 13th 1836; The Brighton Gazette 19th March 1840, 14th January 1841.*
[22] *The Charter May 5th 1839 and June 30th 1839; Lansberry H.C.F. (ed), Government and Politics in Kent (Woodbridge: the Boydell Press 2001) pp128-138; Killingray. D, 'Grassroots Politics in West Kent since the Late Eighteenth Century' Archaeologia Cantiana - Vol. 129 2009 pp33-54; Chalklin, C, Tunbridge Wells, pp71-72; see also Gamage, R., 'Recollections of a Chartist', in the Newcastle Weekly Chronicle, August 16 1884, published online at http://www.visionofbritain.org.uk/travellers/Gammage/12; George Dutch's personal statement (full version) at the Imperial War Museum (Documents 7651).*

The 1840s marked a significant stage in the development of Tunbridge Wells and one which has a direct bearing on the evolution of the socialist movement in later years. In 1845 the town's first railway station opened at the end of what is now Goods Station Road, so connecting the town to Tonbridge, London and the national railway network. The line extended to the current Central Station a year later, but the freight facilities remained at the site of the original terminus.

This in turn meant that industries established themselves in the area and the town accordingly grew northwards. Some new districts suffered from extreme overcrowding and as late as 1909 nearly one thousand people lived cheek-by-jowl with slaughterhouses and workshops in the small area between Calverley, Camden, Victoria and Goods Station roads. The area which developed along and between Camden and Goods Station roads a few years later had a better reputation, although some poor quality and crowded tenements built around courtyards existed here. These streets played host to some of the larger industrial concerns, such as the Baltic Sawmills and, much later, the Municipal Electricity Works.

Part of the Post Office staff at Tunbridge Wells in 1903

Society continued to become more mobile. The Post Office became a major employer in the town. Short distance travel remained by road and horse-drawn coach and wagon builders thrived. 1,267 men, women, boys and girls worked in the town's transport industries by 1911. The two railway companies, the South Eastern and Chatham and the London, Brighton and South Coast, then had 246 employees in the town. Perhaps surprisingly, the Borough's Medical Officer reported that the town had over forty factories and three hundred workshops in 1914.[23]

---

[23] *Many of these figures are taken from Cunningham J. (Ed), 400 Years of the Wells and Cunningham, J., (Ed) The Shock of War: Tunbridge Wells: Life on the Home Front 1914-1919 (Tunbridge Wells 2014) p73.*

It seems likely that the growth of these new districts played a very important part in giving their inhabitants a distinctive working-class identity. Photographs show a landscape of factory chimneys rising above terraced streets, workshops and railway sidings, something very different to the more familiar images of the town's Commons and Pantiles. The pubs in this part of Tunbridge Wells often carried the names of the occupations of their customers, such as the Bricklayers Arms, Victoria Street, or reflected the friendly societies to which they belonged, such as the Foresters, Camden Road, or the Oddfellows Arms, Tunnel Road. Methodist and Baptist chapels, rather than Anglican churches, quickly sprang up in these streets.

It should be no surprise that the meeting which marked the revival of Cooperative ideas in the town, though now organised on the business-like lines of the Rochdale Pioneers, took place in the Joiner's Arms on Old (now Goods) Station Road in April 1857. By 1859 it was meeting in the Basinghall Schoolrooms, a more suitable venue given the strength of teetotalism. The Society decided to dissolve on Friday September 28th 1860, instead becoming a branch of the National Industrial and Provident Society. Crafts, such as tailoring and blacksmithing, unionised, and these had a far from parochial outlook. In 1862 the town's shoemakers collected a pound to support a strike of London stonemasons. The Tunbridge Wells Section of the Amalgamated Cordwainers – presumably the same union – made a donation to help defray the costs of the International Working Men's Conference in Geneva in 1866.[24]

The growth of working class organisations of all types, and the desire for premises free of both alcohol and religion, drove the demand for the construction of a series of institutes, some of them partly funded by landowners or industrialists. The most architecturally impressive example, the Friendly Societies Hall of 1878 in Camden Road, in later years became the postal address for most of the town's trade unions, the Trades and Labour Council headquarters and a popular venue for socialist meetings, though the choice of name suggests that friendly societies still had considerably more support than trade unions at the time of construction. Others which will play a role in this story include the

---

[24] *Tunbridge Wells Gazette, Tonbridge Chronicle and Kent and Sussex Advertiser April 24th 1857 and May 1st 1857, National Archives FS/8/8/239b, Reynolds Newspaper March 16th 1862, See the International Workingmen's Association Minute Book 1864-66.*

Dudley Institute. Many of these establishments contained a hall for public lecturers, a reading room or library and perhaps a games room.

The 1860s saw greater attention being paid to the political and economic status of the female half of the population. Class determined much. Before 1882 all the property of a married couple was legally owned by the husband. Working- and middle-class women alike faced the loss of their children on the breakdown of a relationship. Those from the wealthiest backgrounds found themselves barred from many professions and university courses. Most people turned a blind eye to domestic violence unless it took place in public. Three Tunbridge Wells women, Matilda Briggs and her two daughters Elizabeth and Caroline, signed the country's first petition to demand the right to vote in 1866. Matilda may even have been influenced by socialist ideas as Robert Owen had been a family friend in her youth. Sporadic campaigns for women's suffrage continued for the rest of the century, though the *Courier* concluded in 1873 that prospects for it in the town were not good.[25]

Tunbridge Wells throughout this period remained a town very much tied to the surrounding countryside. Connections strengthened in the mid-1860s with the construction of the network of railway lines which ran through rural districts from Tunbridge Wells West to East Grinstead, Brighton and, fifteen years later, Eastbourne. Considerable numbers of agricultural labourers lived in the town. The number of those whose earnings primarily came from working the land rose from 140 in 1841 to 517 at the time of the 1911 census, though many others would join them at harvest time. One historian has concluded that what became known as the Revolt of the Field, or the rise of rural trade unionism, was most successful in Kent.

In 1872 a group of agricultural labourers met at Shoreham, near Sevenoaks, to form a union. This became the Kent Agricultural Labourers' Union and built branches across the county. By the end of the year it had eighty branches and five thousand members. It had a branch in Tunbridge Wells although it was not one of the more active ones.[26] The union soon expanded into Sussex and so became the Kent and Sussex Agricultural Labourers Union. By

---

[25] *Killingray. D, Grassroots Politics p41; Carwardine, A., Disgusted Ladies: the women of Tunbridge Wells who fought for the right to vote (Leicester: Matador 2018) pp17-44.*
[26] *Figures for agricultural labourers from Chalklin, Royal Tunbridge Wells p65; Cunningham, J., The Shock of War p16.*

1877 it had 251 branches and 13,000 members. It also sought to organise workers in brickworks and other industries, though it is not clear whether this happened at Tunbridge Wells. The union raised the wages of agricultural workers significantly, but in 1878 failed to prevent farmers from locking out union members after the harvest had been gathered in. However it still had over 10,000 members in the mid-1880s and 8,500 in 1888.

Although tactical mistakes and the agricultural depression which took hold after 1873 clearly weakened its bargaining power, the union almost certainly paved the way for the eventual emergence of socialism in rural Kent and would have given those forced to leave the land for towns an understanding of industrial organisation. Nearby towns, villages and even hamlets with active branches included Tonbridge, Wadhurst, Frant, Hadlow, Eridge, Capel, Hildenborough, Golden Green and Castle Hill. In later years the union became the London and Southern Counties Labour League. Its well-written weekly newspaper, the *Kent and Sussex Times*, provided a platform for radical ideas – even quoting Hyndman extensively in February 1886 – and this circulated widely in most towns and villages, including Tunbridge Wells.[27]

Haymaking at Dunorlan Farm,
the Home Farm for the estate of that name, around 1910

[27] *Smethurst, J.B. and Carter, P., Historical Directory of Trade Unions: Volume 6 (Ashgate Publishing Ltd, 2009); Groves R. Sharpen the Sickle !, pp83-85; Kent and Sussex Times March 27th 1886; Arnold, R., 'The Revolt of the Field in Kent 1872-1879' Past and Present No. 64 (August 1974) pp71-95.*

The prevailing distress in the countryside ensured that the stream of new residents into towns such as Tunbridge Wells continued unabated. The Union turned to urging its members to emigrate to Canada or Australia. At the same time, challenged by growing resistance to their rule, landowners, their bailiffs, larger farmers, and their allies in the Church of England set out to shore up their position.

Reports from the election of November and December 1885, fought on a widened franchise which gave votes to many rural men for the first time, detail an astonishing campaign of intimidation. Conservative employers dismissed those they knew to be Liberal supporters or trade unionists in the weeks before the election. Were a Liberal MP to be elected, a general reduction of wages and the eviction of the poor and elderly in the villages would follow. On polling day agricultural labourers were taken from their cottages to the polling stations in pairs while the pillars of the Tory establishment kept watch outside. Such intimidation drove radical thinkers from the villages, and it is no surprise that several of those who played leading roles in the SDF's branch, such as James and Elizabeth Milstead and the Pay brothers, moved to Tunbridge Wells during these decades. Many of the others, including David Geer and Tom Jarvis, were the children of those who had relocated from the countryside.[28]

Life on the land has always been hard and poorly paid. By the 1880s the sense of desperation was palpable. A lengthy poem by John Ullathorn, a seventy-year old inhabitant of Speldhurst, three miles from Tunbridge Wells, captures this sense of dismay. Writing in 1886, Ullathorn reflected on the changes he had witnessed in his lifetime. Workers had been driven from the land by machinery and forced into living in attics and 'back slums', working in factories and workshops or otherwise sent to 'the grave, to the Union [i.e. the workhouse] or to prison'. Radical conclusions, though not revolutionary, followed, and he urged landowners to voluntarily redistribute the land to prevent unrest as 'all waste places and all the waste lands, are crying aloud for the unemployed hands'. A dash of millenarianism followed - 'so let the industrious classes look up, their day of redemption at hand'. At the same time the author recorded his disappointment that workers would 'strike... or shirk'. The final page of the pamphlet in which the poem was published recorded the bills presented to Parliament in support of the

---

[28] *The Kent and Sussex Times January 2nd 1886.*

provision of smallholdings and the provision of allotments by landowners at Folkestone and New Romney, both in East Kent.[29]

Tunbridge Wells continued to grow quickly, if at a slightly slower rate than previously. Much of the new housing followed the railway lines north and west of the town centre. The population reached 24,309 in 1881 and 29,296 a decade later. Even this fails to capture the full picture as by this stage a number of suburbs, outside the boundaries of the town, took much of the new population. These nestled in a hilly patchwork of woodland, hop gardens, orchards and small farms. Rusthall New Town, on the far edge of the long-established village, remained outside the town for administrative purposes until 1900. Hawkenbury, home to railway workers and brick-makers, developed from a cluster of shacks into a significant area of working- class housing. High Brooms, the newest arrival, had only come into existence over the last few years and consisted of a handful of streets set in scrubland about a mile north of the town centre, adjacent to one of the region's biggest brickworks and the town's gasworks and sewage farm. This district had been somewhat remote before the opening of its railway station in 1893. This was followed by urbanisation which eventually linked it to both Tunbridge Wells and Southborough. Except for a handful of shopkeepers and ministers of religion, the population consisted almost entirely of working-class families, and the settlement had much in common with the industrial villages which sprang up in the Lower Medway Valley between Rochester and Maidstone at about the same time.

High Brooms Brick & Tile Works

---

[29] *Ullathorn, J., A New Poem: dedicated to the Landowners and the Unemployed (Tunbridge Wells: A K Baldwin Grosvenor Works 1886).*

James Richards, who had served as a Trades and Labour councillor before the First World War, later recalled that in his youth some of the landlords in High Brooms had failed to do their duty in the way of providing the necessities of modern civilisation. Others noted how tensions arose between local men and those recruited to the brickworks from Staffordshire and South Wales, and between those families who lived in the company's houses and workers who lived in other parts of Tunbridge Wells. High Brooms gained a reputation for lawlessness, and the lack of proper roads or sewerage, due to its location outside the boundaries of Tunbridge Wells, meant a lot of people avoided it.[30]

As we reach the 1880s it is worth taking a closer look at the lives of working people in Tunbridge Wells. One thing that stands out is the seasonal nature of many jobs. The men and boys employed at the High Brooms Brick and Tile Works enjoyed a 'season' from April to October of plentiful (if back-breaking) work, after which most would be laid off for the winter. The building trades employed more people than any other sector of the local economy, with 1,324 recorded in 1911. Work came to a virtual halt in very cold weather, as paint and cement would not dry. The few carpenters, painters, paperhangers and others who remained employed through the winter only worked during daylight hours, their pay being cut accordingly. Many labourers would have moved from job to job through the seasons but the amount of work available in the colder months never matched that in the warmer.

Agricultural work, of course, followed the same pattern. More thoughtful observers recognised that the spikes in unemployment affected everyone. The town's Liberal newspaper noted the 900 people thrown out of work during the winter of 1884-1885 reduced the amount of money circulating in the town by £900 a week, damaging shopkeepers and other tradesmen. This argument seems sophisticated for the time, and the next year's Trades Union Congress made exactly the same point. Thus every winter the number of unemployed would rise dramatically and the SDF, by urging the council to employ as many men as possible to clear snow and ice from the street in the short term, could combine such calls

---

[30] Savidge, A. (revised by Bell, C.), *Royal Tunbridge Wells: A History of a Spa Town* (Speldhurst: Oast Books 1995) p188;   Richards, J., *High Brooms, a Bit of the History of the Place and Its People*, (Tunbridge Wells 1937).

to alleviate the misery caused by capitalism in the short term with demands for its eventual abolition.[31]

Even when there was enough work to go round, human life remained very cheap. Wholly avoidable accidents regularly took their toll. Every few months the local press reported that a workman had died or suffered serious injury. One of the worst cases came in late 1893 when a painter fell to his death due to his ladder snapping in two. At the coroner's inquest one witness gave evidence that it was rotten and considered it to be twenty years old. The manager of the firm disputed this and claimed that he had bought the ladder no more than two years ago. Further investigation found that it had been carefully puttied to disguise its condition. Arguments followed as to whether it had been bought in this state from the Baltic Sawmills or it had been poorly mended by the firm. This death followed a fatal fall in the same part of the town in June in very similar circumstances.[32]

A shunting accident at the gas works c 1910

Death particularly stalked the town's railwaymen, especially those shunting wagons in goods yards. One young man, Edgar Godstone, died while working in the South Eastern company's depot on Goods Station Road in September 1885. The death of another shunter, aged 72, in the same yards three years later led the *Advertiser* to question why better provision could not be made for

---

[31] See the example of the Aylesford and Burham brickworks which in 1867 employed three times as many during the summer than the winter. Hann, A., The Medway Valley, a Kent Landscape transformed (London: University of London 2009) p48. For the building trades, see Cunningham, J. ,The Shock of War' p16. The best description of the building trades can be found in Robert Tressell's Ragged Trousered Philanthropists, written about 20 years later (Lawrence and Wishart 1968). See also The Tunbridge Wells Journal December 25th 1884; Harris, J., Unemployment and Politics: A Study in English Social Policy 1886-1914 (Oxford: The Clarendon Press 1972) p59.

[32] The Courier June 2nd 1893, & November 10th 1893. These incidents bring to mind the fate of Philpot in the Ragged Trousered Philanthropists.

those who had given decades of service to the company, Across Britain 422 railwaymen were killed and 5,560 injured in 1907.[33]

Although the work may have been physically less arduous, those employed in retail, mainly women and children, had the disadvantage of working extremely long hours for little pay. Many of these workers also suffered from the various abuses linked to the 'living-in' system, and this ruined the health of many. Even the home could often prove unsafe. The *Tunbridge Wells and Tonbridge Express* reported a meeting of the town's Improvement Commissioners at which two types of mortar were displayed in jars, the second consisting of 'common earth, a little sand and lime only'. A house on the Beulah estate, built using this material, had recently collapsed, killing a man, and two others, one on Eridge Road and the other on Upper Grosvenor Road, had 'split right up'.[34]

For those who fell out of employment, whether through injury, age or, in the case of younger women, pregnancy outside a stable relationship, life became extremely bleak. Some turned to infanticide or abandoned their children. Between January and May 1885 the bodies of three babies were discovered on the Commons. The town's Coroner condemned it as a scandal. A week later, a walker there found an abandoned three-year old boy and the Board of Guardians called for such children to be photographed to help find those who had abandoned them. (This was principally to relieve pressure on the rates rather than for their welfare.) Others committed suicide.

In March 1886 a pregnant former barmaid from Southborough, now without any means of support, poisoned herself. A month later, two widowed women in their sixties from Rusthall walked into Brighton Pond, near the West Railway Station, in an attempt to drown themselves. Both were rescued though one died later, the other being charged with the wilful murder of her companion as well as attempting suicide. The first of these charges seems to have been dropped later. The newspaper reports noted that they had no food or money left in the house.

As will be seen later, William Willis-Harris, the first Branch Secretary of the SDF at Tunbridge Wells, killed himself in 1899, an act partly driven by the fear that he and his family faced either

---

[33] *Tunbridge Wells Advertiser September 15th 1885, April 20th 1888;*
Jones C, *Tunbridge Wells in 1909 (Tunbridge Wells Civic Society 2008) p42.*
[34] *Tunbridge Wells and Tonbridge Express March 10th 1885.*

penury or the workhouse. Although it is an impressionistic observation, infanticide and suicide both seem to have been more common in Tunbridge Wells than in other nearby places, and this undercurrent proved awkward to those who persisted in trying to think of the town as the Modern Jerusalem.[35]

Chronic overcrowding also took its toll on the town's working class. This problem long pre-dated the formation of the SDF's Tunbridge Wells branch. Thomas Benge Burr, an early historian of the town, requested the Abergavenny family release land south of the town for smallholdings as early as 1766. A vivid account from 1869 noted that a man, his wife and seven or eight children occupied one room of an old cottage. The baby slept in a fish basket, red herrings ornamented the ceiling and heaps of rotten rags lay in the corner.[36]

We lack a comprehensive survey for Tunbridge Wells along the lines of Charles Booth's report on London or Seebohm Rowntree's work on York. However some made telling comparisons with other parts

The area between Calverley, Camden and Goods Station Roads (within the white line) was home to nearly one thousand people in 1909. See Jones, C., 1909

---

[35] *These examples were reported in the Kent and Sussex Times, March 13th 1886, April 10th and 17th 1886; Tunbridge Wells and Tonbridge Express May 12th and 19th 1885; Kent and Sussex Times May 16th 1885 and June 13th 1885.*
[36] *Savidge, A., Tunbridge Wells p.99.*

of the country. Sidney Webb, a leading member of the Fabian Society, claimed in 1902 that parts of the town had higher levels of infant mortality than London and many of the industrial towns in Lancashire. A report by Dr. Edward Burnet, the town's Medical Officer, found that eleven families of three and one family of four lived in one-room tenements, and 130 families of between three and eight people lived in two-room accommodation. He recognised that this overcrowding stemmed from the higher rents, relative to income, than working people experienced at the time in London.

The solution clearly lay in the local authority providing municipal housing at affordable prices, yet a scheme supported by the town's socialists and other progressives in the late 1890s foundered, largely through the opposition of slum landlords, some of whom sat as councillors. The council supressed Dr. Burnet's report for two years until the socialists obtained a copy in 1915. Problems with affordability and overcrowding lasted until an increase in house construction after the First World War eased the situation somewhat. Since the provision of adequate housing ceased to be a political priority such problems have returned and blight the town today.[37]

One intriguing aspect of the Tunbridge Wells district in the decade before the Social-Democrats formed a branch is the revival of direct action, primarily incendiarism. Eric Hobsbawm and George Rudé suggest that arson as a weapon of social protest had become largely extinct after about 1860, the few attacks after this date often being blamed on tramps and vagrants. This does not appear to have been the case in West Kent. In May 1876, labourers in the vicinity of an arson attack near East Peckham, which destroyed £2,000 of property, refused to offer any assistance unless they were first guaranteed payment for their services. Similar things had happened during Swing. On 25th September 1877 the Tunbridge Wells brigades had a pair of arson attacks to deal with, one at Langton Green and the other at Pembury, the first being three miles west of the town and the latter the same distance to the east. None of the three men arrested were convicted. Incendiarists also targeted property at Fordcombe in August 1884 and near Paddock Wood in September 1887.[38]

---

[37] Savidge, Royal Tunbridge Wells p99,159; The Courier October 8th 1902; The Tunbridge Wells Advertiser June 4th 1915.
[38] The Courier May 26th 1876, 28th September 1877; The Tunbridge Wells Gazette August 22nd 1884; Tonbridge Free Press September 24th 1887.

Even more remarkably, what had been a weapon used primarily in rural areas became an instrument of terror in Tunbridge Wells and its suburbs. This first became apparent at Rusthall. The *Tunbridge Wells Advertiser* reported in April 1883 that a cottage, then being extended, had caught fire in very suspicious circumstances. The adjacent Morning Star public house had also twice been set alight very recently. About six weeks later a fire again broke out which destroyed the same cottage and its neighbours. These houses were built mainly of wood, and the barrels of tar used in the renovation work had proved an effective accelerant. At the very least, these incidents suggest a deep-seated grudge, and it is possible that the motive may have been a belief that the buildings encroached on the Common, an issue of public concern that year.[39]

The use of arson will recur later in this book. The SDF faced accusations of involvement in a series of such fires in the late 1880s. Yet, with the passage of time, such individual methods of protest would fade away, to be replaced by collective action.

The Morning Star public house and adjacent cottages (to the right of the fountain)

---

[39] *The Tunbridge Wells Advertiser April 20th 1883 and June 1st 1883, The Tunbridge Wells Journal May 31st 1883 and November 8th 1883.*

PART A BUILDING A BASE FOR SOCIAL-DEMOCRACY

CHAPTER 2 AGAINST GOD AND GOVERNMENT

By the 1880s a number of radical causes, such as land reform, women's suffrage and republicanism, had won converts in Tunbridge Wells. A handful of women and men even considered themselves to be socialists. The next few years would see the formation of branches of the National Secular Society and then the Social-Democratic Federation. Many of those who first became politically active as secularists later joined the SDF. The following chapters will explain how, for the first time in Tunbridge Wells, they won mass support for what might today be termed ultra-radical, or even far-left, political ideas. In 1889 John Stone-Wigg, the Chairman of the town's Improvement Commissioners, complained that the place had 'a vast deal of rowdyism, of rough element and socialism.... more than many towns twice its size'.[40]

The National Secular Society focussed on challenging the intellectual basis and institutional power of organised religion. In the context of mid-Victorian Britain this meant Christianity. It also supported other popular causes. Its journal, the *National Reformer*, carried a report from the area in January 1881. Sir William Hart-Dyke, from a West Kent landowning family, organised a petition in Tunbridge Wells against 'perpetual pensions', which guaranteed the descendants of military heroes or statesmen an income from the government. 255 local people had signed by that stage.[41]

Charles Bradlaugh

The Democratic Federation, the direct forerunner of the SDF, was formed at a conference in London on 8th June 1881. Few people in Tunbridge Wells seem to have noticed. Yet the long and convoluted struggle by Charles Bradlaugh, the dominant figure in the NSS, to represent the electors of Northampton, electrified radicals of all stripes in Great Britain, not least in the Kent town. Bradlaugh first won the seat in June 1880 but, as an atheist, refused to swear the oath of allegiance. The

---

[40] *The Courier January 18 1889.*
[41] *The National Reformer January 9th 1881.*

33

Conservatives barred him from making an affirmation as an alternative. By-election followed by-election, each of which he won. He finally took his seat after the 1885 General Election when the Liberals were returned to power. The NSS thrived on this publicity, and, in 1881 – very much in the *early* 1880s – some local sympathisers formed a branch at Tonbridge and Tunbridge Wells. The action may have been taking place some distance away from Kent, at Westminster and the East Midlands, yet arriving 'fresh from London and the Bradlaugh agitation', certainly won bragging rights for William Willis-Harris, later to be the first Secretary of the SDF's Tunbridge Wells branch.[42]

Henry Albert Seymour was one of the most ardent secularists in Tunbridge Wells. He wrote to the *National Reformer* on 8th May 1881 to announce that he and some friends had formed a local branch of the NSS and that this would meet in three days' time. Other founder members included Thomas Russell, from Rusthall, and Quebes Austin of Tonbridge. The first meeting, held at the Prince of Wales public house, passed a resolution in support of Charles Bradlaugh's right to sit in Parliament, thanked Bradlaugh's supporters, including William Gladstone and John Bright, and condemned those on the Tory benches who had blocked him. It therefore clearly aligned itself with the Liberal Party.[43]

The next few meetings passed relatively uneventfully, troubling the pages of neither the local nor the radical press. Although denying the existence of God outraged many in mid-Victorian England, secular organisations generally recruited from the ranks of the 'respectable' and fairly sober lower-middle and skilled working classes. The press, of course, tended to portray freethinkers as immoral and dangerous chancers with a liking for drink. As Secularism formed a current within the wider Radical movement, debates on issues other than theology ensued. Charles Bradlaugh, a Radical Liberal who had dominated the national organisation from the mid-1860s, saw nothing wrong with the profit motive in manufacturing and believed in the philosophy of self-help. This led him to oppose socialism and trade unionism. At the same time he chaired the Land Law Reform League and supported land

[42] *Justice November 4th 1899, Crick p25-6*
[43] *The National Reformer April 17th 1881, May 13th and May 22nd 1882*

redistribution so as to alleviate rural poverty and break the control of the aristocracy in both Great Britain and in Ireland.[44]

Some leaders of the freethought movement, such as George Jacob Holyoake, were socialists, though in the early 1880s few were Marxists. Holyoake had been a follower of Robert Owen in his youth and remained an advocate of cooperation until his death in 1906. In the 1880s many secularists re-forged the link with a revived socialism, though now in a form more inspired by Marx and Engels than by Owen and his contemporaries. Debates reflecting these differences certainly took place in the pubs of Tunbridge Wells.[45]

These rather dry early meetings failed to attract the disaffected youth of Tunbridge Wells and the numbers enrolled in the NSS remained low. A new approach followed. From November 1881 leading members of the branch gave recitals, sang songs, and impersonated local preachers. Activists gave provocative lectures with titles such as 'Christianity, the curse of mankind'. For a while these tactics worked. Audiences increased. Leading Secularists, such as G W Foote, visited the town, and as the *National Reformer* reported, caused quite a stir. From March 1882 the branch rented premises on Camden Road which they named the Secular Hall and crowds of several hundred sometimes attended. Rather entertainingly, Seymour used nearly every report he submitted to praise his own performances, though we learn little about the success or otherwise of other contributors. The branch also printed and distributed placards advertising events at the Secular Hall and the occasional outdoor rally.[46]

The churches and chapels quickly struck back against this challenge to their authority. The religious lobby had an opportunity to pounce at Easter 1882. Seymour had created and displayed a poster which broke the law on blasphemy. The authorities initially merely removed the word 'Holy' from them. The Commissioners' Police Committee then ordered Seymour's arrest. He duly appeared before the Tunbridge Wells Magistrates, to be charged and bailed. The NSS initially regarded this as a matter of persecution and

[44] *Royle, Radicals, esp. p263, Crick, M., The History of the Social-Democratic Federation (Keele: Ryburn Publishing 1994) p19*
[45] *See Royle, E, Victorian Infidels and the chapter 'Hyndman and the SDF' in Hobsbawm, E Labouring Men: Essays in the History of Labour (London: Wiedenfeld and Nicolson 1964)*
[46] *National Reformer November 13th 1881, November 27th 1881, March 12th 1882 and March 19th 1882*

agreed to pay for Seymour's defence. Foote also faced a prosecution at the same time relating to his newspaper, the *Freethinker*, and at the NSS's conference at the end of the month Bradlaugh concluded by appealing for funds for the two cases.[47]

Seymour, however, whose knowledge of the Scriptures had been praised by the *National Reformer* in May, seems to have fallen from favour by the time the case reached the Maidstone Assizes in July. He had been accused of a second charge of blasphemous libel, which he seems to have concealed from the leadership of the NSS, and this coloured their attitude towards him. This stemmed from a second placard, intended as retaliation against Salvation Army attacks on him, and it could not be effectively defended. His lawyer persuaded him to change his plea to guilty. His punishment consisted of being bound over with a £100 surety, a very lenient outcome. At the end of July the *National Reformer* used Seymour's case as a morality tale; a very young and inexperienced secretary of a provincial society had overreacted to a personal attack, and warned its readers not to fall into the same trap. They followed this by issuing a circular to all branches of the society telling them how to produce material which would not fall foul of the law.[48]

Canon Hoare, the Vicar of Holy Trinity, and the most high-profile cleric in the town, weighed into the debate between the NSS and representatives of the Church which followed. Despite the adulation shown for him at his death, his attitudes were often extremely sectarian, and many had reason to despise him. Few in either camp changed their views. The Secularists fell behind with the rent, and bailiffs seized the hall. Most venues in the town, having been leant on by local clerics, refused to hire their premises to atheists. Membership fell as rapidly as it had risen, and the remaining activists met in the front room of Seymour's house at 1 Wood Street. Yet the town's police acted in a fairly even-handed manner. During one meeting on the Common, they refused to arrest the visiting lecturer, a Mr Thurlow, and prevented their opponents from interfering with the meeting. The development of a tradition of free speech later gave the socialists a real advantage in Tunbridge Wells when compared to other towns.[49]

[47]*National Reformer, May 14th 1882, June 4th 1882, July 2nd 1882.*
[48] *National Reformer July 23rd 1882, August 2nd 1882.*
[49] *National Reformer July 2nd 1882.*

Wood Street, with Henry Seymour's former house on the left

In the last weeks of 1882 the self-appointed guardians of the town's morals over-reached themselves and gave the Secularists another martyr. Their new victim, Edward Cherill Edwards, had a confectionary shop in Camden Road. To challenge the Sunday trading laws he opened his shop on Sundays. In December he was fined by the town's magistrates. He responded in a letter to the *Advertiser*. The Local Board, which had prosecuted him, included the owner of the High Brooms Brick and Tile Works, John Smith Weare, and a number of others who employed domestic servants, all of whom expected their employees to 'pursue their vocation on Sunday', and, indeed, would dismiss or prosecute them if they failed to do so.[50]

Such blatant hypocrisy meant that Edwards' case briefly became something of a *cause celebre* for *Reynolds Newspaper*, a London radical publication. One editorial noted that workmen were preparing the route for Queen Victoria to open the new Royal Courts of Justice in London on the same Sunday that his prosecution cited. Capitalising on this, Seymour established a support fund in January 1883 and wrote to the *Advertiser* and the *National Reformer* calling for contributions. The large Secular Hall in Balls Pond Road, London, raised £1 7s 6d at a meeting at the end

[50] *Tunbridge Wells Advertiser December 15th 1882, January 5th 1883.*

of the month in support, and the London Executive of the NSS called on other branches to contribute.[51]

Unfortunately this did not end the matter. Edwards endured twenty-three further prosecutions until June 1883 when the Police Committee went too far. Several other traders, many of whom were not secularists, joined Edwards in court charged with infringing the Sabbath laws. The magistrates fined Edwards the tiny sum of 6d, made the Committee pay the costs, and the charges against the other defendants were immediately dropped. Edwards' travails continued and only concluded in 1898 when an unsympathetic landlord evicted him. He challenged this but lost, and the ensuing legal costs seem to have ended his career and forced his move from the town to Hastings.[52]

The attacks on Seymour and Edwards came at a good time. The town's Working Men's Liberal Association formed in early 1882 and immediately attracted three hundred members. The officers of the branch came from working class backgrounds; many were active trade unionists. Their causes ranged widely: they discussed international affairs and also campaigned for the removal of the existing Corporation, to be replaced with democratic elections and men of their own class. The Conservative *Courier* derided this demand as ridiculous. A faction within the Association sided with the Secularists. In July 1882 twelve of its members signed an open letter supporting Seymour. Significantly, three of the twelve, George Stevens, John Potter and William Bournes, all later played a role in the SDF's branch. Seymour himself narrowly missed out on being co-opted on to the Association's committee by 21 votes against 25.[53]

The Working Men's Liberal Association's relationship with the future SDF branch was to be very significant for several decades. Both won much of their support from people living in the Camden Road and St John's Road districts. They also saw themselves as heirs to the decades-old radical tradition derived in part from the French Revolution. This renewed itself over successive generations: the Chartists of Kent flew the Tricolour in the 1830s and 40s, while

---

[51] *Reynolds Newspaper, December 10th & 17th 1882; National Reformer November 26th 1882.*

[52] *National Reformer July 1st 1883, June 22nd 1884; Letters from Henry Seymour to Reynolds Newspaper January 16th and 30th 1898.*

[53] *Tunbridge Wells Gazette February 3rd 1882; The Courier March 3rd 1883, July 28th 1882; The Courier February 2nd 1883; Arnold, R.,The Revolt of the Field p74.*

a group of emigrants from the Kent and Sussex Labourers Union marched under this flag before leaving the country in 1879.[54]

In this context the Social-Democrats use of the Phrygian Cap atop their own red flags, their adoption as the *Marseillaise* as their most popular anthem until supplanted by the *Red Flag* in the early twentieth century, and even the decision to hold rallies around what they called the 'liberty tree' on the Common near Mount Ephraim as late as 1905, showed the hold such symbols continued to have. Both showed an active interest in international affairs. Members of the Working Men's Liberal Association continued to defect to the socialist camp into the twentieth century. The two groups though could make common cause in opposing Tory military adventures or the introduction of tariffs on imports. The SDF's branch, however much it criticised the Liberal Party, always regarded the Conservatives as its main opponents, something not always true of its equivalents elsewhere.

Seymour now decided that he wished to become a lecturer for the NSS. Although his speeches seem to have been popular locally, such as one given to the Maidstone branch in August that year, the national leadership of the Society remained unimpressed. In September the *National Reformer* rebuked him, saying that his sweeping generalisations 'by a few strokes of logic or comparative mythology' showed that 'yours is one of the cases in which much more careful and special study is needed if you aspire to become a Freethought speaker'.

Six months later the paper accused him of misunderstanding or, worse still, deliberately distorting Bradlaugh's views. To make the situation worse, one local cleric echoed such criticisms by contrasting Charles Bradlaugh and George Foote, whom he admitted were 'clever men', with those secularists who 'live, move and have their being in Tunbridge Wells [and] number many very poor specimens of erring humanity'.[55] These criticisms clearly stung and two years later he attacked Charles Bradlaugh as a 'contemptible hypocrite'. They probably also precipitated his move

---

[54] *Justice August 19th 1905. The Liberty Tree may have been linked to the revival of this tradition in France during the early 1880s, rather than a direct continuation of earlier traditions from the French Revolution of 1789. See Judt, T, Socialism in Provence 1871-1914 (New York University Press 2011) p62; Arnold, R., The Revolt of the Field.*

[55] *National Reformer August 5th 1883, September 12th 1883, March 2nd 1884; The Tunbridge Wells Advertiser June 1st 1883.*

away from the mainstream radicalism of the NSS towards revolutionary politics and anarchism.[56]

The arrival of two London secularists, Constance Howell and William Willis-Harris, gave the local movement a boost. Constance Howell had registered as a member of Tunbridge Wells branch in January 1884. She had been active in secularist circles since the start of the decade, and had written a series of pamphlets for the Freethought Publishing Company. Many of these, in both title and contents, echoed much earlier secularist works, though Howell's were often written for younger audiences. Thus her 'Biography of Jesus Christ', published in October 1883, copied the title of a much earlier work by D. F. Strauss, which first appeared in an English translation by George Eliot in 1845.

Even today it is strong stuff, much of which used detailed theological arguments to outline the contradictions in the Bible. Howell argued that the achievements of Jesus proved minor compared to Galileo, Darwin, John Stuart Mill, Voltaire and Paine, as well as two of the leading contemporary secularists, Foote and Bradlaugh, but ignores Owen, Holyoake, Marx, Engels and other leading socialists. The National Reformer considered it a 'remarkable little book' and recommended that 'older Freethinkers would do well to read it carefully and circulate it widely'[57].

William Willis-Harris may well be the 'W.H.' recorded as a member of the Tunbridge Wells branch in February 1884. He had moved to the town by March that year. William Willis-Harris's father, William Jewitt Harris, had been a successful Greenwich upholsterer and cabinet-maker. He later retired to a villa in Sidcup, then a very desirable outer London suburb. He died in January 1883, leaving the large sum of £10,734 15s 6d to his children.

In February 1883 William Willis-Harris wrote to the *National Reformer* to describe his recent experiences at the Probate Registry of the High Court where he had insisted on his right to affirm in respect of his father's will, something conceded only grudgingly. Similar problems dogged a Rusthall secularist, Henry Russell - presumably the brother of Thomas (mentioned above) – when the

---

[56] *The Anarchist April 1885*
[57] Royle, *Infidels* p15, p113; Howell. C, *A Biography of Jesus Christ*, (London; Freethought Publishing Company 1883); *National Reformer October 7th 1883*.

town's Coroner threw him off a jury when has asked to affirm rather than give a religious oath.[58]

William Willis-Harris' inheritance enabled him to establish his own business and he decided to move to Tunbridge Wells rather than remain in the Capital. While in London he had trained as an art decorator, learned to paint 'plain or ornamental signs' and to work as a glass and fascia writer. *The Courier* announced on 28th March 1884 that he had purchased a house decorating business, Everest and Sons, from Jane Everest, the widow of the former proprietor. This well-established firm had its shop at 15 Grosvenor Road, a prestigious shopping street, and a separate paint shop at 7 Kensington Road, in the Camden Road district. His decision to relocate may have been influenced by other members of his family, as one of his sisters would marry in the town in 1885. William seems to have been living with his girlfriend, Ada Bigsby, by the time he moved to Tunbridge Wells. They married there in the autumn of 1886.[59]

Revived by new members such as these, the NSS branch decided to arrange a free-speech rally on the Common that summer, writing to neighbouring branches to ask for their support. Twenty to thirty Brighton secularists agreed to attend, with smaller numbers from Chatham and Maidstone. Toby King, a well-known radical from Hastings, attended and fought off some of those who tried to break the meeting up (King was an early influence on many of those who would go on to form trade unions and socialist organisations in Hastings). Arthur Hickmott, a Sevenoaks shopkeeper and secularist lecturer who would later work closely with Tunbridge Wells' socialists, also came. Several gangs tried to break up the gathering, although the police maintained order for about forty-five minutes, before the hostile element became overwhelming. The NSS's George Standring, the principal speaker, nevertheless concluded that it had

---

[58] *Letter to the London Standard, July 13th 1897; National Reformer February 17th 1884. In 1843 William Jewett Harris had gained a footnote in history as one of the jurors sworn in at the trial of Daniel M'Naghten, who had killed Edward Drummond, Private Secretary to the Prime Minister, Robert Peel. M'Naghten's acquittal was important in establishing principles concerning the defence of insanity in criminal trials For his background see the Morning Chronicle March 4th 1843; 1883 Probate Calendar (online); National Reformer February 18th 1883. For the discrimination against atheists in civil proceedings see Royle, Radicals, Secularists and Republicans, p24; The Courier March 16th 1883..*
[59] *See advertisements in the Courier October 22nd 1886 and Tunbridge Wells Advertiser June 22nd 1888; and the Marriage Certificate of Karl Marx Willis-Harris and Catherine Andrews, St James' Moss Side, Manchester, 2nd February 1918.*

been a success as it had established a foothold in 'a most bigoted and priest-ridden town'.[60]

The presence of William Willis-Harris and Constance Howell meant that socialism would have two powerful advocates in the Tunbridge Wells branch. Throughout 1883 and 1884 the *National Reformer* had discussed the subject on a near-weekly basis, despite occasional editorial attempts to end the debate. Provincial societies followed this lead. A meeting of the Maidstone branch – about seventeen miles away – took place in June 1883 under the title 'capitalism or socialism', one of a series with similar titles. Arthur Field, later to play a very significant role in Kent's labour politics, read the Democratic Federation's *Socialism Made Plain* at a NSS meeting there the same year. A debate between Hyndman and Bradlaugh in April 1884, which was reported word for word in the *National Reformer* and printed as a best-selling pamphlet, meant that few secularists could avoid taking sides.[61]

Secularists throughout Britain were already studying political economy, primarily as a result of reading an American work on land reform, Henry George's *Progress and Poverty*, which sold 100,000 copies in Britain by 1881.[62] As mentioned above, Bradlaugh had long championed this cause, but had moved away from supporting land nationalisation towards a gradualist form of peasant proprietorship.

Such growing moderation failed to impress younger radicals. George Bernard Shaw, on the cusp of his career as playwright and author, became a friend and collaborator of William Willis-Harris and Henry Seymour around this time. He later recalled the men of his generation, previously 'pupils of Mill, Spencer, Compte, and Darwin, roused by Mr. Henry George's Progress and Poverty, left aside evolution and freethought, took to insurrectionary economics [and] studied Karl Marx'. Another observer believed that four-fifths of his fellow socialists of the 1880s had come to Marxism via Henry George.[63]

---

[60]*The Courier June 20th 1884;   The National Reformer June 22 1884, January 18th 1885 and February 1st 1885; The Courier May 11th 1906.*
[61] *National Reformer July 1st 1883; Crick, M., The History of the Social-Democratic Federation (Keele: Ryburn Publishing 1994) p35.*
[62] *Crick, History, p19.*
[63] *Royle, Radicals p196-7; Shaw, G.B., 'The Transition to Social Democracy' in Essays in Fabian Socialism, p46 (London: Constable and Company 1949);. Crick, History, p19.*

Marxist ideas became more widely distributed across Britain when the SDF published *Justice,* a weekly newspaper, from the beginning of 1884. Most newsagents boycotted it[64]. However, J.G. North of 35 High Street, Tonbridge, five miles from Tunbridge Wells, stocked it from April that year, suggesting a local appetite for the paper. Intriguingly he is listed in the directories around that time as a hairdresser, so selling radical papers may have been a side-line. In later years the shop became North's Circulating Library. It may have been possible to buy the paper in Tunbridge Wells slightly earlier than this.

A group within the NSS branch, including Henry Seymour, opened the Science Library, a secularist meeting space and shop, at 98 Camden Road, by no later than December 1883. It is likely that William Willis-Harris and Constance Howell funded it, although *Justice* only named the shop as an agent from May 1884. The name echoed the Halls of Science established across Britain by secularists and socialists from the 1840s onwards. Canon Hoare later spoke of his disgust at first discovering these premises:

'We must not leave the people to the propaganda of the Infidel. I used not to know its practical workings, but I have seen something of it now. I will tell you what I saw in my own parish not many months ago. I walked down one of the principal streets and there I saw a great placard in one of the shop windows. It said 'No God and No Government. Anarchy before God and Man.'

Hoare may not have realised the implications of these words. Adapted from a slogan of the French socialist Louis Auguste Blanqui, it would have horrified Charles Bradlaugh almost as much as the Canon. Seymour aired his differences with Bradlaugh in the American anarchist paper *Liberty* in October 1884. One book from the Science Library's collection has survived in London's Senate House Library: a copy of the English translation by the American anarchist Benjamin Tucker of Proudhon's *What is Property?* Other secular, radical, socialist and anarchist books, periodicals and pamphlets would also have been available to buy or borrow. As well as selling *Justice* the shop also acted as an agent for the Socialist League's *Commonweal*.[65] In October the SDF's paper *Justice* carried

---

[64] Crick, *History, p34; Lee and Archibold p58.*
[65] *Liberty, December 15th 1883, October 25th 1884; The Anarchist June 1885; Justice May 31ˢᵗ 1884, January 3ʳᵈ 1885; and a letter from Henry Seymour to the Socialist League, 28ᵗʰ January 1885 (International Institute of Socialist History, Socialist League archive).*

43

its first report from the Tunbridge Wells area. This meeting, at Somerhill, a Jacobean mansion to the south of Tonbridge, featured speakers ranging from trade unionists to aristocrats. The Liberal Party had organised several such gatherings in the district. They hoped to win the support of working class voters by promising to widen the franchise. A handful of sellers of *Justice* joined them. Their intervention proved successful; 61 copies of the paper sold and eleven given away. The sellers were still as much secularists as socialists at this stage, Sir Julian Goldsmid, who was Jewish and owned the grounds in which the event took place, laid claim to be a veteran defender of religious freedom. This immediately drew a rebuke - 'what about Bradlaugh?'[66]

A new division then opened up within the town's Secular Society, and one which might surprise those who consider Tunbridge Wells irredeemably conservative: a split between Marxism and individualist anarchism. Both sides spent more time on these causes than on religious questions during 1885. The National Reformer records no NSS rallies or public meetings that year yet The society's membership remained healthy (It is not easy to estimate numbers because subscriptions could be renewed throughout the year, but 51 renewals were recorded between June and October 1885).[67]

It took time for some young men and women to decide which form of revolutionary politics to endorse. George Bernard Shaw remembered his former acquaintances who would 'plan the revolutionary programme as an affair of twenty-four lively hours, with Individualism in full swing on Monday morning, a tidal wave of the insurgent proletariat on Monday afternoon, and Socialism in complete working order on Tuesday'.

Whether Willis-Harris ever considered himself an anarchist is open to question – in 1897 Seymour claimed that he had once done so, though Willis-Harris denied it. The Science Library soon closed, as the two men decided to set up a London printing firm, the International Publishing Company. This published *the Anarchist*, Britain's first such English-language periodical, from March 1885. Seymour had editorial control, though William Willis-Harris provided most of the money. George Bernard Shaw wrote one of the

---

[66] Royle, E., Radicals, Secularists and Republicans (Manchester University Press 1980) pp23-34,; Justice October 4th 1884; the Tonbridge Free Press August 16th 1884 and October th 1884.
[67] The National Reformer June 28th 1885, August 30th 1885 and December 27th 1885.

longest articles for the paper's first instalment, something which later embarrassed him. Seymour recruited Edward Cherill Edwards to the anarchist cause and may have influenced a few others. Edwards, however, also joined the SDF.[68]

William Willis-Harris, Henry Albert Seymour and George Bernard Shaw also joined the Fabian Society,, then a small and rather select socialist organisation, Seymour doing so on 5th June 1885, shortly after his move to Islington in north London. Willis-Harris remained in Tunbridge Wells. Yet Seymour's move did not cut him off entirely from radicalism in Kent. For its first few months, *The Anarchist* carried a lot of items from the county, such as stories of farmers having their property seized at Biddenden and Ashford, and Seymour continued his correspondence with old acquaintances Edward Cherill Edwards and Toby King.[69]

By this time socialism had gained greater ground than anarchism in secular circles in Tunbridge Wells. Constance Howell published her *Afterlife of the Apostles, written for young freethinkers* in September 1884. This pamphlet is full of pointed observations: no profession had debased itself as much as the clergy; the Bible consisted of 'falsehoods and curses'; and the Christian faith allowed no love for the natural world which 'gave such joy to the secularist'. She hoped for a time when churches and chapels would be demolished or turned into secular halls, something suggested by Richard Carlile, a radical journalist, as early as 1822. At the same time she recognised that early Christian communities had attempted to establish a form of 'social communism'. The *National Reformer* again praised her work as an effective piece of propaganda which might usefully be read by Secular Society branches when no lecturer could be secured. She seems to have joined the SDF at around this time.[70]

[68] Shaw, G. B., 'The Transition to Social Democracy' in *Essays in Fabian Socialism*, p42 (London: Constable and Company 1949); Reynold's Newspaper July 11 1897; the London Standard, July 13th 1897; Fabian Society Minute Books 5th June 1885; Weintraub, S., Bernard Shaw Diaries (Pennsylvania University Press 1986) p322, p206. Edward Cherill Edwards' son Edward Peter Edwards also joined the SDF and stood for the party at a ward by-election in Hastings in 1909, not long after the magistrates of that town had fined him for obstruction while campaigning for socialism. I am grateful to Trevor Hopper for this link.
[69] The Anarchist August 1885, January 1886; Liberty January 3rd 1885.
[70] Howell. C, The Afterlife of the Apostles, written for young freethinkers (London: Freethought Publishing Company 1884); Royle, Infidels, p134.

A few working-class men and women from secularist backgrounds also convinced themselves that socialism represented the future. Tom Jarvis, a 'raw recruit of provincial atheism' then living with his

parents and siblings at 11 Duke's Road, may have been the most important of these. In 1899 he recalled that William Willis-Harris had personally convinced him to join the SDF. The two may have become acquainted through work, as Jarvis was a house painter. In years to

Duke's Road, Tunbridge Wells.

come he served on the SDF Executive and was probably the best public speaker of the early recruits to the branch. One intriguing coincidence is that he represented the Federation at an event held in Paris in 1899 to commemorate the life and work of Blanqui, the man who had inspired the Science Library's poster in 1885.[71]

Samuel Price, a painter of 24 Kirkdale Road, Tunbridge Wells, had joined the Secularists before June 1885 and, together with his wife, became members of the SDF shortly afterwards.[72] In 1889 a Mr F Russell of Rusthall, who must have been related to Henry and Thomas, wrote a letter to the *Courier* which suggests that he had also joined the socialists in the mid-80s.[73]

A handful of others also became members in 1885. In contrast to Tom Jarvis, they do not appear to have been particularly interested in the freethought movement – they may have been on the fringes of it, but certainly never took a leadership role. David Geer, the eldest of six siblings, joined in 1885.[74] He had been born in Tunbridge Wells, although his family, like that of Tom Jarvis, came from rural Sussex. This may reflect a pattern seen elsewhere, as historians have sometimes pointed to the second and third generation families

---

[71] *Justice November 4th 1899; The Tonbridge Telegraph December 17th 1887.*
[72] *The National Reformer June 23rd 1886; The Tonbridge Telegraph December 17th 1887.*
[73] *The Courier February 1st 1889.*
[74] *CPGB Archive, Dona Torr papers.*

which had moved from country to town as forming the backbone of the socialist movement. Geer later suggested that his socialist views were widely known in the town in the early 1880s, perhaps even before the branch of the NSS had been established. He first appeared in the town's press as a schoolboy for winning a prize for a religious essay. At eleven he had started work as an errand boy and afterwards trained under his father, a journeyman carpenter. One formative experience came when he nearly fell to his death while working on the roof of St Peter's Church. On 8th July 1882 he married Mercy Roberts, a union which lasted over six decades. Being teetotal, he preferred to socialise at the Oddfellows' Lodge rather than the pub.[75]

Other members of the Geer family, in particular his nephew Albert Charles Geer, also played a leading role in local socialist, cooperative, trade union and ultimately Labour Party politics over many decades. One of his closest friends, Thomas Cox, then living in Garden Street, also appears to have joined the SDF early. James Sutton and David Bartholomew also became members around this time.[76]

This conversion of a handful of young men and women to socialism in Tunbridge Wells coincided with a broader radicalisation on the street and in the workplace. Two extremely lively labour disputes followed each other in quick succession in the summer of 1885. The first came in July when cab-drivers employed by a Mr Waghorn, the town's principal cab proprietor, took strike action. One driver had been dismissed and prosecuted, allegedly for embezzling a fare. In revenge the men constructed an effigy of Waghorn, attached a placard reading 'midnight shadow' to it, and hired a band of five musicians to accompany them. One demonstrator carried a loaf of bread on a stick as a visual prop to illustrate his contention that Waghorn wished him to starve. A threat of prosecution led to the plan to burn the effigy being dropped, but a crowd of thousands of people joined the march. Such a demonstration would have offered a perfect opportunity to sell *Justice*.[77]

---

[75] *Geer's parents were born at Guestling (near Hastings) and Heathfield. For the point about generations, see Berger, S., The British Labour Party and the German Social Democrats (Oxford: Clarendon Press 1994) p135; The Tunbridge Wells Advertiser November 1st 1901; The Courier July 10th 1942.*
[76] *The Courier January 17th 1947.*
[77] *The Tunbridge Wells Gazette July 10th 1885; the Tunbridge Wells Journal July 9th & July 16th 1885; Tunbridge Wells Advertiser July 10th 1885.*

47

Another industrial dispute started later the same month between the town's Journeymen Tailors' Association and their employers. The principal local Liberal newspaper, the *Tunbridge Wells Advertiser*, initially blamed the tailors for demanding a 25% increase in pay, but the Association disputed this, arguing that an 1876 agreement had been broken, on the advice of a London agent, and that their pay would therefore be reduced significantly. The employers' hand had been strengthened by the greater use elsewhere of machinery in making clothing, so driving down its cost. Many were outworkers, making clothes in their own homes, while others worked in small workshops. "Justice", one correspondent to the *Advertiser*, blamed the masters for the unrest, claiming that their conduct could only lead to a breach of the peace. The tailors had been given a week to accept the lower prices or to leave the town and seek work elsewhere. The lockout saw picket lines established at shops throughout the town. About 70 members of the Association took part in the dispute, and even non-members supported it.

The tailors' dispute quickly turned violent. Crossing a picket line meant running the gauntlet of an angry mob. Racial prejudice also came into play, shown by the anti-Semitic abuse directed against a group of Jewish non-strikers, reflecting the attitudes of many trade unionists during this decade who rather unfairly blamed those fleeing persecution in Central and Eastern Europe for driving down rates of pay.

In later decades, at least in London, Jewish tailors were far more likely to join a trade union than those from other backgrounds. Such divisions only weakened the union's position. The dispute proved acrimonious enough to keep the police and magistrates busy for months; one participant received a month in jail as late as January 1886 for assaulting a member of the union who had refused to strike.[78]

After these two disputes had settled, public interest turned to the plight of the town's unemployed. In August 1885 one local

---

[78] *Reynolds Newspaper August 16th 1885; Tunbridge Wells Gazette July 24th 1885 and August 15th 1885; the Tunbridge Wells Journal August 13th 1885; Harris, J., Unemployment and Politics. p29; Tunbridge Wells Advertiser July 17th & 24th & August 7th 1885; The Tunbridge Wells and Tonbridge Weekly Express and West Kent Journal January 26th 1886; Tunbridge Wells Advertiser August 7th 1885; see Shukman. H., War or Revolution: Russian Jews and Conscription in Britain 1917 (London: Valentine Mitchell 2006) p54.*

newspaper complained that large numbers of 'vagrants' were coming into the town, swelling the population. Many of these may have been looking for work in the surrounding orchards and hop gardens, and a handful to beg. By the end of 1885 and the start of 1886 almost a thousand men were out of work.[79] Unemployment always increased during the winter in Tunbridge Wells but for the first time those affected decided to do something about it. The *Tunbridge Wells Gazette* reported that on Christmas Eve 1885:

> *'the unemployed working men of Tunbridge Wells [had] adopted a novel method of bringing their straightened circumstances before the public, a procession perambulating the streets, headed by a banner bearing the words "Gentlemen: are the unemployed of Tunbridge Wells to starve in a land of plenty?" It was said that two thousand of the unemployed would take part in the "demonstration" – an exaggeration, of course, the procession numbering all told probably about a hundred. It was accompanied by men with collecting boxes who scoured the footways and penetrated into business establishments in search of alms as the grim line of hungry-looking men passed at a funereal pace through the streets. The procession attracted a deal of attention and the collectors appeared to be doing well'.[80]*

Over a period of several weeks a number of other protests took place. Although the Tory press derided the participants as loafers 'who stood on the street corner day after day', with few 'respectable' men among them, one local employer believed that most of the men had worked in the building trade and the Liberal *Advertiser* believed that most of them were *bona fide* working men. The paper also complimented the 150 or so participants on the orderly way in which they conducted themselves. A meeting at the Town Hall to arrange relief followed, but the money raised was limited to those deemed deserving.[81] However, action reaped dividends, as 400 gained temporary work, though at low wages, carrying out tasks like clearing the snow from the streets.[82] This though was insufficient, and as late as March 1886 the unemployed again paraded to obtain relief from householders. The authorities intervened, with the magistrates warning the participants that their

---

[79] *The Maidstone and Kentish Journal, Rochester and Chatham Journal and South East Advertiser January 2nd 1886.*
[80] *The Tunbridge Wells Gazette December 25th 1885'*
[81] *The Tunbridge Wells Journal December 24th & 31st 1885; Tunbridge Wells Advertiser December 25th 1885.*
[82] *The Tunbridge Wells Journal January 14th 1886.*

actions amounted to intimidation and that they faced arrest if they continued.[83]

These hunger marches in Tunbridge Wells echoed others across Britain that grim winter. Similar protests took place in London, Manchester, Birmingham, Leicester, Great Yarmouth, Northampton, Grimsby, Nottingham, Sheffield, Norwich, and, perhaps most significantly, at nearby Hastings. On occasions windows were broken and in London the protests degenerated into riots.[84] Whether the Tunbridge Wells marches had been organised by members of the SDF, or inspired by reports from *Justice*, is not known.

By the end of 1885 many people across Britain associated the party with organised processions of the unemployed. One of the largest and most violent, a procession to Hyde Park in February 1886, had been organised by the SDF's metropolitan branches. The Tunbridge Wells press covered the London protests in some detail and so brought the socialists some publicity, whether positive or not,[85] The growing unemployment problem may have converted some in Tunbridge Wells from individualist Liberalism to Marxism; Constance Howell's *A More Excellent Way* specifically criticised Bradlaugh's attitude towards those out of work as part of her contention that socialism had taken on the progressive mantle previously held by the NSS.[86]

Although the SDF now possessed a nucleus of supporters in Tunbridge Wells and it had become clear that its causes – in particular unemployment – had become more resonant, the NSS became the first to benefit. Those who had joined both organisations took the lead. Tom Jarvis became Secretary and organised a series of political and religious meetings - details of which we know little - in a rented room owned by a Mr Spratley, a cabinet-maker, in Tunnel Road, north of the town centre, in the autumn of 1885.

Despite this increase in interest, the NSS still faced opposition. Mr Spratley bore the brunt of this. He was in poor health and had sub-let part of his premises to a wheelwright. The wheelwright then

---

[83] *The Courier March 19th 1886; The Tunbridge Wells Journal March 18th 1886.*
[84] *Shaw, G. B., 'The Fabian Society; in Essays in Fabian Socialism p133 (London, Constable and Company 1949) p131; Harris, Unemployment p55.*
[85] *The Tunbridge Wells Gazette February 26th 1886.*
[86] *Howell, C., A More Excellent Way.*

invited his secularist friends to make use of it. The workshops then burned down. When other tradesmen had suffered similar misfortune, the town's clergy had organised relief, so as to save them from destitution and the workhouse. They rejected Spratley's claim on the ground that atheistic meetings had been held on his premises. A leading member of the Secularists, clearly sympathising with Spratley, wrote to the *Advertiser* to confirm that Spratley had no knowledge of these meetings, and condemned the 'narrow-necked' followers of Christ for failing to follow the examples set by him and the Good Samaritan. It is not clear whether Spratley received anything. [87]

In October the *Courier* reported that Charles Bradlaugh, Annie Besant, and Foote were going to give a series of lectures in the town. Any ruptures caused by Seymour had clearly been mended by his departure from the town. A few weeks later, Jarvis wrote to the *National Reformer* to say that the branch had held a meeting at the Clarence Hotel, elected new officers, and that meetings would be held at the same venue until further notice.[88] Under him the branch maintained a constant flow of reports to the national organisation, something that the SDF's branch would replicate once established. A series of monthly public meetings was planned. A meeting on Home Rule for Ireland followed. The struggle for Irish home rule unified the radical left, members of the Liberal Party, the SDF and secularists all being committed to it. It is likely that supporters of all these organisations came to this well-attended meeting.[89]

The NSS branch's programme for the rest of the spring generally reflected the interests of Jarvis and the other socialists. An outspoken, and perhaps rather eccentric, Anglican clergyman, Reverend Stewart Headlam, was booked to give a lecture on land nationalisation in February. His local connections may have secured him as speaker, as he had lived in Tunbridge Wells for twenty years and his sister still lived in the town[90]. Headlam had made enemies in the Church through his work with the Guild of St Matthew, a Christian socialist organisation and his willingness to appear on secularist platforms. He also championed female music hall performers and other performing artists, professions often

[87] *The Tunbridge Wells Journal November 19th 1885; Tunbridge Wells and Tonbridge Express November 10th 1885; the Tunbridge Wells Advertiser November 6th & 20th 1885.*
[88] *The Courier October 9th 1885; The National Reformer January 3rd 1886.*
[89] *The National Reformer January 10th & 24th 1886.*
[90] *The Tunbridge Wells Advertiser November 20th 1908.*

regarded as little better than prostitution. Reinforcing his radical credentials, he had assisted in drafting the Democratic Federation's manifesto in March 1883, which a year later became the basis for the SDF's programme, and became active in the Fabian Society,.

A death in the family meant that he had to pull out, being replaced by his colleague Frederick Verinder, the Secretary of the Guild of St Matthew and President of the English Land Restoration League. Verinder lectured on the ideas of Henry George, and explained the biblical basis for holding land in common.[91] In March the secularists discussed theories in biology. Secularists and socialists had used concepts from evolution, initially those of the French biologist Jean Baptiste Lamarck from the 1840s and more recently Charles Darwin's account of human evolution, to undermine the Biblical account of creation.[92]

The meeting in mid-April 1886 proved an even clearer pointer to the future. A member of the NSS gave a reading from Karl Marx's *Wage Labour and Capital*. This early article by Marx had been translated into English and serialised in *Justice* from December 1884 to February 1885 and then republished widely in pamphlet form. A 'very interesting discussion' followed the lecture.[93] This pamphlet is a good introduction to Marxist economics, and it led some members to tackle more substantial books such as the first volume of *Capital*. Tom Jarvis may have taken the lead in this; his letter on the labour theory of value to *Justice* in March 1889 shows how well he had grasped Marx's ideas.[94]

A few weeks before this April 1886 meeting, which can be seen as a milestone in the transformation of the Secular Society into a branch of the SDF, the town's press first reported the latter organisation in a local context following an incident at the High Brooms Brick and Tile Works. It is not clear quite what had happened previously, but the owner, John Smith Weare, accused two employees, Samuel Oakland and James Piper, of working to rule – whether as part of an organised industrial dispute or not is unclear - and of belonging to the 'Social-Democrat party'. This can only be a reference to the

---

[91] *The Courier February 26th 1886; the Tunbridge Wells Journal February 25th 1886; Orens, J, R., Stewart Headlam's Radical Anglicanism (University of Illinois Press 2003) p85-86, p90; Lee and Archibold History p51.*
[92] *Royle p20, Infidels; Hale, P.J Political Descent, Malthus, Mutualism and the Politics of Evolution in Victorian England (Chicago: 2014) p175, p181, p261.*
[93] *The National Reformer March 14th 1886 and April 18th 1886.*
[94] *Justice March 2 1889.*

SDF. Weare dismissed both men on the spot. Neither lived at High Brooms and they felt that this had been held against them.

In normal circumstances this incident would not have made the local newspapers. With no effective legal protection, workers could be hired and fired at will. However a building at the works, rented as a mission hall from the company, burned down within hours of their dismissal. This structure had been used to provide a range of services for local people and as a chapel by the district's Primitive Methodists. Little remained of the building and the damage reportedly cost £1,200. Shortly after the fire, police arrested the two men at the Black Horse public house in Camden Road, Tunbridge Wells. The two found bail of £50. A few days later they appeared before the magistrates at Tonbridge, the High Brooms district then being outside the boundaries of Tunbridge Wells.

In the event they were lucky. A shopkeeper in the Silverdale Road area who had sold two men a pint of oil and some matches could not identify the men in the dock as her customers and, following a suggestion by their solicitor, W C Cripps that the fire could have been an accident, the men were acquitted. The fact that they had assisted in putting the fire out may have helped their case, and it is likely that Weare had made enemies in the area, as he earlier had among the Secularists as a result of his role in the prosecution of Edwards. A large crowd, many of whom must have come from High Brooms or Tunbridge Wells to Tonbridge, attended the hearing and cheered the verdict, though the officials present suppressed this as quickly as possible. There is no evidence that the SDF's members had contact with either men, or even had been active in the High Brooms district, yet it is significant that the employers in the town already regarded the new political party as a threat. The association between arson and socialism, reinforced by several subsequent incidents, would dog the branch for the next few years.[95]

W C Cripps

---

[95] *The Tunbridge Wells Gazette February 19th 1886 and February 26th 1886, The Tunbridge Wells and Tonbridge Weekly Express and West Kent Journal February 23rd 1886 and March 2nd 1886, The Tunbridge Wells Journal February 18th 1886. For social crimes see Rule, J., "Social Crime in the Rural South in the Eighteenth and Early Nineteenth Centuries," Southern History 1 (1979): 135–53.*

THE CAPITALIST'S TEN COMMANDMENTS.

I.

I am Capital, thy Master, that brought thee out of the Land of Liberty into a State of Slavery. Thou shalt not become thine own Master nor have any other Masters but me.

II.

Thou shalt not create any wealth, nor any likeness of any wealth that is in Heaven above, or that is in Earth beneath, or that is in the waters under the Earth, unless I can make a profit out of it. Thou shalt bow thyself down under my oppression and serve me, for I, Capital, am a jealous Master and visit the poverty of the fathers upon the children unto the third and fourth generation of those that create wealth for me, and show mercy unto the thousands of sycophants that love me and help me to share the spoils of Labour.

III.

Thou shalt not produce wealth for thyself, for I, Capital, will not hold him guiltless that attempts to do so in vain.

IV.

Keep the Labour Days, and sanctify them, as I, Capital, have commanded thee, lest I throw thee out of employment. Four-and-a-half days thou shalt work for me, and one-and-a-half for thyself. But the seventh day is a rest day for Labour to recoup his strength. In it thou shalt not do any work, thou, nor thy son, nor thy daughter, nor thy wife, unless they be menial servants or administer to my comforts. And remember that thou art my slave, therefore do not attempt to enjoy thyself lest thou over-exert thyself and be unable to produce a profit for me next week.

V

Honour Landlordism and Usury, my co-partners, as I, Capital, have commanded thee, that thy days may be short in the Land in which thou art born.

VI.

Thou shalt commit murder for my sake only.

VII.

Thou shalt give thy daughters in prostitution and thy wife in adultery to me.

VIII.

Thou shalt not steal, that being the right divine of capital.

IX.

Thou shalt bear false witness against thy neighbour—if he be a Socialist.

X.

Thou shalt not desire the full produce of thy labour, neither shalt thou covet the Land of thy birth, nor the stored-up wealth of past generations, nor the idleness, luxury, and privileges of the wealthy, nor anything that is in possession of the capitalist.

(With apologies to Moses.)

W. WILLIS HARRIS.

Socialism and free-thought in Tunbridge Wells can fairly be said to share the same roots. As will be seen, some in the party felt overt atheism made the job of converting the working class British and Irish to socialism far more difficult. In the late 1880s, William Willis-Harris had a spirited attempt at re-writing the Ten Commandments, and this was published as part of a pamphlet in 1893. Others in the branch followed his example. Kathleen Kough moved seamlessly from London freethought in the 1890s to socialism in Tunbridge Wells a decade later, returning to London to become, among other things, Assistant Secretary and a Vice-President of the NSS in 1911. In May 1914 the then Vicar of Holy Trinity, Reverend D J Stather Hunt, claimed to have no problem with socialism as such, but considered the Tunbridge Wells variant unacceptably anti-religious.[96]

---

[96] *The Tunbridge Wells Gazette September 10th 1886; Royle, Radicals, p146;, The Tunbridge Wells Advertiser May 8th 1914; The Courier June 12th 1914.*

Many of those attracted to secularism and socialism in Tunbridge Wells lived in the streets between Goods Station Road and Camden Road. One of these, Commercial Road, is pictured above c1906, while the picture below gives a good impression of the area.

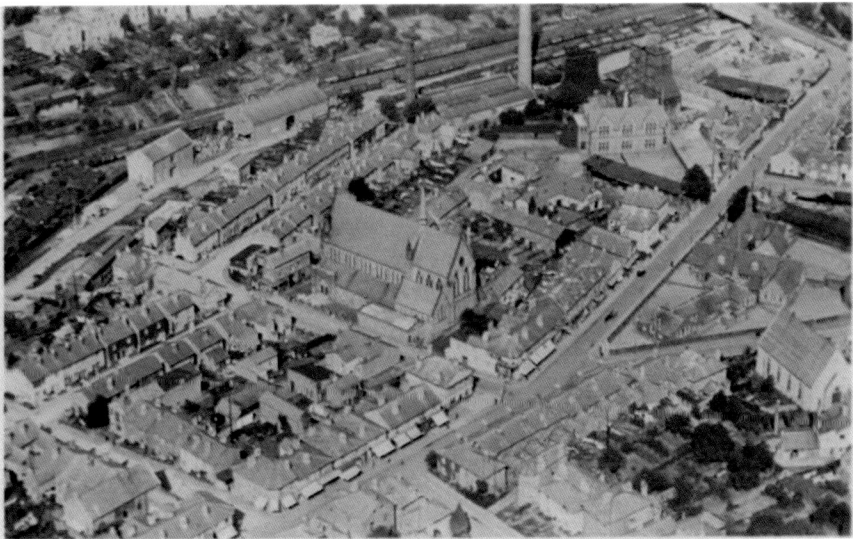

CHAPTER 3   PLANTING THE RED FLAG

Tunbridge Wells had begun to change by the spring of 1886. The unemployed were organising themselves to demand relief, trade unions had struck the previous summer and the National Secular Society's supporters discussed Marxist economics. This organisation, together with the Working Men's Liberal Association, had encouraged considerable numbers of artisans, labourers and tradesmen to become politically active. *Justice* and *Commonweal* circulated in the town. Yet local politics remained either Conservative or Liberal. William Willis-Harris, David Geer, Constance Howell, Tom Jarvis and their friends began to realise that for the first time they had enough support to build a branch of the Social-Democratic Federation. They wrote to the party to organise a series of lectures that summer. Constance Howell later wrote of the way in which they prepared Tunbridge Wells for the new gospel. Members placed the party's penny pamphlets on seats on the Common, dropped leaflets on country roads, handed material to crossing sweepers and placed it in passing wheelbarrows.[97]

Henry Albert Seymour's International Publishing Company printed flyers for distribution around the town. The branch advertised their meetings on eye-catching posters with large black lettering on a red background, and Seymour may well have printed these too. Of even greater significance was their decision to print a range of socialist and anarchist books, including what appears to be the first version of the *Communist Manifesto* to be published in book form in the British Isles. This was a somewhat idiosyncratic effort, largely based on Helen Macfarlane's translation of 1850, and credited to Karl Marx with the assistance of Friedrich

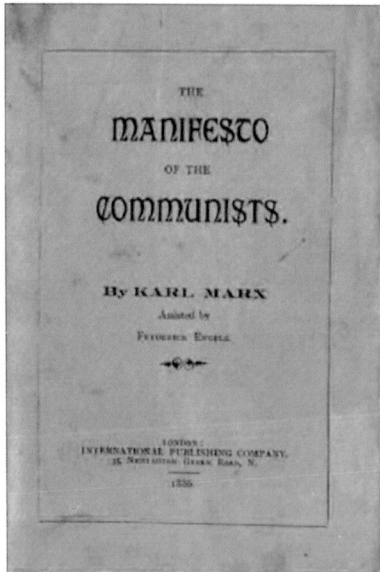

The International Publishing Company's version of the Communist Manifesto, printed in 1886. Reproduced with permission of Dave Cope

[97] Howell, C, A More Excellent Way p 180, p217-8.

Engels. They published this in 1886, suggesting that copies would have been distributed at Tunbridge Wells at early SDF meetings. Residents of the town would therefore have had early access to what would become so familiar a text to future generations of socialists.

These developments in Kent would have delighted the party's leaders. The SDF wished to break out of London to become a national organisation, part of its transformation from a collection of radical associations and clubs into a new, avowedly socialist, party. It therefore put a lot of effort into establishing a foothold in a number of towns and cities across England and Scotland and by early 1886 had established provincial branches at Salford, Bolton and Edinburgh. In contrast to these places, London speakers could travel down to Tunbridge Wells for the day, rather than having to pay for overnight accommodation. Its position on the Kent and Sussex border meant that it could act as a base for building the movement across the south-east. Other characteristics gave the new branch a fair chance of success. The party suffered from chronic poverty, and having William Willis-Harris and Constance Howell, two members with spare money, gave the branch a real advantage. A tradition of free speech on the Common, taken advantage of by religious and political groups for decades, meant that socialists did not face persecution there as they did in many other places.[98]

Careful preparation paid off. On 10th July 1886 *Justice* announced that two meetings would take place the next day, a Sunday. Tom Mann, one of the leading socialists and trade unionists of the late nineteenth and early twentieth centuries, lectured twice at 11.30am and 3.00pm. *Justice* reported that his speeches drew a good response:

'The first Socialist lecture delivered in Tunbridge Wells was given on Sunday morning by Thomas Mann, who lectured on 'social democracy' on the Common to above 350 very attentive listeners. In the afternoon he had an audience of from 1,200 to 1,500 and was well received, his subject being an 'eight-hour day'. During the day we sold all the literature we had, i.e. 81 Justices, 25 Christian Socialists and 234 one-penny pamphlets. All the Justices went in the morning and there was a great demand for

---

[98] *Crick, History, p45, p47; Brown, S., in Cunningham, J., Ed., The Nonconformist Churches and Chapels of Tunbridge Wells (Tonbridge: Royal Tunbridge Wells Civic Society Occasional Papers No. 2) P17.*

57

more, the literature being literally scrambled for. The series of lectures which will be delivered at Tunbridge Wells promises to be very successful and there is every possibility that a strong branch will be formed'[99].

Mann proved an excellent choice as debut speaker. A contemporary described his performances as 'relentlessly energetic, mentally mercurial and fiercely and torrentially denunciary'. The growth in audience size for the afternoon meeting suggests that some had been sufficiently impressed to bring their friends and relatives with them; audiences may also have been swelled by those leaving religious services or staying in the hotels which lined Mount Ephraim. The speeches certainly proved impossible for the local press to ignore. A month after his speech, he responded to a hostile article carried in the Liberal *Tunbridge Wells Advertiser*. A copy of his letter, sent at some point in the 1940s by David Geer to Dona Torr, Mann's biographer, has survived in the archives of the CPGB.[100]

Tom Mann

A summer and autumn of open-air lectures followed. Unfortunately we know little about them other than the title and the name of the guest speaker. Some tackled economic themes from a Marxist perspective, such as 'why are the workers poor and the idlers rich?', 'the iron law of wages', 'living to work' and 'working to live', together with others on unemployment and international affairs. A handful discussed political theory, such as one on the 'fallacies of political democracy'. A NSS speaker lectured one Sunday in July, possibly as no socialist could be booked, though the lectures on the Ten Commandments and the Roman Catholic Church received merely a

---

[99] *Justice Saturday July 17th 1886.*
[100] *Saunders, W., Early Socialist Days (London: Hogarth Press 1927), p53; CPGB Archive, Dona Torr papers.*

'patient hearing'. A better response greeted another secularist that September. The SDF's own meetings almost certainly far exceeded the expectations of the branch's founders. Similar crowds to those which had greeted Tom Mann attended on 25th July, despite heavy rain. 14s 6d worth of literature was sold. At another of the meetings, in early September, sales amounted to 170 copies of *Justice* and 36 pamphlets. To put these figures in perspective, it was a matter of rejoicing for the Hastings branch of the same party twenty-one years later when sixty copies of *Justice* were sold. Meetings could on occasions be a lively affair. John Fielding's lecture on 8th August was interrupted by a man described in the report to *Justice* as a 'well-fed exploiter'. Angered by the speeches, he made a desperate attempt to disrupt proceedings by calling for 'three cheers for the Queen'. This failed miserably, being very effectively countered by an enthusiastic 'three cheers for the proletariat'.[101]

Constance Howell's *'A More Excellent Way'* contains a fine description of one of the meetings held in the late summer of 1886. Although the Common is now far more wooded, and the growth of road traffic means that livestock has long vanished from it, the location, on the slopes near to the Mount Edgcumbe Hotel, is instantly recognisable:

[The] Common was not an ordinary common; it was an extensive stretch of moorland, grassy and covered in some parts with bracken, gorse and blackberry bushes; at this time of year it was generally a good deal burnt by the sun, but there had been rain lately and the landscape was green and fresh...

[The speaker] and his friends walked along the upper road that headed the common, and presently came in sight of what they called his pulpit. It was a flat piece of rock that jutted out from a mass of rocks and overhang a small valley where most of his audience were assembled. They were there ready, waiting for him, standing in a compact crowd; and further off, on slopes and knolls, were groups sitting or lying on the grass; and opposite to the "pulpit", on a rising ground stood other thick rows of people; and scattered about the rocks near to where he was to stand were more men and boys. Altogether, there must have been over a couple of thousand persons. A pile of literature, which the lecturer

---

101 *Justice July 24th & 31st 1886, August 7th ,14th& ,21st & 28th 1886; The National Reformer July 25th 1886, September 11th 1886; The Courier October 1st 1886.*

had brought with him, lay upon the grass in readiness to be sold; and several members, distinguishable by a crimson rosette, were moving among the crowds with handfuls of pamphlets and doing a good trade...

He had understood beforehand what sort of audience it would be; it was of all classes, all ages, and both sexes, but the majority were men of business, professional men and men of independent means. The artisans and labourers formed the mass in the dell,

A photograph of the Common showing how much more open it was before the practice of grazing livestock ended

and also formed the background, standing on the rocks up against the blue sky; while the better-off people were those opposite to him on the rising ground and slopes. The former were loudly friendly, the latter silently hostile. And there was another numerous section who were neither friends nor enemies, but curious or indifferent; there were boys playing noisily, there were giggling girls, there were nurses with perambulators and crying babies; and there were dogs barking and even a tame goat bleating'[102].

Most importantly, it is clear that progress followed week after week. Reports flowed into headquarters every few days and would have been in stark contrast to the limited progress made elsewhere. Mark Bevir has recently calculated that the SDF's membership across the British Isle in the 1880s averaged 580, with only about 100 members outside London, though this may be an under-estimate. Membership figures for revolutionary parties are notoriously inaccurate even today, but close analysis of one branch, London's Marylebone, suggests that only one-third of the 150 paper members were paying their regular subscription. This is perhaps inevitable for any organisation recruiting so much from the ranks of the unemployed, and Tunbridge Wells probably had a similar

---

[102] *Howell, C, A More Excellent Way pp176-180.*

proportion of paying members. Others may not have been able to regularly pay their dues but were active in other ways. Any figures for branch membership should therefore be approached with caution. However, with this qualification, it is interesting that *Justice* reported that 58 people had joined the branch by the end of August, with 18 enrolled in the previous week alone. By mid-September the branch had apparently grown to 98 members.[103]

However questionable these figures may be, they suggest that the branch had become one of the largest in Britain, something backed up by the much more reliable records of literature sold. For a medium-sized, often rather conservative town, this should be recognised as quite an achievement. In early September Henry Mayers Hyndman, speaking to a London audience, used the success of the branch at Tunbridge Wells, together with its equivalents at Northampton, Glasgow and Manchester, to lay claim to be the leader of what could now be considered a genuinely national movement. Yet its enemies soon began to take notice. Bands of thugs were sometimes hired to break up socialist meetings and Constance Howell suggests that there were boycotts of firms employing socialists and the blacklisting of activists by the end of that summer.[104]

Social Democratic
FEDERATION

(Tunbridge Wells Branch.)

TWO LECTURES

Will be delivered on

Tunbridge Wells Common

ON SUNDAY, SEP. 5, 1886,

BY

HUNTER WATTS.

11. 30. a.m. Living to Work.

3. 30. p.m. Working to Live.

You are requested to give in your name to join the branch after the lectures.

International Publishing Company, 35 Newington Green Road, London, N.

An early handbill printed by Henry Albert Seymour in London. From the collection of Andrew Whitehead and used with permission

Who joined the branch in its early days? Most recruits were skilled male workers, such as carpenters and painters, who came

---

[103] Bevir, M, *The Making of British Socialism*, (Princeton, Princeton University Press 2011) p111; Crick, *History*, p37p111; *Justice* August 28th 1886, September 18th 1886.
[104] *Reynold's Newspaper* September 12th 1886; Howell. C. *A More Excellent Way*, p272.

overwhelmingly from the building trades. As such they would have had personal experience of seasonal unemployment. At the same time they had a degree of individual freedom not afforded to men like the park keeper mentioned above. Only a handful came from the very poorest and most lived in the terraces of the Camden Road district rather than the town's worst slums. Most seem to have been in their twenties and thirties. Almost all, it appears, could be considered hard-working, respectable and fairly sober working men by the standards of mid-Victorian England.

What about the women? As Dr Anne Logan has shown, females outnumbered men in Tunbridge Wells. This was not the case in the SDF branch and this remained the position throughout its existence. There are some economic reasons: women more often worked in service or retail than men, and would have put their jobs at risk had they joined the party. The SDF from its foundation was the first political party in Britain to allow women to join as full members and always believed in the enfranchisement of all adults. Several women played leading roles in the development of the branch – Constance Howell and Ada Willis-Harris from the start – but in almost all cases they came from wealthier backgrounds than many of the leading male activists. Women in the two major parties could only join ancillary organisations, such as the Tory Primrose League (which allowed both sexes to enrol) and the Women's Liberal Associations. As will be shown, though, this theoretical commitment to equality sometimes failed in practice.[105]

The branch took questions of gender seriously. Constance Howell, who would later write a novel about the fight for women's suffrage, used arguments advanced by both secularists and socialists such as August Bebel and Friedrich Engels to conclude that organised religion was the tool used to condition both the male working class and all women from early childhood to accept a status as second-class citizens. She also wrote about the prejudice faced by women who wished to become doctors. Perhaps the most telling statistic is that four of the 19 women mentioned by Karen Hunt as leading female Social-Democrats were members in Tunbridge Wells, while

[105] Logan, A., 'Home and Away: Politics and Suffrage in the First World War'; Royle, E, Victorian Infidels: (University of Manchester 1974) p294; Eustance, C. L. Daring to Be Free: The Evolution of Women's Political Identities in the Women's Freedom League 1907 – 1930 (Unpublished doctoral thesis, University of York, 1993) p39-40.

two of the others formed close relationships with the branch in later years.[106]

The men seem to have been fairly enlightened. William Willis-Harris, in an article on the hypocrisy of 'respectable' attitudes towards prostitution, hoped that the socialist revolution would abolish the economic dependence of women on men. There is no evidence within the branch of the misogynistic attitudes encountered elsewhere in the party, though, as these frequently appeared in print, some women may have been discouraged from joining by them. Things may have been worse in other parts of Britain. Margaret Llewellyn Davis, General Secretary of the Women's Cooperative Guild in the 1880s, observed that men in the south proved to be far less hostile to women taking on political roles than their northern equivalents.[107]

By late August the branch had sufficient members to both maintain its activity in Tunbridge Wells and to send small bands of missionaries into the surrounding countryside and neighbouring towns. At this time of year harvesting was at its height and the days were still long enough to allow lengthy walks through the district. George Meek, later to establish socialism in his home town of Eastbourne, recorded his experience of the harvest in Tunbridge Wells in the mid-1880s, when hop and fruit pickers, many from the most deprived districts of London, filled the town's cheaper lodging houses and pubs. In July, *Justice* carried a report about the plight of seasonal fruit pickers in Kent and Surrey, some of whom lived in the neighbourhood but most came from the 'back streets of London'. It is worth mentioning that the East End of London, which provided so many seasonal hop pickers, would through the strikes of the match workers, dockers and gas labourers, lead the way in establishing what is often termed the New Unionism, organising those working in jobs often derided as unskilled. In this context, Constance Howell's observations are significant:

'Some of the pickers were villagers; whole families shut up their houses for the day, put on their worst clothes and went "hopping", returning to their cottages at night. But in other parts, the workers were brought down from London, and it was these who were most to be pitied... The "hoppers" were helpless in a manner which

---

[106] Howell, C., A More Excellent Way p21-22; Gaffin, J. and Thoms, D Caring and Sharing: the Centenary History of the Women's Co-Operative Guild (Manchester: The Cooperative Union 1983) p6.
[107] See in particular, Hunt pp 48-50 and pp119-20; Royle pp 246-50.

concerned themselves, for they were too poor to resist and combine. Hathaway and his friends found them a very mixed company; some were densely ignorant and stupid, while some had heard about Socialism in London, and had glimmerings of what it meant. All received their visitors well, and accepted the literature distributed by them'.[108]

Constance Howell became the first of many socialist authors to visit the hop gardens. Her near-contemporary Margaret Harkness included a similar trip in her novel *In Darkest London,* first published a year later, More famous novelists, including Jack London and George Orwell, later joined the hoppers in Kent. The annual migration of the hop-pickers from London, in decline by the 1950s, is now often shrouded in nostalgia, but Howell's descriptions of the poor living conditions endured by the migrants are borne out by other sources, and her observation that, as it had been a good growing season, some children had made their hands so sore by picking fruit that they were forced to go to hospital, is credible. Conditions had improved somewhat by the middle of the twentieth century, with slightly better housing and some rudimentary medical facilities being provided by the authorities and charities.

Activists from London helped with this work. In August George Bateman spoke at the market in Tonbridge and at 'Swanborough Common' – possibly Southborough or even Swanley. William Willis-Harris, George Bateman and Hunter Watts travelled to East Grinstead a week later. The branch also undertook rambles to distribute material from field to field. In mid-September Ada Bigsby, Tom Jarvis and William Willis-Harris took the train from Tunbridge Wells to East Farleigh, one station before the county town of Maidstone, and 'walked through the hop district distributing Socialist literature'.[109]

The last visit to a village came with a lecture on land nationalisation at Rotherfield, a few miles south-west of the town, in mid-October. Rotherfield had played a significant role during the Swing Riots, with bands of labourers carrying a document declaring, in a proto-socialist phrase, that 'every man should live by his labour', and it is interesting to reflect on whether any of the agitators of 1830 would themselves have been in the audience fifty-six years later. The new

---

[108] *See Meek, George, Bath-Chair Man, by Himself with an introduction by H G Wells (New York, E.P. Dutton and Company 1910) p51; Justice July 31st 1886; Howell, C, A More Excellent Way p213.*
[109] *Justice August 28th 1886 and September 4th 1886.*

socialist gospel had been put before a number of audiences, whether consisting of locals or London migrants, in several places in the Wealden countryside. Only the extremely brave, or those with slightly more economic independence than usual, such as some tradesmen, would have attended these meetings, as the hostility shown towards the Liberals at the 1885 election would in turn be directed against the SDF and other socialists. Merely being in the audience at a socialist meeting in a late 19th Century village was often enough to be dismissed and evicted from a tied cottage.[110]

Two months of hard work culminated on 19th September in Hyndman's first known visit to Tunbridge Wells, and the opening the same day of a Socialist Hall, the first of three in the lifetime of the branch. Hyndman lectured on the 'social revolution' to a well-behaved crowd of about 1,500 on Tunbridge Wells Common. According to some reports the majority in the crowd had come out of curiosity rather than to support him and that even the Tonbridge Division Secretary for the Conservatives had turned up. The sources differ enormously in respect of the amount of socialist material sold; *Justice* claimed that 15s was collected and £1 6s 9d of literature was sold, yet the *Courier* claimed that the collection and sale did not get much interest.[111]

H. M. HYNDMAN.

In contrast to the public speeches on the Common, only members of the SDF and their families, together with a handful of journalists, were invited to the opening of the Socialist Hall, located in a densely-packed district between the Central Goods Yard and Quarry Road. The building, derided as having no architectural interest by one critic, had sufficient capacity for 120 people, and seems to have been full on this night. Other socialist halls established at about the same time had areas devoted to a library and a store operated on

---

[110] *Justice October 30th 1886; Hobsbawm, E. J., and Rudé, F. E., Captain Swing; Justice September 18th 1886; Pye, D. Fellowship Is Life: The National Clarion Cycling Club 1894-1994 (Bolton: Clarion 1995) p38.*
[111] *,Justice September 25th 1886; The Tunbridge Wells Journal September 23rd 1886; Tunbridge Wells Gazette September 24th 1886.*

Cooperative principles and this may well have been true of the Tunbridge Wells one.[112] Constance Howell recorded the appearance of its interior in some detail.

> *'The hall was a wooden building over a stable, and when the local Salvation Army occupied it, it had been little better than a shed; but the Socialists had hired it for a year; and they had mended and painted and whitewashed, had made a temporary ceiling, and had furnished the room with forms and a platform and table, entirely by voluntary labour. Across the rafters were stretched red cloth, on which were painted, in black and white letters, the mottoes "Work for All and Overwork for None", "Educate, Organise, Agitate", "Liberty, Equality, Fraternity" and "Vive la Revolution Sociale".*
>
> *The opening night was quite a gala night. As [the speaker] ascended the rather damaged steps, a red light was burned, the piano inside struck up the Marseillaise, and he entered a pretty-looking hall hung with colourful lanterns, ornamented with portraits of Karl Marx and Ferdinand Lassalle and of those speakers of the [SDF] who had suffered for the cause, and densely filled with an enthusiastic audience who cheered him lustily'*[113].

The newspaper accounts confirm most of these points and record that Ada Willis-Harris marked Hyndman's arrival at the Hall by playing the *Marseillaise*. The *Courier* reported his speech in some detail, in particular his call for a red international to seize all the machinery of the Metropolis. Hyndman then declared war on the middle and upper classes and concluded by attacking some of the leading landowners of the district, suggesting some local knowledge (he may indeed have played cricket for Sussex with some of them in the 1860s).

According to Constance Howell, the meeting ended with the singing of Edward Carpenter's then-new socialist anthem *England, Arise*. In an intriguing coincidence, the baptism of Siegfried Sassoon, who briefly re-enters this story in 1917, took place at the church of St Stephen's, a temporary building immediately adjacent to the Socialist Hall, on Sunday 10th October, exactly three weeks later and a day on which meetings would also have taken place. Sassoon,

[112] See Saunders, W., *Early Socialist Days* pp14-15.
[113] Howell, C, *A More Excellent Way* p187.

a great admirer of Edward Carpenter's work, later wrote to him to thank him for helping him to come to terms with his sexuality.[114]

The contempt shown towards the SDF soon turned to fear. On 8th October, two adjacent shops, 107 and 109 Camden Road, had paraffin poured through the letterboxes. The attacker then dropped in bits of burning newspaper. These fires extinguished themselves before much damage was done. Several doors further down, at Mr Rundle's furniture warehouse at number 127, about a gallon of oil was poured into the premises and pieces of burning silk pushed through. Again this failed to spread, though this was merely a matter of luck. A bottle of paraffin was found on the doorstep of this shop, though it could not have held the quantity of accelerant used. This was wrapped in a draper's bill, to which the words 'socialism', 'fire' and 'treason' had been added in red and black letters, probably in an effort to replicate the Federation's handbills and posters.[115]

The town's newspapers carefully avoided blaming the branch directly for the crimes, though they trawled carefully through the events of the last few weeks. The SDF had written to the Local Board to request relief works for the unemployed; the Board's response was negative. This, some supposed, might have motivated a supporter to commit such crimes. The *Courier* condemned the revolutionary harangues being delivered on the Common. Two speakers in particular, Andrew Hall, and John Burns, came under attack. Hall, in a particularly militant speech,

107 and 109 Camden Road today

had allegedly called for a raid on Tunbridge Wells with an armed Socialist force and Burns – later to become a Liberal Party cabinet minister – apparently had more knowledge than an innocent person would have of the affair. Both men were unusual amongst the leading members of the party as they came from working class

---

[114] *The Courier September 24th 1886; The Tunbridge Wells Journal September 23rd 1886.*
[115] *Tunbridge Wells Journal October 14th 1886.*

backgrounds[116]. The authorities had become interested by this stage, perhaps even at the Home Office, though no official record has been found. Burns noted that detectives had followed him down on the train from London. One of the key speeches given on the Common in *A More Excellent Way* starts with the orator addressing his audience as 'friends, ladies and gentlemen, policemen and detectives', and this may have been taken from real life.[117]

The authorities in Tunbridge Wells seemed to have had little idea about who may have been responsible. Some noted that a leading member of the branch – possibly Edward Cherill Edwards - occupied a shop in the row that was attacked, making SDF involvement unlikely, and others pointed out that the three tradesmen in the working-class district of the town, all unconnected to one another and none of them involved in any political activity, made poor potential targets.

The SDF almost immediately issued a pamphlet. Sadly no copies of this have survived, although some passages were reproduced in the local press. It singled out the *Courier* as a 'local Tory Rag', condemned the 'rowdies' employed to break up their meetings and denied involvement in the arson attacks, apparently suggesting that a member of the Local Board, the police, or even someone employed by that paper might have been responsible instead. William Willis-Harris also wrote to *the Tunbridge Wells Journal* to express his indignation at the attempts to link his organisation to the 'bogus outrage at a most wanton and villainous attempt at murder on the Camden Road'.

Provincial newspapers across Britain, from Cornwall, Devon and Dorset to Shipley and Manchester, carried reports which associated the Federation with the outrages. The *Beverley and East Riding Reporter* noted that the Social-Democrats had opened a hall in the town, although most examples omitted this fact. The police minute books for the year, which are stored in the Town Hall, do not suggest that they saw the socialists as credible suspects. The police offered a reward of £25 for information leading to an arrest and conviction, though no arrests appear to have been made.[118]

---

[116] See Howell, C, in *a More Excellent Way* and Rowbotham, S, and Weeks, J, *Socialism and the New Life: the personal and sexual politics of Edward Carpenter and Havelock Ellis (London: Pluto Press 1977) p63.*

[117] *The Courier October 22nd 1886; Howell, C., A More Excellent Way p180.*

[118] *The Courier October 13th & 29th 188;, Tunbridge Wells Journal October 14th 1886.*

To this day the arson attacks remain a mystery. In hindsight the wording on the paraffin bottle has rather more in common with bonfire night, with socialism, fire and treason replacing gunpowder, treason and plot, than with any serious revolutionary message. The youth of Tunbridge Wells had long amused themselves by setting light to the furze on the Common, and this may have been an escalation of such behaviour. A youthful prank, though with potentially extremely serious consequences, may well be the most likely explanation. Events over the next couple of years, as we will see, add weight to this possibility.

Despite this, William Willis-Harris's fear that *agents provocateurs* may have been responsible is not entirely fanciful. Henry Hyde Champion much later wrote that, two days after the acquittal of the Federation's speakers following the Trafalgar Square riots, a mysterious visitor had turned up at his rooms claiming to be the caretaker of a warehouse full of kerosene on the banks of the Thames. Had they been convicted, every drop would have been poured into the river to burn all the shipping in it.

Likewise, George Bernard Shaw noted that agitators who 'preserved friendly relations with the police' had 'threatened to set London on fire' simultaneously at 'the Bank, St Paul's, the House of Commons, the Stock Exchange and the Tower' during the lengthy occupation of Trafalgar Square in 1887. Accusations of incendiarism had dogged the socialist movement since the Communards of Paris had resorted to the tactic out of desperation in their fight for their city in 1871, and a speaker at a public meeting spoke of an unsuccessful socialist plot to burn down Vienna.[119]

Whatever the explanation, publicity, even of this dubious nature, brought benefits. According to *Justice*, 2,000 people had listened to the speaker on 3rd October, five days before the arson attacks, their audience doubling to 4,000 a fortnight later. These figures may have been generous as the *Tunbridge Wells Journal* claimed that between 2,500 and 3,000 attended on the 17th.[120] Not all of those listening can have been hostile, as the collection of 17s 6d at this

---

[119] *Champion, H., H., Quorum Pars Fui – An Unconventional Autobiography (originally printed in 1908) and the very useful introduction by Andrew Whitehead, Society for the Study of Labour History: Bulletin No. 47 (Autumn 1983) p27; Shaw, G. B., 'The Fabian Society; in Essays in Fabian Socialism p133 (London, Constable and Company 1949); The Courier October 29th 1886; The Tunbridge Wells Journal October 21st 1886; Howell, C., p272.*
[120] *Justice October 9th & 23rd 1886; the Tunbridge Wells Journal October 21st 1886.*

second meeting demonstrates.[121] Both the arson attacks and the growing crowds attending these meetings led to further action being taken against the socialists. There were calls for political gatherings on the Common to be banned. Others organised anti-socialist meetings, with the town's Debating Club discussing the motion that socialist economics were wrong-headed and likely to have a pernicious effect on the minds of the young and inexperienced. More heat than light resulted. One speaker had at least read the Federation's 'Socialist Catechism', but most of the others merely parroted the right-wing view that poverty was self-inflicted.[122]

Workmen clearing snow from the streets of Tunbridge Wells, date and street unknown. This was the standard form of relief offered to alleviate winter unemployment.

---

[121] *The Courier October 22nd 1886.*
[122] *The Courier October 29th 1886; The Tunbridge Wells Journal October 21st 1886; Howell, C., p272.*

CHAPTER 4   THE RADICAL ALLIANCE
AND THE COOPERATIVE SOCIETY

One of the great divisions of mid-Victorian radicalism concerned the question of the unemployed. Those who became socialists tended to argue that the nature of capitalism meant that there could never be enough work for all. Others, many of whom remained members of the Liberal Party, and including several leading secularists, considered the workless to often be the author of their own misfortune. All parts of the socialist movement believed that society, whether acting at the municipal level or through the state, had a duty to provide public works to alleviate unemployment, whereas more individualistic opinion felt that such intervention could undermine personal liberty if it went too far. These men looked towards emigration as an alternative way of reducing unemployment, something which the Kent and Sussex Agricultural Labourers Union had long championed locally but which the Social-Democrats consistently opposed. Both, even if for different reasons, supported schemes such as co-operation, and, in some cases, collective action through trade unions.

As the nineteenth century drew to a close, the socialist perspective tended to gain ground, the Liberal Party itself adopting a more interventionist position with the Newcastle Programme, though their failure to put this into practice when in government after 1892 lost them support. William Bournes, a veteran trade unionist from Tunbridge Wells, shows this evolution. A native of Chatham and a generation older than many of those who first embraced socialism in Tunbridge Wells, he joined the House Painters and Decorators Union in the late 1870s. The branch elected him Vice-Chair in 1885. In October 1892 he spoke in opposition to socialist plans to tackle unemployment, though a few years later he joined the SDF and became one of the branch's leading members.[123]

The SDF, therefore, had every reason to throw itself into a campaign against unemployment. On Friday 18th November a delegation led by a Mr Hobbs, an out of work painter, walked to Pembury to lobby the Guardians of the Tonbridge Union Workhouse. The following Tuesday about 100 or 150 people assembled at the Social-Democratic Hall. Banners, some of which had previously been displayed in the Hall, included 'we want work and not charity', 'work for all' and 'over-work for none' – the latter being a reference

---

[123] *Tunbridge Wells Gazette May 15th 1885; The Courier October 28th 1892.*

71

to the Federation's manifesto demand for an eight hour day. The group was led by the Federation's 'huge' red flag, followed by a black flag. Two police officers accompanied the procession. From Camden Road the marchers made their way to the upper-middle class Broadwater Down, returning via the Frant Road and Pembury Road. Some felt that this black flag had a sinister meaning, possibly even being an anarchist symbol, though it had long been used as an emblem by the unemployed.

These marches lend support to the number of members claimed by the SDF at Tunbridge Wells. Both the *Tunbridge Wells Journal* and the *Maidstone and Kentish Journal* wrote that most of the participants were members of the SDF. The march ended with a meeting at the Town Hall. Some nonconformist ministers attended in support. In an attempt to distance the unemployed from the socialists, the meeting's Chair stated that if the unemployed became 'in any way associated with the Social Democrats', the 'hearts and the pockets' of the town's richer citizens would close. Arguments and barbs against Canon Hoare followed. At the end of the meeting, 150 of those present, mainly socialists, held their own impromptu rally on the Common.[124]

The pressure continued. A socialist delegation visited the Local Board on 1st December to further press the case of the unemployed. The Board accepted that the situation had become so bad that some works would be commissioned. Despite this positive response, the protests continued. In early December a torch-lit procession of the unemployed threaded its way through the town's streets. Work commenced on a new sewage plant in Rusthall, and 150 men gained jobs there. The branch used this success to their advantage, their 'agents' being sent to this location to recruit new members a month later.

Many others still found themselves out of work. In a repeat of the previous winter, groups of unemployed demanded relief in an intimidating manner, in one case by putting their foot in the door until relief was offered. The Board threatened that arrests could follow. Some of this pressure bore fruit, and in the East Ward, workmen started to transform an area previously used as a

---

[124] *Justice November 27th 1886; Tunbridge Wells Journal November 18th 1886; The Courier, November 24th 1886; the Tunbridge Wells Journal November 25th 1886; Torr, D. Tom Mann and His Times Volume One: 1856-1890 (London: Lawrence and Wishart 1956) p226.*

municipal dump into what would become the Grosvenor Recreation Ground.[125]

A second strand of the branch's work was to offer practical solidarity. They intended this to contrast with the meagre charity offered by the rich and the churches. The SDF requested that its members in work contribute to a fund to provide free breakfasts for the children of the town's unemployed. In practice, much of the money came from William Willis-Harris. Between 100 and 190 breakfasts were served each week at the Social-Democratic Hall from January to March 1887, by which stage seasonal unemployment had eased. The SDF repeatedly argued that local government and the state had a duty to feed the children of the poor, many of whom arrived at school too hungry to learn. This small-scale scheme in Tunbridge Wells emphasised the practicality of the concept.[126]

To the credit of all concerned, the SDF and the Working Men's Liberal Association tried to find common ground, recognising that the Tories would take advantage were left-leaning members of the working class to be divided into two hostile camps. Two organisations, the Radical Alliance, formed at the end of 1886, and the Cooperative Society, established about a year later, forged links between the Social-Democrats, working class left-leaning Liberals and trade unionists. Their fates were very different. The first collapsed amid much acrimony while the second became one of the town's leading businesses. Within a few years a Trades and Labour Council would follow and again prove a success.

The Committee of the Radical Alliance drew its membership entirely from political activists, the seats being split evenly between the Liberal Party, the Social-Democratic Federation and another group of radicals, some of whom may also have been Liberals. There were no positions specifically for trade unionists though the Alliance's Chair, Mr Scrace, was a leading local activist in the Amalgamated Society of House Decorators and Painters. Ordinary meetings took place at the Friendly Societies Hall in Camden Road. Perhaps inevitably this led a shareholder in the hall to complain that the building was drifting into the hands of Radicals and Secularists.

---

[125] *Tunbridge Wells Local Board Minute Book No. 15, Justice December 11th & 25th 1886;, The Courier January 14th 1887; the Tunbridge Wells Journal January 18th 1886.*
[126] *Justice January 22nd & 29th 1887, February 5th ,12th & 26th 1887 and March 5th 1887; Crick, History, p36.*

73

The Alliance had its own flag, combining the Liberal shade of blue and the Socialist shade of red. Both parties had permission to display their own banners at meetings. Both sides seem to have considered it a platform for disseminating their own politics, which could only cause difficulties, though the factions agreed on one rule, that anybody found to be a Conservative would be expelled.[127]

The Friendly Societies Hall

The organisation's first campaign, to which both sides were committed, was to win a public library for the town. By 1887 Tunbridge Wells had fallen behind other towns in Kent and Sussex in this area. Tonbridge, its much smaller neighbour, had opened its first public library in 1882.[128]

A series of public meetings, supported by both the SDF and the Liberal Party, followed. The former came in for much criticism. Some residents felt that public libraries might give socialism a platform, while others only supported them to 'educate the people so they did not listen to the rantings of socialists'. That contributor claimed that the municipal libraries at Birmingham and Manchester had ensured that socialism made little impact there.[129]

Tensions between the Socialists and Liberals grew when the SDF decided to run William Willis-Harris as a candidate for the School Board election. One SDF member attacked the petty-mindedness of other members of the Committee in March for not supporting him.

[127] *The Courier January 5th 1887; the Tunbridge Wells and Tonbridge Weekly Express, the West Kent Journal December 21st 1886.*
[128] *Barker-Read, M, The Tonbridge Local Board in Chalklin, C. W. [Ed.] Mid Victorian Tonbridge (Kent County Council 1983) p7-8.*
[129] *The Courier January 19th 1887; the Tunbridge Wells Journal January 20th 1887; Hobsbawm, E., 'Man and Woman: Images on the Left' in Uncommon People: Resistance, Rebellion and Jazz (London: Weidenfeld and Nicholson 1998) p99.*

In the event he gained 569 votes, a very respectable showing, though not enough to win. [130]

The Alliance, did however, work together to organise a meeting on in favour of Irish Home Rule in mid-April. Unfortunately the audience, at between one and two thousand, fell below expectations. The meeting took place at the usual SDF venue below the rocks near the Mount Edgcumbe Hotel. The organisers arranged a stellar line-up of politicians and activists, including the Irish Nationalist MP for Kilkenny, Mr Chance; the SDF's Tom Mann, and two Liberals, F W Verney, who had stood for the Tonbridge Division of Kent, and J Haysman. The organisers had put a lot of work into preparing the site, erecting a stage and bench covered in green fabric and painting banners carrying shamrocks and slogans including 'Ireland Free shall be our Jubilee'. The SDF erected a red flag surmounted by a cap of liberty in a prominent position near to the Liberal Party's blue banner.

Differences between the speakers, though, led to discord. Tom Mann spoke at length about the record of successive Liberal and Tory governments in Ireland, including a series of pointed remarks about the coercive measures introduced by Gladstone in the first few years of the decade. Heckling from the Liberal camp increased when he turned to calling for a 'Social Revolution' which would guarantee the freedom of both Ireland and Great Britain. A march from the Common through Lime Hill Road to the town centre followed. Local Conservatives lined up to oppose it although the confrontation did not turn violent. The day's proceedings concluded with a meeting at the Friendly Societies Hall. A resolution against coercion passed, though the SDF's attacks on Gladstone came in for criticism, By way of a rejoinder, Tom Mann reminded the Chairman that the SDF had been invited to take part in the meeting as equal partners with the Liberals.[131]

The Tory Party viewed the controversy with delight and flooded the *Courier* with letters designed to put pressure on the Liberal Party to cease co-operation with the Socialists. One claimed that 'the dynamiters and assassins in America' - an attempt to link the SDF with bombings allegedly carried out by anarchists in Chicago – were now 'involved in the meetings of Mr Gladstone's new party'. It seems

[130] *The Tunbridge Wells Journal March 31st 188;, Justice April 16th 1887.*
[131] *The Tunbridge Wells Gazette April 1887; the Tunbridge Wells Journal April 28th 1887; Justice April 30th 1887.*

likely that leading local Liberals used financial pressure to force its working class activists to oppose the Federation. William Willis-Harris wrote to the moderately Liberal *Gazette* and the Tory *Courier* to highlight the hypocrisy of censoring socialism at an *anti-coercion* meeting. He attacked the 'Whigs' – a pointedly archaic description – and called on radicals within the party to join the Socialists to form a strong party along the lines of the German SPD. Only the Tory paper printed his letter.

The non-socialists in the Alliance hesitated for a few weeks but then decided to expel the SDF's members of the Committee. This was explained by saying that, as the SDF had not pledged to support the Liberal Party, they might leave them 'in the lurch' at a future election. Following this decision, Tom Jarvis and David Geer wrote to the town's press to argue that as the word radical derived from the Latin 'pertaining to the root', radicalism had evolved into socialism.[132]

Vitriolic attacks followed. Many were laughably ill-informed. The Treasurer of the Tunbridge Wells branch of the Salvation Army circulated a pamphlet in April called *Christianity or Infidelity; which?* This purported to be written by a local secularist who had found God, and was rapidly debunked. Two months later a local evangelical minister, Mr Cowley, attacked socialism as a sham and the work of Jesuits, an interesting but unconvincing claim. There are occasional hints of violence being deployed to force the socialists to abandon meetings; the branch praised one speaker in July for dealing with the opposition in a 'very able manner', and this may not have been purely verbal.[133]

In response, Constance Howell wrote a long letter to the *Courier*. When transcribed, Marx became 'Marie', something which can only have been deliberate. She noted that many of the town's working class had read Gronlund's *Cooperative Commonwealth* and recommended that local tradesmen and gentlemen should read Engels, 'Larsalle', Bebel, Gronlund, Kropotkin, Reclus and Hyndman. The letter ranged over a number of topics; the temperance movement, popular at the time, provided no solution to poverty, as if all men became teetotallers there would no longer be a

---

[132] *The Courier April 27th 1887; Letter from Willis-Harris to the Courier May 29th 1887; Letter from Willis-Harris to the Tunbridge Wells Gazette May 6th 1887; Tunbridge Wells Gazette May 20th 1887, Tunbridge Wells Journal May 19th 1887.*
[133] *The National Refor;er, April 24th 1887; The Courier June 22nd 1887; Justice, July 9th 1887.*

competitive advantage to it and wages would fall, a theme later developed by her in *A More Excellent Way*. Being both a woman and a socialist, it is clear that the *Courier*'s editor refused to take her views seriously.[134]

The SDF's annual conference was far more positive. The annual report highlighted the branch's victories, in particular the marches of the unemployed, their success in getting the Rusthall sewage farm built to provide jobs, and their role in organising the meeting in favour of Irish home rule.[135]

Harry Quelch

For the second successive year the branch sent emissaries to nearby towns and villages in the summer months. At the same time they maintained the pattern of two meetings on the Common most Sundays. Members of the SDF twice lectured at Rotherfield in July. They also visited the hop gardens, which had been damaged by severe gales, in August or September. Other venues and times in Tunbridge Wells were tried. Harry Quelch spoke outside the Grosvenor Hotel, near Willis-Harris's shop, as well as twice on the Common one Saturday. The branch formed a close working relationship with Quelch which lasted several decades. Twenty-six years later David Geer, together with the much younger Katherine Veals, joined his funeral procession, reportedly a quarter-mile long, from his former house in Nunhead to his grave at Camberwell Cemetery at Forest Hill.[136]

The most significant efforts involved an attempt to establish a presence, and perhaps an independent branch, at Tonbridge. Regular meetings took place at the Angel Hotel, then one of the town's principal public houses, from September 1887, and these continued for several weeks. On 15th October *Justice* carried reports from meetings at both towns (a lecture by a Mr Hobart had been disrupted by some 'Tonbridge rowdies'). No other town in south-east England outside London was mentioned. They also pushed for

---

[134] *The Courier June 17th 1887*.
[135] *Justice, August 13th 1887*.
[136] *Justice, September 27th 1913*.

support for the town's unemployed at a public meeting, leading the Tonbridge Local Board to create a register of those out of work.[137]

This work of the socialists briefly revived the Tunbridge Wells and Tonbridge branch of the National Secular Society. About 1,500 people listened to two open-air lectures in October. A leading local clergyman 'listened to the logic and scientific arguments adduced' and failed to counter the speaker's points. Yet when Stewart Headlam spoke at the Friendly Societies Hall a few weeks later it was now on behalf of the Social-Democratic Federation rather than the NSS. About 200 attended. Arguing that all parishes should be centres of democratic socialism, he called for land nationalisation and for an eight hour day. It is hard to resist the conclusion that by this stage the majority of local secularists had joined the socialist movement.[138]

An interesting insight into these meetings comes from the diaries of George Bernard Shaw who visited the SDF branch in December to give his lecture on 'the rent of ability'. Unlike others, who travelled to and from the town the same day, he decided to spend some time in the town. His diary entry reveals that he left London by the 2.45 train from Charing Cross, spent the night at the house of William and Ada Willis-Harris, where he read Gronlund's *Ca Ira* and wrote some letters, before returning to London on the 9.55am train.[139]

The branch again became embroiled in controversy. Tom Jarvis delivered a letter to the Commissioners for their meeting on Wednesday 2nd November 1887. It concluded that:

> *'We would point out to all that the responsibility for any rash actions which hungry men and women may be driven to take rests entirely with you. The class to which you belong imagines that it gains by low wages and excessive competition and some of you probably have become wealthy by swindling the poor out of their wages and rackrenting the hovels they inhabit. These truths we are daily pointing out to those that suffer and it is in your interests*

---

[137]*Justice, July 30th 1887, August 13th 1887, September 10th 1887, October 15th 1887, January 21st 1888..*
[138] *The National Reformer, September 11th 1887 and October 3rd 1887; The Tunbridge Wells Gazette November 25th 1887.*
[139] *Justice, December 17th 1888; Weintraub, Diaries p322..*

to see that the wretched condition does not drive the poor to desperation'.[140]

Contempt, ridicule and some bravado greeted it. The Commissioners debated whether to let it lie on the table or consign it to the wastebasket. The town's papers were no more positive. The *Tunbridge Wells Gazette* condemned its impudence, though it crowed that it 'will show the working classes who their so-called friends are, and by what unscrupulous means they are seeking at their expense to advance their objectionable tenets'.

In the weeks that followed, the local press printed a series of articles about 'socialist outrages' – many of them actually the work of Irish republicans or American anarchists. The *Tonbridge Telegraph* pointed to a 'socialistic armoury' in Chicago comprising of at least one hundred muskets. A series of marches and occupations by London's unemployed the same month ended in bloodshed.

The Commissioner of the Metropolitan Police banned demonstrations in the capital, had hundreds of special constables sworn in and soldiers mobilised to restore order. In the ensuing riots, at least two men died and over a hundred were wounded. A week later Alfred Linnell, almost certainly a bystander rather than a participant, was killed at yet another demonstration in London.[141]

The events which followed seem almost to have been inevitable. On Tuesday 30th November a fire broke out in a house, 81 Upper

Bloody Sunday, Trafalgar Square, 13th November 1887

---

[140] *The Tonbridge Telegraph, November 5th 1887.*
[141] *The Tunbridge Wells Gazette November 4th 1887; The Tonbridge Telegraph, November 19th 1887; Crick, History, p47; Roberts, A. Salisbury: a Victorian Titan (London: Phoenix 2000) p470.*

79

Grosvenor Road. This was immediately assumed to be arson. A second attack followed the same week, though details are sparse. Fire then claimed a villa called Hollybank in Crescent Road on 5th December. This may have been intended to send a signal to Canon Hoare, a neighbour. Hoare retaliated by denouncing socialism at the next meeting of the town's Tradesmen's Association. The fire brigade recorded the cause as unknown, yet the *Tunbridge Wells Gazette* believed that someone had used a ladder to climb onto the roof, remove tiles, pour an accelerant in and set light to the property.

A nearby property, owned by Mr Vigor, had paraffin and matches thrown through the letterbox, though with little damage. The same method was used at an empty property owned by a contractor, Mr Judd, in Queens Road and, potentially most seriously, to try and burn down the Baltic Sawmills in Goods Station Road. Other suspected arson attacks over a few days hit the premises of a coal and coke dealer (probably adjacent to the South Eastern Railway's yard nearby) and a jeweller's shop somewhere in the town. The *Tonbridge Telegraph* concluded its report by stating that many feared for the safety of property in Tunbridge Wells and that the police had offered a £50 reward for information leading to the conviction of the perpetrators.[142]

The SDF, of course, denied any involvement. They repeated the tactics used so successfully the previous winter, with lobbying of the Town's Commissioners and the Poor Law Guardians at Pembury Workhouse. Yet they capitalised on the fear generated by the arson attacks. A delegation consisting of David Geer, Tom Jarvis and Samuel Price, accompanied by a crowd hovering outside, visited tradesmen who were also Commissioners. They stated that they wished to merely cause inconvenience, rather than loot shops or break windows, but the authorities warned Jarvis that his speeches came close to incitement to riot and that he faced prosecution if he failed to moderate his tone. Yet, despite the *Courier* claiming that unemployment only affected 150 or 200 that year, the board relented and agreed to the Federation's demand that it raise a loan for public works. This sum of £3,200 ensured that 70 or 80 men gained work for a few weeks.

---

[142] *The Tonbridge Telegraph December 3rd 1887;, The Tunbridge Wells Gazette December 9th 1887; the Tunbridge Wells Journal December 1st & 8th 1887; The Tunbridge Wells Gazette December 9th 1887; The Tonbridge Telegraph December 10th 1887.*

The less fortunate could still hope for a free breakfast. William Willis-Harris and Constance Howell made the biggest contributions to pay for these, though a list of other subscribers included David Geer, Albert Geer, W Mason, W J Tubbs, W Eastland and a supporter from Tonbridge, T Potter. Many of these were either already active or were to play a leading role in the branch for years to come. William Willis-Harris, burnishing his secularist credentials, contrasted the way in which socialists had cooperated to provide free meals to the needy with the 'pseudo-Christianity with which we are sated'. Money had long been poured into churches but not to alleviate the deprivation suffered by so many of the town's working class children.

Such work had an impact on their opponents. The Local Board joked -uneasily – about what to do with flags left over from the Jubilee celebrations, one member suggesting that the black ones had already been given to the SDF. A public meeting heard that the town had a 'tendency towards socialism', though one commissioner hoped it was untrue that one street was now populated exclusively by members and supporters of the party.[143]

The branch celebrated the turning of the year in fine style. Constance Howell, Ada Willis-Harris and Mrs Price organised what they intended to make an annual supper and 'reunion'. This was a rare division of labour on traditional gender grounds. The men painted the banners, which read 'vive la revolution sociale' and 'liberty, equality, fraternity'. A journalist from the *Tunbridge Wells Advertiser* attended, along with forty or fifty members of the branch. A single long table covered in 'various substantial viands' ran the length of the building. From the report it seems a convivial occasion; the growing enthusiasm given to the successive toasts to 'the workers of the world', 'the red flag', 'the prisoners of the cause in all parts of the world' and 'most enthusiastically the social revolution', suggest that the ale and wine flowed freely. At the end, William Willis-Harris declared that 'the blood of the martyrs should be the seed of the socialist cause' and condemned Government coercion in Ireland and England.[144]

---

143 For the above paragraphs see *The Tonbridge Telegraph December 17th 1887, The Tunbridge Wells Journal, December 15th & 29th 1887, Justice January 7th 1888* and *February 4th 1888; Tunbridge Wells Advertiser January 27th 1888; Tunbridge Wells Advertiser January 8th 1888; The Courier February 3rd 1888*.
144 *Tunbridge Wells Advertiser January 13th 1888; Justice, January 7th 1888.*

81

A special meeting followed a few days later, addressed by an English socialist, A S Headingly, and Aleksandr Lavrenius, an anarchist 'comrade from Russia'. Headingly outlined the way in which the demand for an eight hour day had been made in different countries, rejected calls to limit immigration and declared that once international socialism was established, war between countries would be eliminated. Headingly remained interested in Russia and twenty years later translated a speech by Leon Trotsky into English, though after 1917 he became extremely anti-Bolshevik. Lavrenius's speech is lost to posterity, though something of the man can be gauged by his subsequent activity. Eighteen months later the French authorities jailed him for a bomb plot, and after his release, he travelled to the United States.[145]

Willis-Harris's relationship with Henry Albert Seymour had changed by this stage. *The Anarchist* had deteriorated as Seymour's racial theories and hobby horses made their appearance. Dividing domestic news into 'Keltic' and 'Teutonic' may have been no more than a harmless eccentricity, but his comment in September 1887 that Jews had murdered millions through usury makes uncomfortable reading (and would have lost support in the émigré communities in the East End). Many secularists, socialists and anarchists felt his advocacy of free love had handed ammunition to their opponents. The *Anarchist* had also delighted in attacking the National Secular Society, Socialist League and SDF. A rival anarchist publication, *Freedom*, also took much of the market.

Seymour, who seems to have been most comfortable as a big fish in a relatively small pond, lost no time in attacking it. He also fell out spectacularly with Benjamin Tucker, who had been a big influence on Seymour in previous years. Seymour warned any remaining readers in June 1887 that the International Publishing Company would soon become a one-man operation. The paper only appeared sporadically after this. In March 1888 he told subscribers that William Willis-Harris owned much of the plant and planned to sell it. Interestingly, he praised Willis-Harris for his sacrifice of time and money and declared their friendship intact 'apart from their respective opinions'.[146]

---

[145] *Justice, January 14th 1888*; Kendall, W., 'Russian Emigration and British Marxist Socialism' in the International Review of Social History, December 1963 (Cambridge University Press), pp 351 – 378 p359.
[146] *The Anarchist, June 1887, September 1887, March 1888*

Some good came from this. Seymour's swallowing of pseudo-scientific ideas of race may well have spurred William Willis-Harris to write one of his most important articles, published in *Justice* in April 1888. This article, on the political implications of Charles Darwin's concept of the survival of the fittest, rejected what he considered the misapplication of laws governing nature to human society. Whereas the capitalist could claim that natural selection justified poverty and exploitation, the roots of these were in fact social and economic. Socialism and scientific advance would eliminate them. Co-operation rather than competition would improve physical and intellectual ability.

Imperialists would not have enjoyed his suggestion that adaptation to environments meant that those who came from malarial parts of America or from the West Coast of Africa were better fitted for them than white Europeans. His position is still controversial, though reports of studies such as the one by scientists at America's Princeton University in July 2016 into yeast fungus which concludes that altruism is a better survival strategy than selfishness, still give the debate relevance.[147]

In the context of his own time, Willis-Harris's conclusions have recently been compared to those of Peter Kropotkin, remembered both as an anarchist and a scientist. A series of articles by Kropotkin from 1890, which had much in common with the article by Willis-Harris, led to one of his most important books, *Mutual Aid,* in 1902.[148] There may not have been a direct link, though Kropotkin lived in England throughout this period. As a revolutionary, he may have read *Justice* and the article. If he had done so, the exchange of ideas flowed both ways. In July, William Willis-Harris used one of Kropotkin's earlier works – probably *The Conquest of Bread* - to attack Malthusianism, arguing that instead of starvation there would soon be a 'reign of plenty' under socialism. He argued that evolution was leading to greater intellectual capacity in the population at large, and he even predicted a time when food could be produced synthetically in laboratories.

---

[147] *i, July 27th 2016.*
[148] *Justice, April 28th 1888; see also Hunt, Equivocal Feminists p70; Hale,P, J., Political Descent, p225, p258.*

It is a pity that these points were raised in no more prestigious a forum than the letters page of the *Tunbridge Wells Advertiser.* William Willis-Harris's article set the terms of debate for the rest of the branch's existence. It will be shown that they studied Mutual Aid in the first decade of the twentieth century and rejected the arguments put forward by a pro-eugenicist lecturer on the eve of the First World War. [149]

William Willis-Harris's recovery of some of the capital sunk into the

The view from Upper Stone Street, Tunbridge Wells, in about 1906

International Publishing Company, as well as his decision to move his business from Grosvenor Road to Upper Stone Street, also freed up some money. The impending birth of his first child, named Vera Zassulitsch Willis-Harris after the Russian revolutionary Vera Zasulich perhaps stretched his finances. He also downsized his business and no longer needed the paint shop in Kensington Street. This came at a good time.

The previous autumn, a meeting had been held at the Town Hall to form a Cooperative Society. At this, Willis-Harris argued that this would be more successful than the two previous attempts to set up such a society. A number of others, including William Bournes, spoke in favour of the proposal, in particular as it might allow working class families to be less dependent on credit when out of work. It seems likely that Willis-Harris transferred the Kensington

---

[149] *Tunbridge Wells Advertiser July 13th 1888.*

Road premises to the new society shortly afterwards. The Cooperative also agreed to purchase the adjacent building and constructed meeting rooms on the first floor. Hundreds enrolled in the first few months of its existence and it rapidly attained a secure financial position.[150]

The growth of the Cooperative Society beyond Kensington Street is one of the most important and long-lasting legacies of the SDF's first years at Tunbridge Wells. Within a few years it had become the town's largest retailer and over the next quarter-century it opened branches across the town at London Road and St James Road and in suburbs such as High Brooms, Rusthall and Southborough. The society also established two large and well-equipped bakeries at High Brooms and Tunnel Road and had a coal depot and sidings at

Kensington Street, Tunbridge Wells.
Now part of a re-aligned Victoria Road.

the Central Goods Yard. Road and rail transport followed, with the society constructing stables at the Tunnel Road site and having its own carts and railway wagons.

The Society retained its independence until April 1946, when it merged with the Brighton Society. At the time of writing, the

---

150 *The Courier September 30th 1887; Tunbridge Wells Advertiser March 30th 1888.*

Cooperative, much merged since then, still retains a store in Silverdale Road, established before the First World War, though on a slightly different site. Yet the cultural impact of the Society is as important as its commercial success. Annual children's fetes and parades, meetings of the branch of the Women's Cooperative Guild – which met weekly by 1892 - and the performance of music, songs and plays in the rooms above the Kensington Street shop gave it a role far beyond the merely political. At the same time, Social-Democratic Federation members, especially David Geer and Tom Jarvis, played a leading role in the organisation, in particular on the Education Committee, and socialists and trade unionists regularly used the meeting rooms for lectures and debates.[151]

Yet, as one correspondent to the *Tunbridge Wells Journal* reflected, many in the town hated the light. A referendum in March determined the library question. A series of meetings in February, supported by the SDF and the Liberal Party, again made the case for a positive vote. However the opponents of the scheme won by 1,003 votes. William Willis-Harris came in for some particularly personal attacks. There was some controversy over the validity of the poll. Of the 4,800 householders in the town, 1,500 were not wealthy enough to qualify for a vote, and, of the 3,322 ballot papers distributed, 150 were not delivered. Remarkably the referendum settled the matter for three decades or so and the town only provided a free public library in the 1920s. [152]

[151] Richardson, W., *Brighton Cooperative Society – The People's Business* (Brighton c1984) p60, 151; *Kelly's Directories (various)*.
[152] See *The Courier* March 16th 1888; *Tunbridge Wells Journal* March 15th 1888; *Tunbridge Wells Advertiser* March 19th 1888; *Justice* March 10th 1888; *The Tunbridge Wells Journal* February 17th 1887; *The Courier* Febru,ary 3rd 1888.

CHAPTER 5   A FIGHT FOR THE FUTURE OF SOCIALISM:
THE TUNBRIDGE WELLS BRANCH
v. HENRY HYDE CHAMPION

The differences between William Willis-Harris and Henry Seymour had little long-term effect on the development of socialism in Britain, but a more significant dispute came to a head at around the same time. The historian Andrew Whitehead has summarised the career of Henry Hyde Champion succinctly and effectively. By the late 1880s he had become one of the most famous socialists of his day, as one of the four members of the SDF put on trial after the riots of February 1886. Soon afterwards he began to have doubts about the direction of his party. In September 1887 he announced, through his own journal *Common Sense*, that he had left the SDF's Executive and would no longer write or lecture for it. He followed this declaration with several pages of cutting criticism. Some of this, such as its numerical weakness (he believed that it only had 689 members), may have been justified, other aspects less so. Champion also argued that an attempt at seizing power through physical force would not succeed, something which the SDF sometimes toyed with at this time, and – in a manner which would not have endeared himself to people like William Willis-Harris and Constance Howell - opposed the hostile attitudes shown towards Christianity. At the same time he argued that he wished to remain a member of the Federation and to reform it from within.[153]

Unsurprisingly this created a lot of controversy. Herbert Burrows accused Champion of trying to damage or sell out the SDF in an exchange which Harry Quelch, as editor, tried to keep out of *Justice*. Allegations of financial impropriety which had swirled around Champion in 1885 re-surfaced. On October 18th Tom Jarvis wrote a long letter to *Common Sense*. He made clear that he spoke only for himself, and had not consulted the Tunbridge Wells branch, but felt that they would decide not to take any copies of the paper at their next meeting. The SDF's Tunbridge Wells branch had, as mentioned previously, sold Champion's earlier *Christian Socialist*. More provocatively, he suggested that one letter, signed merely T.M., might well have been concocted by Champion himself. In

---

[153] *For Champion and the Tunbridge Wells branch, see Champion, H., H., Quorum Pars Fui and in particular the introduction by Andrew Whitehead; see also Clayton., J., The Rise and Decline of Socialism in Great Britain (London: Faber & Gwyer 1926) p68; Common Sense September 15th 1887.*

conclusion he hoped that all would do their best for socialism and that the truth would prevail.[154]

This argument may not have been greatly important were it not for other developments. Around this time the work of the few thousand socialists active in Britain had begun to influence the much larger trade union movement. In hindsight it is clear that both needed each other. From the late 1870s many unions – such as the Kent and Sussex Labourers' Union - found themselves in difficulties, unable to oppose wage cuts, with falling membership and some of them spending more money than they raised. Higher unemployment, while it gave opportunities for socialist propaganda, reduced the effectiveness of collective bargaining. Some trade unionists took inspiration from the SDF and the Socialist League, which both argued that reducing the working day to eight hours would cut joblessness. In London the idea of an eight hour day won mass support from trade unionists and lively debates followed at the Trades Union Congress that year. Seeing new possibilities, Henry Hyde Champion now openly argued for an alliance between socialists and trade unionists to build a new mass movement, working through the National Labour Electoral Association's London organisation to this end. His work soon led to a split in this organisation between his supporters in the metropolis and others, such as Thomas Threlfall, who wished merely to increase the number of trade unionists standing for the Liberal Party.[155]

The SDF's national leadership has often been blamed for failing to take advantage of the opportunities presented by an alliance between socialists and the unions. Their reading of Marx led them to conclude that trade unions could only marginally improve pay and conditions for the working class. At best they could engender solidarity and lead their members towards socialism. Some Social-Democrats and several trade union leaders did their best to antagonise each other. Yet, largely driven by the work of provincial activists across Britain, the party began to take a more positive view of trade unionism. It seems surprising that leading local Social-Democrats had not already joined trade union branches though this may reflect the dominance of the Liberal Party within the trade

---

[154] *Common Sense October 15th 1887, November 15th 1887.*
[155] *Duffy, A.E.P, 'The Eight Hour Day Movement in Britain 1885-1893 in the Manchester School, Volume 3 Issue 6 September 1968; Common Sense September 15th 1887;, Pelling, H.M., 'H H Champion, pioneer of labour representation' in The Cambridge Journal January 1953 Vol VI No 4 p226-8.*

union movement and the moribund state of many union branches before 1889.

The records for each branch of the Carpenters and Joiners Union survive and have been digitised. David Geer joined the branch on May 18th 1889 though his friend Thomas Cox only did so in October 1892. Other Social-Democrats, such as Tom Jarvis, became members of the Painters and Decorators Union. They used the town's Cooperative Society to demonstrate the case for limiting the working day: the society now closed on Wednesdays yet business thrived. The eight hour day, they argued, would therefore not ruin industry and commerce. In contrast to the middle-class leaders in London, they quickly realised the benefits of a broad labour movement embracing both the trade unions and the socialist parties. In March 1888 William Willis-Harris ran in the local elections, but as a 'Social-Democratic and Labour', rather than a purely SDF candidate. He won 532 votes in the School Board election, which again left him at the bottom of the poll. He had been disqualified by a minor administrative error from standing for the Board of Guardians – many of the candidates had developed a type of gamesmanship sought to prevent their opponents from being allowed to stand on spurious grounds, but Willis-Harris felt that his disqualification was specifically due to his politics.[156]

The Social-Democrats of Tunbridge Wells and Henry Hyde Champion both therefore accepted the logic of a 'labour alliance', but strongly disagreed on how to bring it about. Champion, while still a member of the party, travelled the country to ask Liberal and Conservative candidates to support an eight-hour working day in return for his endorsement as 'labour' candidates. This drew charges of unprincipled opportunism. He made such efforts in many parts of the country but the Tunbridge Wells branch would have been most aware of his efforts in various parts of Kent. In a pamphlet with the pointed title *The New Labour Party*, he recorded that the Liberal candidate for the Thanet parliamentary by-election that summer, Edward Knatchbull-Hugessen, had been persuaded to support a maximum eight hours of work for miners and some other industries. Indeed Knatchbull-Hugessen had agreed in private to support a number of demands, such as universal male suffrage, the payment of Members of Parliament, the right of public demonstrations and some works to relieve unemployment, but

---

[156] See Crick pp75-91; *The Tunbridge Wells Advertiser March 30th 1888, April 27th 1888.*

refused to make this public. Champion's agent told a meeting about this agreement and released a manifesto supporting the candidate. The Conservative won. The affair seems to have caused the SDF some embarrassment as the minutes of the annual conference recorded that the handful of their members in the area had supported Champion's position. Weeks later he repeated the offence by intervening on the side of the Liberal candidate at the by-election in Maidstone. For a party committed, at least on paper, to revolution and at the very least to independence from the two major parties, Champion had watered down its principles to an unforgivable extent.

For the Tunbridge Wells branch this appears to have been the last straw. At some point in the next few months they wrote to the party's Executive to demand Champion's expulsion. The correspondence regarding this does not appear to have survived. Champion used the *Labour Elector* to pour scorn on the SDF, claiming that the issue of his expulsion had engaged the whole attention of the party, which two years ago had been both feared and respected. The Tunbridge Wells branch got their wish in November, though Champion claimed that the twelve-strong majority had not reached the two-thirds required for such a decision. To avoid any doubt, he sent in a letter formally resigning from the party. Perhaps significantly, the Labour Electoral Association had also passed a resolution a few weeks earlier, aimed at Champion, which barred anyone who was not a trade unionist and working man from membership. This, however, failed to weaken his grip on the organisation in London.[157]

Although this unpleasant affair had taken much time and effort, some things changed for the better. In April the branch started to use a different newsagent who agreed to display *Commonweal*, and presumably *Justice*, in his or her window. It started a series of lectures on the Common in June, having delayed them for a couple of months for the election campaign. Socialism still sold well in Tunbridge Wells. Hyndman's lectures on the collapse of the middle class and on the movement in Paris attracted audiences from all backgrounds. The Social-Democrats collected donations of 9s 6d at one meeting in July and sold a hundred penny pamphlets and received twelve shillings in August. For all this activity, the branch

---

[157] *For the course of events, see Justice, August 11th 1888; Labour Elector July 1888, November 1st 1888, December 1st 1888; Pelling, 'Champion' pp228-9; Kent Times and Tribune December 15th 1888.*

seems to have stagnated somewhat when compared to the previous two years.[158]

The strike of matchworkers at Bryant and May's factory in London that June proved a welcome distraction. At first glance, this workforce made unlikely industrial militants. The majority of workers in the factory were young women or girls and, like most workers regarded as unskilled, they had no formal union organisation. Their plight had been recognised in a radical paper, *The Link*. In it, Annie Besant, who had moved from secularism to the Fabian Society,, exposed the tyranny of an avowedly 'Christian and Liberal' employer. Besant suggested that sympathisers might consider a consumer boycott in June and repeated this suggestion in subsequent months. The workers, themselves, however, decided that a strike might be more fruitful and 1,400 of them walked out in the first days of July.

Annie Besant

The Tunbridge Wells branch secured Harry Quelch, editor of *Justice*, to address a meeting in solidarity, chaired by Tom Jarvis, outside the Grosvenor Hotel. Despite being on a newsworthy subject, one source suggests that only 50 or 60 attended, all of them working class. Bensley Lawrence, the engine-man and time-keeper at the Baltic Sawmills, had been murdered the previous night and this seems to have caused widespread shock and perhaps reduced attendance.[159] The meeting collected 14s for the dispute and passed a resolution:

---

[158] *Justice, March 24th 1888, June 27th 1888, August 10th 1888, October 20th 1888; The Courier April 13th 1888; Tunbridge Wells Advertiser March 30th 1888, June 22nd 1888; Letter from William Willis-Harris to the Socialist League, 13th April 1888 (International Institute of Socialist History, Socialist League archive); The Tunbridge Wells Gazette June 22nd 1888.*

[159] *Perhaps significantly his killers, William Gower and Charles Dobell, said they had murdered him as he was a 'masters' man' who had unfairly deducted pay from Gower for lateness. They also admitted carrying out the arson attacks of 1887. Tunbridge Wells Gazette October 10th 1888; The Courier October 19th 1888; Tunbridge Wells Gazette November 23rd 1888; Tunbridge Wells Journal November 22nd 1888; The*

'This meeting of Tunbridge Wells workmen expresses its hearty sympathy with the girls and women now on strike against the tyrannical impositions of Messrs Bryant and May and emphatically protests against the mean trickery of fines and stoppages [of pay] by which they were robbed of a portion of the miserably scanty wages.

This meeting also urges all working men and women to rally to the support of these downtrodden members of their class in order to enable them to form an organisation and to secure better conditions of labour in the future'.

There are a number of intriguing links and questions. By this stage a large number of the strikers had gone 'hopping' in Kent to support themselves. Some may have been present. Tunbridge Wells proved generous in supporting the dispute, eventually collecting a total of £2 8s 9d, though 3s 6d of this had been used to print handbills. The branch collected a further 17s 9d after the strike was won and forwarded this to London to establish a permanent trade union. William Willis-Harris, whose political evolution from secularism to socialism had come earlier than Annie Besant, looked to the consumer boycott as a useful tool. In August he wrote to *Justice* to ask that bodies including the SDF, the Socialist League, the Fabian Society,, the Cooperative Societies and the London Trades Council should work together in future to coordinate such boycotts. By contrast, he showed relatively little interest in strike action.[160]

A reminder of the branch's heroic first few months came with the publication of *A More Excellent Way* in late summer. This had been completed several months before but Swan Sonnenshein, which published a lot of radical books, initially declined the manuscript on the grounds that the 'great majority of socialist books are, commercially speaking, a failure'.

Constance Howell therefore agreed to pay for the costs herself, paying £81-16s-6d for a thousand copies to be produced. Costs

Illustrated Police News October 27th 1888, December 22nd 1888; Kent Times and Tribune July 28th 1888
[160] *The main sources for this section are The Link: a journal for the Servants of Man 23rd June 1888; Raw, L., Striking a Light: The Bryant and May Matchwomen and their place in history (London: Continuum 2011) esp. p7, pp89-90 p122, p139; Justice, July 21st 1888; The Tunbridge Wells Gazette July 20th 1888, The Tunbridge Wells Advertiser July 27th 1888, Justice, September 1st 1888; McCarthy, T. The Great Dock Strike 1889: the story of the labour movement's first great victory (London: Wiedenfeld and Nicholson 1989) p66.*

were increased further by a late change to one chapter and her desire to commission an expensive cover – consisting of a red flag and a cap of liberty – which at one stage she wanted Walter Crane, one of the more prominent artists in the socialist movement, to design.[161]

Harry Quelch gave the novel a somewhat mixed review in *Justice*, though he paid tribute to the branch for struggling manfully for socialism in the most discouraging conditions. He concluded that the book was worth reading and might convert some to the cause, though he disliked its aggressive atheism and argued that 'it is a matter of little moment from the socialist point of view whether [workers] swear by Jesus Christ or Karl Marx, or both'. Henry Hyde Champion's *To-Day* was much more hostile. This may not only have been as a result of the enmity between him and the Tunbridge Wells branch. The journal had given negative responses to virtually all other contemporary 'realist' socialist novels and plays, such as *Out of Work* by Margaret Harkness and Edward Bellamy's *Looking Backwards*, and even afforded George Bernard Shaw's classic *An Unsociable Socialist*, which it had itself serialised, a mediocre review. Interestingly, Champion many years later claimed to have been the subject of seven separate novels, although he could not recall the name of any of them. The review would have done nothing to mend relations between the two sides.[162]

Responses in the provincial press were often better. The *Courier* reviewed the book, and *Justice* reproduced this. It complimented the thrilling tale and interesting narrative and noted that the author intended to 'advocate the claims of socialism, in all the forms of which she is evidently well-versed'. This review even praised the leading character as noble, though unsurprisingly declared that we cannot admire his teachings. Similarly positive reviews from the *Women's Penny Paper* and the *Scottish Leader* were carried in *Justice* in March 1889.

In October that year Swan Sonnenshein produced a shilling version of the book, which *Justice* recommended that all members should buy and induce others to do so. Perhaps the most interesting review was the *Spectator*'s, which believed that it was 'so much of a novel with a purpose that it can hardly be considered a novel at all. It is

---

[161] *Swan Sonnenshein Archive (University of Reading) Correspondence, Volume 8, 879, 903, Volume 9 353, 512, 763, 791.*
[162] *For these reviews see To-Day June 1888, August 1888 and June 1889. See also Royle, Radicals, p240-1.*

really an exposition of present-day Free-thought and Socialism'. It praised the way it had been written and liked one character in particular who, though conservative in some ways, proved open to the new politics. At the same time the novel fell into the trap of caricaturing some other characters who opposed socialism and secularism.[163]

Whatever the critics felt, it is clear that the publisher's prediction proved correct and the book struggled commercially. The shilling edition did a bit better than its predecessor and from August 1890 the SDF's London headquarters supplied it directly to branches. As a result it probably became fairly well-known within the party, though therefore merely preaching to the already converted rather than recruiting others to the cause. It then fell into obscurity.

Constance Howell's conversation with the keeper at Calverley Park forms a very powerful section of her novel. Although taken much later, this is a postcard of the gates and keeper; and below is a permit to allow access to the park.

Perhaps the most illuminating passages in the novel are based on dialogue between Howell's protagonist and those who opposed socialism. She herself had lodged at Calverley Crescent and her account of a debate with a park keeper, employed to keep men of his own class from the park, is almost certainly taken from real life. Why, for example, did his family occupy a tiny cottage when others lived in

---

[163] *Justice December 15th 1888, March 16th 1889 and October 12th 1889, The Spectator October 6th 1888*

mansions? As the conversation developed, the socialist noted that the park keeper would having nothing to look forward to in old age other than the workhouse and that his children 'had to take their chance in life, and the chances were small'. However, this 'Conservative working man' being so 'used to such a condition of things, that he thought it must be right', remained unconvinced. He let slip that he had listened to the Federation's speakers on the Common, though he made it clear that he feared for his job if his employers found out. In conclusion, the socialist bitterly concluded that under capitalism:

> *"The enemy of the unemployed workman is his fellow who is in employment; and the workman out of employ is again the enemy of the employed, for by the possibility of replacing him he keeps down the employed man's wages. The disinherited classes are not fraternal, they are fratricidal. And the selfish contentment of some is the ruin of the rest."*[164]

What makes such passages all the more interesting is the way in which they anticipate the themes developed by Robert Tressell in the *Ragged Trousered Philanthropists*. The author was a member of the Hastings branch of the SDF and the extensive links between that branch and its Tunbridge Wells equivalent will be discussed later. The Robert Tressell Society's website chose the following passage from his novel for its internet home page:

> *As Owen thought of his child's future, there sprang up within him a feeling of hatred and fury against his fellow workmen. They were the enemy - those ragged-trousered philanthropists, who not only quietly submitted like so many cattle to their miserable slavery for the benefit of others, but defended it and opposed and ridiculed any suggestion of reform. They were the real oppressors - the men who spoke of themselves as 'the likes of us' who, having lived in poverty all their lives, considered that what had been good enough for them was good enough for their children.*

From the late 1980s a few socialist and feminist historians noticed the similarities between the two, without recognising the links between Howell's novel and Tunbridge Wells. One in particular praised the chapters which were set in the town, with the protagonist's arguments for socialism being 'put in a way that is sharp, witty and to the point – as no pamphlet could have been -

---

[164] Howell, *A More Excellent Way*, p218-221

and where the drama of the arguments, the wit in rebuttal, the inanity of the bourgeoisie arguments about socialism give the novel an aesthetic dimension'. She also considered that the novel's feminism echoes Sarah Grand's *The Heavenly Twins*, also a novel by a Tunbridge Wells writer. The latter may be coincidental, though as I have already argued that the influence on Tressell may have been more direct. Sarah Grand herself is often credited with identifying the concept of the 'new woman' during the 1890s and it is telling that Frank Tanner, a London member of the SDF in the early twentieth century, took inspiration from her novels.[165]

The marriage of secularism and socialism soon had a lively practical demonstration in the town. In September thirty members of London's Limehouse branch of the SDF decided to visit Tunbridge Wells. The Limehouse activists at first wandered around the town and the Common and a number perhaps enjoyed the local ales. After a few hours, they decided to attend a service given by the curate, Reverend Watkins, at Hoare's church. They entered the building, refused to remove their hats and red rosettes, and yelled their approval or otherwise at the words of the sermon. After this, the two branches met outside the building, paraded the streets to the *Marseillaise*, and considerable disturbance ensued. Some called for the offenders to be prosecuted for causing a disturbance in a religious building. The Tunbridge Wells branch continued to host other branches over the next few years, such as Wandsworth in 1889 and Battersea in 1891. London branches of the SDF had previously organised similar interventions in churches.[166]

Reverend Watkins

---

[165] *Swan Sonnenshein Archive (University of Reading) Correspondence, Volume 11, p.589; Justice August 2nd 1890; Tanner, F., British Socialism in the early 1900s (Socialist History Society Occasional Publication No. 35, 2014), p25. For more recent reviews see in particular, de la Motte, B, Radicalism, Feminism, Socialism, the rise of the Woman Novelist, pp29-39 in Gustav Klaus, H., [Ed] the Rise of Socialist Fiction 1880-1914 (Brighton: Harvester 1987) and Hapgood, L., 'The Novel and Political Agency: Socialism and the Work of Margaret Harkness, Constance Howell and Clementina Black: 1888-1896' Literature & History, vol. 5, 2: pp. 37-52.*
[166] *The Courier September 7th 1888; Justice September 8th 1888; The Tunbridge Wells Gazette September 7th 1888' Justice July 27th 1889; July 7th 1891.*

The same month, the last recorded meeting of the local branch of the NSS took place. George Standring addressed a large crowd who listened 'with attention and approbation.' Standring had been one of the first people to join the Fabian Society, and the choice of him, rather than a non-socialist member of the NSS such as Foote or Bradlaugh, suggests that this meeting may have been a joint one with the SDF. The size of the audience certainly gives this impression.[167]

Robert Bontine Cunninghame Graham

The Social-Democrats followed this with probably their largest indoor meeting to date, for which they hired the Town Hall. To raise interest, they handed out small red leaflets advertising the speaker as 'Cunninghame Graham MP, late of Pentonville Prison'. The room had only filled up to half its capacity when Ada Willis-Harris played the *Marseillaise* and her husband announced the speaker. Yet all the seats were soon taken. The audience particularly enjoyed the speaker's attacks on the Home Secretary, Henry Matthews, and the Commissioner of the Metropolitan Police, Charles Warren. He gave the speech a Kentish flavour, reminding those present of the roles played by John Ball, Wat Tyler and Jack Cade; then discussed current affairs, using the example of strikes and subsequent state repression in Pennsylvania and Belgium to claim that 'liberal capitalists' could be as repressive as the Russian state. In conclusion, he announced that the branch had just selected Tom Jarvis as the socialist candidate for the Kent County Council elections in January.[168]

The Local Government Act 1888 which established county councils also led to the most significant reform in the way in which Tunbridge Wells ran itself since the 1830s. Existing sanitary boards, responsible for public health, became either urban or rural district councils or county boroughs. Concern that the town might

---

[167] *The National Reformer September 23rd 1888.*
[168], *Tunbridge Wells Gazette November 30 1888; Justice December 1 1888; the Tunbridge Wells Journal November 29th 1888.*

be assigned only urban district council status forced an initially reluctant John Stone-Wigg, Chairman of the Local Board, to petition the Privy Council to obtain Borough status. On January 16th 1889 the town was awarded the charter incorporating it as a Borough and a month later the scroll arrived on a special train. A 21 gun salute and a procession through streets bedecked with flags followed. Reports of the proceedings took up several pages of the local papers and received significant coverage in the national press.[169]

The SDF had little interest in joining the party. This may seem surprising at first, as for the first time in the town's history a working class candidate could stand with some chance of success. They seem to have concluded that, as democratisation would have come in any event, the form which the new local administration took mattered little. The Social-Democrats and Stone-Wigg, as mentioned above, had little love for each other, and the latter emerged as one of the winners of the process, serving as Mayor from 1889 until 1891.

The borough was divided into four wards, each with six councillors. Six aldermen joined their ranks. Several factors still hindered the socialists, as they did in other towns throughout Britain. Voters had to pay rates and faced disqualification if they had accepted poor relief. The reformed electorate therefore only enfranchised 3,594 people in a town of nearly 30,000, which meant that a lot of working age men had no vote. In particular, younger men, often still living with their parents, together with those in lodging houses or who moved address frequently, had no representation. The female majority of the population remained unenfranchised until 1894, and the resulting extension of local election voting rights on the basis of existing property qualifications that year probably further skewed the electorate away from the working class.[170]

The Tunbridge Wells branch felt that the town's resources would be better used on public works instead of expensive ceremonies. Swimming baths, washhouses, a new town hall and summer and winter gardens would improve the lives of working-class residents and attract visitors. They also stepped up their call for a maximum

---

[169] *In a few cases the Government ordered that county boundaries be redrawn so that the entire town came within a single county. Tunbridge Wells accordingly became a wholly Kentish town. See Chalklin, C.W., Royal Tunbridge Wells; a History p84; Beavis, Ian 'Fighting for the Future' in 400 Years of the Wells pp124-6.*
[170] *Chalklin, C.W., Royal Tunbridge Wells; a History p84.*

eight-hour day for all. At the turn of the year, the party organised an open-air meeting at Lime Hill Road to publicise their proposals. Geer, Jarvis and Clifton also looked to the Poor Law Guardians to provide work. The usual parade through the town followed, though the revival of the economy affected turnout. The *Advertiser* claimed that the gathering attracted only 50, though Jarvis counted 120.[171]

Campaigning for the County Council election started with open-air meetings in January. Hunter Watts travelled to the town to assist. Press reports suggest that it proved a thankless task, as few people attended the rallies on a patch of waste ground near the Central Goods Yard or at Lime Hill Road. The bitter winter weather would not have helped.

Yet the branch succeeded in turning the election into a referendum on socialism and trade unionism, and even rebuilt relationships. Scrace, the head of the Radical Alliance, supported Tom Jarvis' call to increase the rate of pay for those working on work designed to relieve unemployment. More surprisingly, Jarvis' opponent, Cheverton, claimed to be 'as much a socialist as anybody' but believed 'in levelling up but not levelling down'. Though a cliché, this may have had some impact.

Jarvis won 71 votes to his opponent's 923. Looking for a silver lining, Jarvis declared that the fact that over 70 people had consciously voted for revolutionary socialism was a positive development. Scrace aside, others to the left of centre had been less supportive. *Justice* claimed that 'Liberals, Whigs, Radicals and Tories' had united against them and that, in light of the restrictive franchise and the bourgeois character of the district, it had been a good result. Yet rejection clearly hurt, and in 1899 Tom Jarvis remembered how *British* workmen – contrasting with their Continental peers - would cheer the speakers on Tunbridge Wells Common or join the processions of the unemployed but not vote for the SDF.[172]

Two months later, David Geer and Tom Jarvis tried their luck again and stood as candidates for the Borough's East Ward. Sixteen men decided to contest the six available seats and so the majority would

---

[171] *The Courier January 1 1889; Tunbridge Wells Local Board Minute Book No. 16 November 7th 1888; Tunbridge Wells Journal December 6th 1888; The Tunbridge Wells Advertiser January 4th & 11th 1889.*
[172] *The Tunbridge Wells Journal January 17th 1889, The Tunbridge Wells Advertiser January 18th 1889, Justice November 4th 1899.*

be disappointed. As with the County election, the contest in this ward turned on trade union matters. Two other candidates, John Saunders and John Mason Junior, also declared that they intended to act as working class candidates. Both supported the payment of trade union rates for all municipal work, whether in-house or contracted out. They also benefitted from being supported by a number of locally influential people, including the Reverend J Irving, something the secular Socialists could not have achieved. Jarvis won 41 votes and Geer 30. On the positive side, Saunders and Mason each secured enough votes to win seats in the ward, becoming the first two representatives of both their class and the labour movement.[173]

The branch reorganised itself. Charles Hugh Barden took over the job of secretary. Barden, a photographer and the son of a local fishmonger and poulterer with a shop on Camden Road, only remained in the town for a few years, before moving to Chichester and later the United States. The limited amount of public activity meant that the branch only wanted six copies of the Socialist League's *Commonweal* per week in the winter months, though it also requested copies of its pamphlet on the Paris Commune. Barden promised to write and ask for more once outdoor work resumed, though he does not appear to have done so, possibly because the Socialist League was becoming increasingly dominated by anarchists.[174]

By 1889 the Social-Democrats of Tunbridge Wells no longer had the south-eastern counties to themselves. The SDF formed a branch in Brighton that year. Others though felt that Henry Hyde Champion's strategy provided a more plausible path to a mass movement of the working class. Maidstone's Arthur Field, for example, until recently a member of the Liberal Party, shared Champion's vision. He wrote to the *Kent Times and Tribune* to support Champion throughout 1888 and in December that year organised a meeting of what he called the Maidstone Labour Party or Maidstone Labour Electoral Association. Champion, George Bateman and William Parnell all visited the county town, yet meetings seem to have attracted just dozens rather than the hundreds seen in Tunbridge Wells. Maidstone, like Tunbridge Wells, nevertheless elected its first

---

[173] *The Courier March 15th, 20th 27th 1889.*
[174] *Letters from Charles Barden to the Socialist League dated March 22nd 1889 and March 29th 1889 (International Institute of Socialist History, Socialist League archive).*

working class representative, Councillor Beale, Secretary of the London and Southern Counties Labour League, in 1889.[175]

The strike of London's dockers in August 1889 is still remembered today as one of the most important disputes in British labour history. The efforts of the Social-Democrats in Tunbridge Wells to support the strikers cannot be faulted. The branch organised rallies, indoor meetings and collections. Geer and Jarvis shared platforms with the Lib-Lab Councillors Mason and Saunders. Scrace and William Bournes spoke on behalf of their union. More remarkably the Mayor allowed the Cooperative Society free use of the Town Hall for one meeting in solidarity. At one rally the collection amounted to almost £7. David Geer collected £6 18s 8d and Constance Howell also donated £5. It is clear that many in the town took a close interest, and even though the dispute at one stage looked like it might turn into a London-wide general strike, which would almost certainly have spread beyond the capital, support remained strong.

Not everything proceeded smoothly. An attempt to hold a meeting at Tonbridge in early September failed when a delegation of socialists was stopped by the police at Quarry Hill, the grounds given being that they might pocket the money collected. Those parading through Calverley Road the same month faced similar allegations, and only the presence of a very well-built docker prevented a bystander from picking a fight with one of the local activists. Support from towns such as Tunbridge Wells proved critical in keeping the dispute going before huge amounts of money made their way to London from the labour movement in Australia (the latter eventually contributed over £30,000 of the total of £48,750 raised in support). Many other groups collected for the cause; a year later the *Kent and Sussex Courier*'s columnist complained that a lot of men working for building firms had given money to 'this

[175] *Champion, Quorum Pars Fui, p28;, Justice, October 10th & 24th 1891, November 21st 1891; Edwards, J., The Labour Annual 1895 (Manchester: Labour Press Society Ltd.) p170; Labour Elector December 1887, November 30th 1889 and December 21st 1889; Aubry, B., 'Arthur Field in Gildart, K and Howell, D , [Eds] Dictionary of Labour Biography Volume XIII, (Basingstoke: Palgrave MacMillan 2010); Clark, P and Murfin, L., The History of Maidstone; the making of a modern county town (Stroud: Allan Sutton Publishing Ltd 1996) p182; Aubry, Field, p71; , Kent Times and Tribune March 10th 1888, June 30th 1888, July 7th 1888.*

disastrous struggle' rather than the regular Hospital Sunday collections. [176]

The victory revitalised the whole labour movement. Trade union membership grew by around 200,000 in twelve months, and the so-called 'New Unionism', embracing the less-skilled workers, meant that industries which had previously been unorganised soon became the base for some of the most combative and active militants.

At Tunbridge Wells the railway workers and cab drivers formed new union branches between 1888 and 1890. Some Social-Democrats, such as Will Thorne and Harry Quelch, worked indefatigably for the new unions. Thorne's trade union, the National Union of Gasworkers and General Labourers, recruited brick-makers, building site labourers, dock workers and agricultural workers, including in the brickfields of Kent, Sussex and Surrey. David Geer, already active in the Carpenters' and Joiners' Union, also joined the Gasworkers and General Labourers in 1890 and a branch formed in the Medway Towns at about the same time.

From the perspective of the Tunbridge Wells SDF, these developments brought dangers as well as opportunities. *Justice* had only half-heartedly supported the strike. Henry Hyde Champion, in contrast, came out of the dispute very well. In Kent many wished to keep away from the rival factions. The longshoremen in the Medway Towns, to which the strike had spread, formed their own trade union, and stayed away from Quelch's South-Side Labour Protection League, Champion's Dock, Wharf and Riverside Union, and also rebuffed overtures to affiliate to the Kent and Sussex Labourers' Union. [177]

The Tunbridge Wells branch again turned to making socialists. The SDF in late 1889 asked the Fabian Society, to run a series of lectures in the town. The Fabians are usually thought to be more middle class than other socialist organisations, yet several hundred working men attended the first lecture by Sidney Webb, while there is no evidence that any wealthier people came. Annie Besant gave

---

[176] *Maidstone Journal and Kentish Advertiser September 10th 1889; The Tunbridge Wells Advertiser August 30th 1889, September 6th & 13th 1889; the Tunbridge Wells Journal September 5th & 12th 1889; The Courier September 1st 1939. For the dispute see McCarthy, The Great Dock Strike 1889; Justice; September 14th & 21st 1889; The Courier September 12th 1890.*

[177] *Thorne, W., My Life's Battles (London: Lawrence and Wishart 2014) pp xxiv, 121.*

the next address, supported by William Willis-Harris. She drew frequent applause from the crowded room. The subsequent lecture by Sidney Olivier - who had also spoken outdoors on the Common and at Lime Hill Road in September – also drew a good response. This is perhaps surprising as contemporaries felt his thought processes to be so complex that his lectures were almost incomprehensible. He also spoke at 'Flying Scotchman' speed. He was speaking in familiar territory. As a boy he had attended Tonbridge School and now lived no further away than Limpsfield, near Oxted, then connected directly to Tunbridge Wells by a railway line. These three lectures later formed part of a collection known as *Fabian Essays in Socialism.*[178]

In January 1890 David Geer, Edward Moore, Henry Reid and George Gabriel addressed a rally of the unemployed in Lime Hill Road. A delegation then visited the Council to call for public works. Even David Geer, recognised for his skill, had been out of work for a fortnight. Controversy followed when Reverend Mountain, the minister of Emmanuel Church on Mount Ephraim, decided to open a subscription list to fund a series of penny dinners for the town's poorest children.[179]

Mountain and the socialists had once worked cordially together. In December 1889 David Geer, Reverend Mountain and William Bournes had all condemned proposals to prevent political and religious meetings from taking place on the Common. Geer later spoke at one of Mountain's free suppers and argued that, even as a teetotaller himself, he could see that abstinence would not remove poverty. Overpopulation was not a problem as the country's wealth had increased twice as fast as its population. He subsequently wrote that 70 or 80 men had been unable to get into the venue, proving that unemployment had not fallen by as much as some had claimed, and that one of the unemployed had been mistreated by a policeman. He also organised a working class relief committee, organised from his house at 56 Western Road, and thanked those

[178] *Tonbridge Telegraph, December 14th 1889; Tunbridge Wells Journal December 12th , 21st & 28th 1889, The Tunbridge Wells Advertiser December 13th 1889, Justice September 14th 1889; Pugh, P. Educate, Agitate, Organise: one hundred years of Fabian socialism (London: Methuen 1984) p20-21; To-Day December 1888; Edwards, J., The Labour Annual 1895 (Manchester: Labour Press Society Ltd.) p184.*
[179] *Tunbridge Wells Journal December 5th 1889.*

who had contributed. £19 15s 10d had been collected, 13s of this had gone towards printing costs, the rest being distributed.[180]

It is not clear whether Mountain had been offended by Geer having discussed politics or by his creation of a rival organisation funded by men of his own class rather than the rich, but their relationship seems to have soured from that time. Mountain organised what he termed 'entertainment for the poor' at his school room, and in the course of this attacked socialism.

Three months of correspondence followed, opinion being split largely on class lines. Radicals such as Scrace sided with the socialists against Elvy Robb, a young and ambitious Tory councillor. The socialists watered down their atheism to the extent that Geer used biblical quotes in support of the contention that labour is the source of all wealth, in particular Saint Paul's belief that 'he that shall not work, neither will he eat'. William Willis-Harris similarly quoted Stewart Headlam and other Christian Socialists to argue that the two movements could co-exist. He also pointed to the provision of free breakfasts in previous years to the children of the unemployed. Unconvinced, Mountain continued his attacks on the Federation, particularly singling out Hyndman and Jarvis, in a letter written in mid-March 1890. Mountain made further enemies, having banned an amateur football team from using a piece of land belonging to the church, perhaps giving the Socialists some new allies.[181]

Hyndman joined in. The SDF hired the Town Hall in March. They attracted a large working class audience. Part way through, Mountain arrived. Hyndman had clearly followed the controversy closely and took the opportunity to deliver a stinging rebuke:

'Having read an extract from Mr Mountain's letter, Mr Hyndman said he had once heard of a man called Jesus of Nazareth, a man who used very strong language... He went forth into the streets of Jerusalem and went up a mountain... and he absolutely said – the Scribes and the Pharisees and Sadducees, who were the capitalists and the landlords of those days – the Scribes and the Pharisees were hypocrites, and those who had laid waste

---

[180], *Tunbridge Wells Advertiser January 10th & 24th 1890.*
[181] *The Courier January 17th 1890, February 5th 1890, February 27th 1890, March 12th 1890; Tonbridge Telegraph January 18th 1890; Tunbridge Wells Advertiser January 31st 1890.*

widows' houses and for a pretence made long prayers, should receive the greater damnation.'

In the rest of his speech, Hyndman repeatedly compared the priesthood of first century Palestine who had rejected Jesus with those contemporary Christians who opposed socialism. An impromptu debate followed, pitting Elvy Robb and Reverend Mountain against Hyndman and Geer. The socialists had the better of the argument and Mountain withdrew. One person in the audience also directed a jibe at the Queen.[182]

Five days later, John Ward, billed as an unskilled labourer from Wandsworth, spoke under the title 'Socialism, the Religion of Humanity'. Unusually a complete version of his lecture survives and is held in the library of the University of Sussex. Christianity stood condemned as 'one of the lowest forms of mockery that has ever blighted the human race' and its creed 'peace on earth, goodwill to men' had become the 'direct instigation of the piling of mountains of human bones and the flowing of seas of blood'. Across the world, Christian countries first sent missionaries and then gunboats, only Islam had proved more rapacious. Babylon and Rome had both collapsed as a result of inequality, and the same fate awaited modern countries. Anchoring his arguments in contemporary politics, the American secularist Colonel Ingersoll received praise for his theological knowledge but criticism for his views on the social sciences. Ward also attacked Bryant and May.

It is clear that Reverend Mountain had opened a hornet's nest. Tom Jarvis, in one of the first of many similar acts of provocation by the branch, wrote to the *Advertiser* to thank him for 'unwittingly having been playing the part of a revolutionary agent'. Yet many in the town seem to have grown tired of the controversy. The last time Mountain spoke on the subject, at the end of March, he addressed a half-empty room.[183]

Some of the most active spirits in the branch began to drift away. William Willis-Harris worried that socialist and labour politicians had become rather too interested in palliatives to address the most glaring symptoms of capitalism and as a result had lost sight of revolution being the ultimate goal. In March 1890 he warned that

---

[182] *The Courier March 21st 1890;, Tunbridge Wells Advertiser March 21st 1890.*
[183] *Ward, J., Socialism; the Religion of Humanity by John Ward (an Unskilled Labourer) (Wandworth Branch of the SDF c1890) ; The Courier April 4th 1890; Justice, March 22nd 1890; Tunbridge Wells Advertiser March 28th 1890, April 4th 1890.*

'the innocent and so easily-gulled British workman' risked being conned by Tory and Liberal politicians who now spoke in support of the reforms which they had vehemently denounced a few years ago. The danger had become even greater now that some politicians claimed to speak for labour yet remained wedded to the two main parties. The SDF's members needed to remember that:

> "However important eight hour bills, free education, improved dwellings and free meals in schools are, they are NOT socialism. Stepping-stones they are to Social-Democracy, and it is owing to the continual pushing of them, both on the platform and in the press by the Socialists, that they are now within the sphere of practical politics.... [Yet] no Socialist should vote for any man who does not recognise the Class War and who will not pledge himself in favour of the Nationalisation of the Land and the Instruments of Production."[184]

William Willis-Harris had Henry Hyde Champion firmly in his sights. Champion had spoken at Maidstone in February and this may have encouraged William Willis-Harris to put pen to paper. Champion's rather fragmented autobiography uses an almost identical formulation to Willis-Harris when taking about the eight hour day – 'in this way we certainly brought that particular reform into the region of practical politics'. Hyndman endorsed Willis-Harris's views in an editorial. William Willis-Harris had come as close as anyone to defining what a distinctively socialist party should stand for. His definition echoed down the years.

The SDF later cited the failure of the Labour Representation Committee to commit to the class war as their reason for withdrawing from it, and in 1908 argued that this omission meant that the Labour Party should be refused membership of the Second Socialist International. The resolution which led to the formation of the British Socialist Party in 1911 similarly declared the need to fight the class war to the finish and the common ownership of production and distribution, and significantly deleted previous references to striving for immediate reforms within the framework of capitalism.[185]

---

[184] *Justice March 1st 1890.*
[185] *Tanner, F., British Socialism p81-2. For the Labour Party's affiliation to the Second International, see Lenin,V., On Britain, (Moscow, Progress Publications 1979) pp95-101.*

However William Willis-Harris had other interests to follow. By February 1890 his family had moved to the small Sussex village of Warnham, just outside Horsham, where William wrote two editions of a book on turkey farming in 1890 and 1893, the first of which was published in Tunbridge Wells. These are of more than passing interest. Essentially a practical guide, they concluded with pointed remarks on the 'robbery of the common lands by laws of the wealthy and avaricious landlords' and condemned those who were sighing for the return to the days of protection.

For several years he exhibited his birds at the annual Agricultural Show in Tunbridge Wells. A monument to his daughter Vera, who died at just two years old, still stands in Warnham's churchyard. Rural life failed to soften his revolutionary zeal, as he named his son Karl Marx Willis-Harris. Finally the family moved to the village of Easebourne, a couple of miles from Midhurst, and won a seat on Pulborough's School Board. He continued to write to the newspapers in Tunbridge Wells and spent considerable amounts of time there. [186]

Constance Howell similarly became a semi-detached member of the branch. She spent some time in Eastbourne in 1888 and in 1890 moved to Bournemouth. Here she corresponded with a circle around the American author Edward Bellamy, whose novel *Looking Backwards* had been well received by socialists and the wider public alike on both sides of the Atlantic. The Nationalist Club in Boston, published an article by her, *Is Our Civilisation a Failure?*, and reviewed *A More Excellent Way*, in October 1889. The reviewer took a positive view of the novel, though he disliked the militant atheism as much as Quelch had.

She also donated large sums of money to the party and to support strikes, giving £20 in April 1889, £10 in October 1890, £20 in May 1890 to support agitation in the Potteries and in March 1892 donated £10 for the London local election campaign and £20 for work amongst the miners of the north-east. This cash funded quite a lot of the Federation's provincial propaganda. [187]

---

[186] Willis-Harris, W., *The Turkey: how to breed and rear successfully. By a Practical Turkey-Breeder (W. W.-H.). Warnham 1890, printed at Tunbridge Wells and Pulborough 1893)*
[187] *Letters between Constance Howell and the Socialist League (International Institute of Socialist History, Socialist League archive); Swan Sonnenshein Archive (University of Reading) Correspondence, Volume 12 (16th November 1889); Lipow, A Authoritarian*

The partial withdrawal of these members, with their energy and their money, marks the end of the first period of the branch's existence. At first glance, the picture appears bleak. It appears that the Socialist Hall had been given up around this time. Business meetings took place in the front room of Tom Jarvis' modest house at 11 Duke's Road, suggesting that the number regularly attending may have been no more than a dozen or so. Veterans of the branch would have remembered the fate of the town's Secular Society.

Occasionally something of the old spirit shone through. In May, Tom Jarvis debated with Elvy Robb, who was reduced to quoting Charles Bradlaugh in support of his position, and made rather optimistic claims that the position of the working class would improve. A month later they made themselves enough of a nuisance for some to call for public meetings on the Common to be banned:

> 'Pedestrians on the Common on Sunday were treated to a couple of discourses on this hydra-headed subject. A member of the SDF mounted the rock in the afternoon and evening and inveigled against capitalism, doing down everything connected with it'.[188]

Three months later the branch raised funds in support of the Australian dock strike, though the amount hardly compared to that collected for the London dispute the previous year. The circumstances of the collapse of the Australian struggle helped the Tunbridge Wells SDF in its dispute with Henry Hyde Champion. Champion, then in Melbourne, claimed it had been grossly mismanaged, and gleefully predicted its failure, thereby losing much trade union support in both countries. His intemperate attacks on Ernest Parke, the editor of a radical London journal, alienated John Burns, Tom Mann, George Bateman, Keir Hardie, William Parnell and Ben Tillett.

Champion's links to wealthy Conservatives again drew attention. Friedrich Engels reflected the views of many in the movement by arguing that Champion, whether consciously or not, had worked in the Tory interest. As the year drew to a close, the branch arranged for Hunter Watts, who had spoken several times in the town, and S D Shallard, later to be the principal lecturer for the Hutchinson

---

Socialism in America: Edward Bellamy and the Nationalist Movement. (University of California 1982) p22; The Nationalist, October 1889.
[188] *Justice, April 17th 1890; Justice, May 31st 1890; Tunbridge Wells Advertiser June 6th 1890.*

Trust, an offshoot of the Fabian Society, to address large audiences in the Town Hall in December.[189]

Services to and from the London Brighton and South Coast Railway's Tunbridge Wells station (after 1923 Tunbridge Wells West), top, allowed Constance Howell and William and Ada Willis-Harris to remain active in the Tunbridge Wells SDF despite living some distance away.
On the left is the simple grave of Vera Willis-Harris which stands in Warnham Churchyard.

---

[189] *Justice, September 27th 1890; Tunbridge Wells Advertiser December 5th &19th 1890; Pugh, Educate pp58-9; Barnes, J., 'Gentleman Crusader: H H Champion and the Early Socialist Movement' in the History Workshop Journal Volume 60, Issue 1, 1 October 2005, Pages 116–138 p133; Pelling, 'Champion' pp230-233*

CHAPTER 6   THE TUNBRIDGE WELLS BRANCH
AND THE RISE OF THE INDEPENDENT LABOUR PARTY

The Tunbridge Wells branch struggled to make much progress in the years between 1891 and 1894. Although they continued to hold public meetings and sell *Justice*, their efforts seem somewhat low key compared to previous years. Despite this, two developments helped set the course of events for several decades to come. The first was the growth of a labour movement across Kent and the second came from a turn by the socialists of Tunbridge Wells towards the trade unions.

It is worth considering how the labour and socialist movement organised itself at this point. It should be remembered that the Labour Representation Committee – the forerunner of the modern Labour Party with its millions of affiliated trade unionists - only formed in 1900. Before then there were, on the one hand, competing socialist groups arguing between themselves, and on the other, activists working for trade union rights who tended to seek Parliamentary representation via the Liberal Party. In 1892 Keir Hardie became the first fully independent Labour Member of Parliament, unaffiliated to the Liberal party. The Socialist League had effectively collapsed by then, leaving the SDF as the only socialist party with a presence throughout Great Britain. Local 'labour parties', often working in conjunction with trades councils and led by leading union members, formed in some places, including Gillingham and Dover. The SDF formed its second Kentish branch, at Sheerness, in 1891.

The SDF still sometimes drew a crowd at Tunbridge Wells. In June 1891 a leading Fabian, Harry Lowerison, spoke twice. Jim Connell, who wrote the words to the *Red Flag,* addressed an open-air meeting that September. The Social-Democrats took leading roles in several local trade union branches and in the Trades Council, and it is noticeable how the local papers gave these meetings more coverage than they afforded the Federation. The Cooperative Society likewise offered a platform for socialist speakers from various organisations. Such work ensured that the socialist movement in Tunbridge Wells did not become moribund.

Crucially the SDF continued to attract new members. Those who joined in these relatively fallow years perhaps proved more committed to the cause than the men and women who had become active in earlier years. The fact that Tunbridge Wells had an organised and active socialist movement also influenced visitors from other parts of the region.

One of those who would go on to build the movement across Kent and Sussex was Eastbourne's George Meek. He was a Liberal Party activist who had only met one socialist before in his home town. In the autumn of 1890 he visited a friend who had moved to Southborough. At dinner the daughter of his host expressed her dismay that her brother had recently joined 'those wicked socialists'. Meek's memoirs are silent as to whether he then made contact with the SDF in Tunbridge Wells, but within a few months he had become a socialist himself, losing a steady job at the Liberal Club as a result. In the summer of 1893 he established a branch of the Fabian Society, in the Sussex resort.[190]

Of more immediate importance, James and Elizabeth Milstead, a brother and sister from Lamberhurst, on the border of Kent and Sussex, joined the SDF in the early 1890s. Both had moved to Tunbridge Wells at an early age to find work. In 1881 Elizabeth, then aged 21, and James, only 15, worked for a baker and confectioners in the High Street, close to the Central Station. The owner of the bakery, Mr Boorman, had himself come from Lamberhurst. Probably on account of their work, they tended to keep a low profile for a few years, though *Justice* on a few occasions recorded donations from James for various industrial disputes and election contests. After the mid-1890s a slightly freer political climate allowed them to take a more prominent role in the party, James became one of the Federation's councillors, and both continued to be active until at least the First World War.[191]

Of all those who joined in these years, we know the most about Rose Bigwood. Her motivation might be considered primarily humanitarian rather than political. Educated by her father, a Baptist minister from West Brompton in London, she had worked as a missionary among the poor at Brighton and Wandsworth before moving to Tunbridge Wells. On arrival, she came into contact with both the Women's Liberal Association and the SDF. Both organisations tried to recruit her. She agreed to teach members of the SDF some French and German, though she had some misgivings about a party still closely associated with atheism, and

---

[190] *Fabian News June 1891; Justice September 19th 1891; Meek, G. p148; Coxall and Griggs pp57-58; Fabian News August 1893.*
[191] *Justice August 2nd 1892 and June 14th 1893.*

was told off for pushing socialist views at a series of university extension lectures.

The decisive movement came in October 1890 when the *Advertiser* published her letter condemning conditions in the Lew, near St John's Church. She singled out properties in Sweetbriar Row and Caley's Cottages, described as 'not fit for a horse or a dog'. To deal with such slums and the attendant overcrowding - two, three or four roomed houses there accommodated large families - she argued that the town council should alleviate unemployment by building better quality homes. The landlords threatened to sue her.

Rose Jarvis (née Bigwood) in 1906 (British Library, used with permission)

David Geer wrote a letter which picked up on her correspondence and invited her to join the party.[192]

Rose soon took up this offer and shortly afterwards married Tom Jarvis. Both Tom and Rose won election to the provincial slate to the Federation's executive, Rose being the only woman ever to achieve this. Over the next few years she spoke at a London demonstration for universal suffrage for all men and women regardless of wealth or marital status, challenged stereotypes of male and female work and argued repeatedly for free school meals on the basis that children could not learn if hungry.[193]

Unfortunately Tom Jarvis' health soon deteriorated and by October 1892 they moved to Pond End Farm, Blackmoor, a village near Liss. *Justice* suggests that they may have worked with William Willis-Harris, who lived fairly close by, to organise a handful of meetings in towns near the border of Sussex and Hampshire. However, as

---

[192] *Tunbridge Wells Advertiser October 24th 1890.*
[193] *Northampton Pioneer, May 1906; Hunt p269-270, Beer, M., A History of British Socialism (London: Bell and Sons 1920) p277; Justice October 4th 1923.*

will be shown, they later moved to a village outside Sevenoaks and again played a full part in the life of the Tunbridge Wells branch.[194]

By 1891 the improvement in the local economy first apparent in the late 1880s had strengthened and work, if hard and poorly paid, at least became plentiful in the warmer months. The establishment of new industries, attracted to places with relatively clean air and water, benefitted the town. This was exemplified by the Photochrom Company of Upper Grosvenor Road, which pioneered colour photography, and the carriage and motor car works of Rock, Hawkins and Thorpe, opened in 1892 on Grosvenor Road. The opening of a second railway route to London in 1888 and the transformation of the branch to Brighton into a double track main line led to a major enlargement of Tunbridge Wells West station over the next half decade or so.[195]

Developers also started work on major new residential estates such as the Madeira and Molyneux Park developments at around this time. Most significantly, a labour bureau opened annually from at least January 1891, which gave the unemployed a chance to cut wood into small pieces for kindling. The low rates of pay for the men employed there angered the socialists and the unions, but there is little doubt that it took the edge off winter unemployment and perhaps helped re-enforce notions of a division between the deserving and undeserving poor.[196]

The SDF therefore turned towards redistributing some of the proceeds of this relative prosperity to their own class. Several members joined the town's Trades Council at its formation in 1891. In September this resolved to demand that workers at the Borough Council would finish at one o'clock on Saturday without loss of pay. When put to the vote the Borough Council overwhelmingly rejected the demand. The Trades Council then announced that union members working on improvements to the Council Chamber would walk out at one o'clock and take the consequences.

---

[194] *Hunt p157-9, 160-1, p207, p243; Fabian News October 1893; Fabian Society List of Members (London: George Standring 1892).*
[195] *Mitchell, V, and Smith, K, Branch Lines to Tunbridge Wells from Oxted, Lewes and Polegate (Midhurst: Middleton Press 2005).*
[196] *Tunbridge Wells Journal February 19th 1891.*

113

WOOD WORKERS' FINE RECORD

Tom Cox, Tom Morris, David Geer and B Evans photographed in 1943. The first three were all active members of the Carpenters and Joiners Union for over 50 years, as well as the SDF.

David Geer and another man, both ringleaders of the strike, failed to persuade the majority to follow them. They were dismissed the following Monday. Yet they had won themselves a platform. Maidstone's Councillor Beale addressed a meeting at the Friendly Societies Hall in their defence. The secretaries of the London Building Trades Society and the Amalgamated Society of House Decorators joined him on the platform. In return the Carpenters and Joiners Union branch collected £1 1s to support a strike in London. The trade union demand for shorter hours was linked by speakers to the need for more working-class representation on the council.[197]

After a period of relative inactivity, the SDF again made headlines in the town's press in early 1892. The Town Clerk's salary had been a long-running sore for some years. Some on the council now called for a near-doubling of it, from £250 to £450 a year. The Federation organised a meeting in protest at the Town Hall in February. This, rather like Rose Jarvis's earlier efforts, led to threats of legal action and, although the branch made no formal apology, they seemed to have been rather cautious for a period.[198]

David Geer achieved rather more, though predominantly as a trade unionist rather than a socialist. In October 1892 he presided over a meeting, supported by its national organiser Mr Matkin, to set up a new branch of the Carpenters and Joiners Union. He had been forced to leave to town to find work, but now set himself up as an

---

[197] *The Courier September 4th 1891, October 2nd 1891, November 2nd 1906; Tunbridge Wells Journal January 23rd 1890, September 10th 1891; Tunbridge Wells Gazette September 11th 1891; The Workmen's Times September 11th 1891; Clarion April 15th 1895; Aubry, B., Red Flows The Medway (Rochester: The Pocock Press 2003) p143.*
[198] *The Tunbridge Wells Advertiser July 5th 1889; The Courier February 5th 1892; Tunbridge Wells Journal January 7th 1892 and February 11th 1892.*

independent tradesman, specialising in shopfronts and fittings. This gave him some financial stability.

In March 1893 Geer broke new ground by speaking at High Brooms on behalf of the Cooperative Society. The same month he signed a letter in support of Louisa Twining's campaign to be elected as a Poor Law Guardian. Twining had long been active in fighting for better conditions in workhouses and continued these efforts at Pembury. Geer signed with a number of other leading trade unionists, Liberal and Tory politicians, Councillor Saunders and even the Reverend Mountain. Such initiatives suggest a degree of flexibility which eventually paid dividends within the town's labour movement.[199]

Through the years 1893 and 1894 the Tunbridge Wells branch seemed to tread water, carrying out little activity other than selling *Justice* and holding a few meetings on the Common. Tunbridge Wells SDF and the Trades and Labour Council both sent delegates to the meetings of a new county-wide organisation, the Eight Hours League of Kent.

Economic factors suggested some scope for reviving the right to work campaign. In January 1893 the two hundred men out of work left 16 families and 72 children facing absolute destitution. Some turned to crime. In March one young mother, Anne Joyce, stole some groceries. The magistrates, accepting that she had been forced to act in this way by poverty, decided that fining or jailing her could only be counter-productive.[200]

Elsewhere, however, things had begun to move. The Independent Labour Party was formed in January 1893 at a conference in Bradford. The Eight Hours League of Kent held a meeting in Dover that July and decided to re-name itself the Kentish Independent Labour Party. Arthur Field carried out much of the organisational work of the new body and with considerable justification claimed fifty years later to be one of the founders of the national party. The Tunbridge Wells SDF also had the right to send a delegate to the ILP's first few Kent conferences. The Tunbridge Wells Cooperative Society joined a group of Sussex societies. In the early 1890s David Geer and James Sutton, as well as their ally William Bournes,

---

[199] *The Courier November 10th 1893; Twining, L., Reflections of Life and Work (London: Edward Arnold 1893)..*
[200] *Tunbridge Wells Journal January 5th 1893, March 9th 1893.*

travelled to represent the town at the conferences of both the Kent ILP and Sussex cooperative societies.[201]

Yet the work often seemed impossible. Arthur Field, in a phrase which like Constance Howell's earlier observations would also not be out of place in the *Ragged Trousered Philanthropists*, concluded despairingly in August 1892 that the workers of Kent were:

> *'Retained in a position of clumsily administered feudalism, they tamely submit to the rule of their robbers and when they start to think and move it is only with the object of substituting a more plausible set of robbers for those now in power. Liberals and Tories, Tories and Liberals, for ever and ever!'*[202]

One surprising exception was Sevenoaks. As the history of the movements in Sevenoaks and Tunbridge Wells are closely tied together it is useful to give a brief outline of events in the former. For any reader not from the area, it should be noted that the two towns are about twelve miles apart and are linked by both the road and main railway line running from London to Hastings. Sevenoaks in the early 1890s had just begun to expand as a result of London commuting (the railway arrived in the 1860s, much later than Tunbridge Wells and Tonbridge), and a limited amount of industrialisation near what is now Sevenoaks Bat and Ball Railway Station but in many ways it still felt like a small market town set high upon the Greensand Ridge.

In June 1892 Arthur Hickmott, previously known to the Tunbridge Wells movement as a secularist lecturer, joined the national Fabian Society,. A few months later, Tom and Rose Jarvis moved to the area. In February 1893 the *Sevenoaks Chronicle* announced that a Sevenoaks Progressive Association had been formed. Weeks later it called for 'genuine', or independent, labour representation in local government and put forward a series of demands, pledging to support any candidate who supported them. In August the Deptford and Greenwich Socialist Society visited and distributed material.

---

[201] *Tunbridge Wells Journal January 5th 1893, March 9th 1893; Justice, July 8th 1893, July 15th 1893 and December 30th 1893; letter from Arthur Field to Herbert Bryan March 7th 1937 (Working Class Movement Library, Salford); the Dover Express 7th July 1893; Hastings and St Leonards Observer June 17th 1893; The Bromley and District Times July 12th 1895; Crick, History, p72.*
[202] *Workman's Times, August 13th 1892.*

The picture then becomes very confused. By the end of August the Independent Labour Party held a meeting in the town. The following month the *Courier* reported that a branch of the SDF would soon be formed in Sevenoaks. Finally, in December, a 'Socialist Labor Society' formed and met at Arthur and Ellen Hickmott's house.[203]

Most of these organisations soon died away, with only the ILP branch surviving for any period of time. It is likely that any chance of the SDF establishing a lasting presence at Sevenoaks collapsed when Tom and Rose Jarvis moved again, this time to Beare Green Farm, Holmwood, a few miles from Dorking. Arthur Hickmott though continued to play a significant role in several organisations.

The Kentish Independent Labour Party elected him treasurer in July 1893 and he won a seat on Sevenoaks Urban District Council as a 'Labour and Socialist' candidate in 1894. In May that year he wrote to *Justice* about rural unemployment and land redistribution in his capacity as Secretary of the Sevenoaks Independent Labour Party. Although it is not clear when he joined the SDF, he had certainly done so by November 1895 as that month he advertised his drapery business in *Justice*, something which only party members had the right to do.[204]

The state of the branch, the region and the wider party during the winter of 1893-4 can now be considered. Ten years had passed since the SDF assumed its current name and first published *Justice* as a weekly paper. At Tunbridge Wells the movement could also be regarded as a decade old, as William Willis-Harris had moved to the town in March 1884. The SDF's branches at Sheerness and Brighton had collapsed over the past few months, leaving Tunbridge Wells, Southampton, Grays and Reading as the only functioning southern branches outside London. Some encouragement came at the end of December 1893 when *Justice* paid tribute to the activists at Tunbridge Wells, alongside those of South Salford, Blackburn, Darwen, Northampton, Aberdeen and Liverpool, for their role in

203 *The National Reformer January 18th 1885 and February 1st 1885; Fabian News June 1892; The Sevenoaks Chronicle February 10th & 24th 1893 and March 29th 1893; Justice, August 19th 1893; The Courier August 28th 1893 and September 6th 1893; Fabian News December 1893.*
204 *Justice, October 4th 1923; The Courier May 11th 1906; Justice, November 30th 1895; Justice, May 5th 1894; ILP News May 1898 p6; Fabian News December 1894, January 1895.*

transforming the SDF from a London-based radical grouping into a national political party.[205]

Otherwise the year 1894 proved most notable for the list of leading activists departing the town. It is also one of the few years for which there is no evidence of new members coming forward. It is not clear why this should have been so. The SDF claimed a doubling of national membership during these twelve months; even if this claim is exaggerated it is clear that the local situation did not match the national pattern. Tom and Rose Jarvis left the district completely, moving to a house in Upper Clapton, London, from where Rose stood for the Hackney School Board election. Charles Barden likewise left the town to run a photographer's studio in the Sussex city of Chichester.

The fall in the membership led the branch to curtail its activities further. They continued to meet weekly at David Geer's house and a number of members contributed financially to support strikes and election campaigns. Yet, for the first time in eight years, there is no evidence of outdoor meetings taking place in the warmer months. The branch's most notable activity came in late April and early May, when Tunbridge Wells' gardens and allotments supplied the flowers for the SDF's vehicles taking part in the May Day parade in London.[206]

Some of the divisions between liberalism and socialism began to crumble around this period. The Women's Liberal Association invited a Fabian Society, lecturer, Mrs Mallet, to address a public meeting at Tunbridge Wells Town Hall in March. Her lecture gave a brief history of the campaign for women's suffrage and called for working women and poor widows to be given the vote, implicitly endorsing the campaign for adult suffrage adopted by the SDF from its foundation. Significantly a number of the town's trade unionists, including Councillor Saunders, William Bournes and Scrace, joined a group of Liberal Party activists on the platform. Bournes paid tribute to William Gladstone, who had recently stepped down as Prime Minister, and expressed his hope that his successor, Lord Roseberry would continue on the same path.

---

[205] *Justice*, June 3rd 1893, December 30th 1893.
[206] *Crick, History*, p86; *Justice*, June 12th & 16th 1894; *Fabian News* May 1894; *Fabian Society List of Members (London: George Standring 1894); Justice*, May 12th & 19th 1894. *Justice gave details of branch meetings most weeks.*

A day later Mrs Mallet spoke on similar themes at Fordcombe, a tiny village a few miles to the west. This might seem a strange choice, but the following year Jane Escombe won election to Penshurst Parish Council, which includes Fordcombe. In time she was successful in pushing for progressive policies including the construction of municipal housing, clean water and an isolation hospital for the district. A working man also won election to the parish council and supported her efforts. Six houses – named Pioneer Cottages – stand on Smart's Hill as an enduring tribute to their work. Socialist ideas had begun to permeate the least likely places.[207]

Pioneer Cottages, Smart's Hill, Penshurst
(British Library, used with permission)

Edith Abbott, active in the Tunbridge Wells Women's Cooperative Guild, echoed these calls by presenting a paper to the organisation's annual congress on the workings of the Poor Law. She pushed for greater female representation on Boards of Guardians, something permitted since their formation in 1834, and perhaps used Miss Twining's victory in Tunbridge Wells as an example. The WCG circulated a copy of her speech to branches throughout the country and 45 Guild members stood at the next election, 22 of them successfully. Unsurprisingly, this developed into a campaign to encourage more women to stand for local government and to grant them the vote at general elections.[208]

Organised labour also made some gains. The Municipal Council Labour Representation League and the Trades Council, again often with William Bournes to the fore, repeatedly demanded that the council use local labour rather than contracting work out and that all should be paid at the standard local union rates. Private firms also faced this demand. In May and June the bricklayers of Tunbridge Wells, Tonbridge and Crowborough took strike action. Some firms immediately conceded the demand for a rise in the hourly rate but others dragged their feet for several weeks before

---

[207]*Fabian News March 1894; The Courier March 9th 1894; Carwardine, A., Disgusted Ladies p64. See also John Boughton's website Municipal Dreams.*
[208] *Gaffin and Thoms, D., Caring and Sharing, pp78-79.*

conceding. However, though prolonged, the dispute seems to have been more peaceful than those in other areas.[209]

Yet socialism proved a sickly infant. The ILP made some inroads. Branches of the new party formed at Maidstone, Chatham, New Brompton, Dover and Northfleet. Rallies took place in a number of market towns and agricultural or industrial villages, including Chipstead Common, Riverhead, East and West Malling, Aylesford, Loose, Snodland, Halling, Burham, East Farleigh and Mereworth, sometimes with the support of London branches. Yet, except for Arthur Hickmott, few avowed socialist or labour candidates achieved great success at the municipal elections that autumn.

Most of the handful of working men who won seats on West Kent's parish councils had stood as Liberals or even Conservatives, much as Champion had previously suggested; and Arthur Field's crushing defeat at Maidstone, where he achieved a mere seven votes despite assiduously seeking the endorsement of organisations such as the Stone Street Working Men's Radical Club, proved to be merely the worst of a bad set of results. Field had fallen out with much of Kent's ILP and seems to have tried to organise a Maidstone branch of the Fabian Society, and a Maidstone Socialist Society, neither of which lasted. At Tunbridge Wells the Municipal Council Labour Representation League struggled to agree to support any candidate, though William Bournes ran for a seat as an independent candidate in the North Ward and won a creditable 218 votes. The Social-Democrats, it appears, lacked the resources to put a candidate forward.[210]

---

[209] *The Courier March 16th 1894, September 7th 1894, May 25th 1894, June 1st 1894 and June 8th 1894.*
[210] *Kent and Sussex Courier July 6th 1894; Sevenoaks Telegraph and Kent Messenger July 7th 1894, September 1st 1894; Tunbridge Wells Journal November 8th 1894, December 8th 1894; Clark, P and Murfin, L., The History of Maidstone p183.*

Workmen improving the services in Goods Station Road (date and photographer unknown but probably in the first decade of the Twentieth Century). The SDF supported schemes such as this to introduce proper sewerage into working class districts as well as to provide jobs. The election of SDF and Fabian Society councillors made it easier to persuade the Council to commit money to such areas.

PART B   TURNING THE BOROUGH RED?

CHAPTER 7   REBIRTH, MOMENTUM AND TRIUMPH

1895

is perhaps the year in which the SDF's branch was at its weakest, but also marks the beginning of its revival. The next few chapters show how, with some outside help, it soon equalled and then surpassed its strength of the late-1880s. Factors such as disillusionment with the moderate course of the Liberal government encouraged many radicals and trade unionists to join its ranks, while it also recruited from a new generation. The same years also saw the town's trade unions strengthen and the formation of a local branch of the Fabian Society.

The local elections at the end of the year showed that support for socialist ideas could win far more votes than had been the case previously. The SDF gained its first councillor in 1897. It is the importance which the branch gave to winning representation for the working class which gives the years from 1895 to 1905 a unifying theme, together with its concentration on municipal, rather than private, ownership of services. The jingoism inspired by the Second Boer War led to a reactionary backlash and reduced the socialist vote significantly, though they retained at least one representative on the council throughout these years.

None of this was pre-ordained. The 1895 *Labour Annual* noted the presence of the Trades and Labour Council and two separate left-wing political organisations. The Municipal Council Labour Representation League met at William Bournes' house in the St John's district and the Social-Democratic Federation convened at David Geer's dwelling in the East Ward. It is telling that neither used a larger space, although the Trades Council, Cooperative Society and individual trade unions regularly filled public halls.

Due recognition should be paid to the work of those who had kept the Socialist branch going against all odds, such as David Geer and James Milstead. Crucially they proved adaptable enough to take advantage of the rising tide of interest in socialist ideas, and advanced new causes such as municipal housing. Although formal activity may have been limited, a thirst for socialist ideas remained, something recognised when F G Miles and Co, a newsagent in a prominent position in Calverley Road, decided to become one of the relatively few official agents for *Justice* in September.[211]

The first campaign of 1895 concerned unemployment. By February the Pembury Workhouse held 547 permanent or semi-permanent inmates, 121 'vagrants' had recently used the casual ward and 757 had received outdoor relief in Tunbridge Wells town alone, demonstrating the inability of even so large a workhouse to provide for all those out of work. The town's relief committee had assisted a total of 1,200 people by March that year. David Geer, acting in his new capacity of Secretary of the Trades Council, called for the construction of public baths.

The handful of councillors with left-leaning sympathies asked the Town Clerk to read a government circular, initially issued by Joseph Chamberlain in 1886, which encouraged local authorities to borrow money for public works to boost employment, rather than relying on the Poor Law. The Trades Council also called on the Borough to commit to employing direct labour rather than contractors. The Borough Councillors rejected a motion to this effect, introduced by Councillor Saunders, by 5 votes to 19. Many of the more ambitious public works proposals suffered the same fate although 313 men obtained temporary work clearing the snow from the streets in January and February.[212]

The summer seems to have been fairly quiet, though with one notable exception. In June the various Cooperative Societies affiliated to the Lewes District – which included Portsmouth, Portsea, Tunbridge Wells and Reigate as well as such Sussex towns as Brighton. Hastings, Arundel and Eastbourne – held their quarterly conference at Tunbridge Wells. David Geer read a paper on behalf of another co-operator, Mr Penn, who had suffered a family bereavement.

The Tunbridge Wells Society had by that stage achieved one of the highest turnovers in the region. In its geographical scope, the meeting can be seen as a precursor of the South Eastern Counties Federation of Socialist Societies, an organisation which a decade later aimed to build links across Sussex, Surrey and Hampshire, as

---

[211] *Justice September 18th 1895.*
[212] *Tunbridge Wells Journal February 7th & 15th 1895 & March 25th 1895; Tunbridge Wells Journal March 14th 1895; Harris, J. p76-77; The Courier April 12th 1895; The Courier March 22nd 1895; Tunbridge Wells Journal March 28th 1895.*

well as Kent, and in which Tunbridge Wells played an even greater role.[213]

A few weeks before the municipal elections an industrial dispute arose at just the right moment to again link the causes of trade unionism and working- class representation. Sir David Lionel Salomons, the owner of Broomhill, had been appointed Mayor of Tunbridge Wells that year. His uncle had distinguished himself in Liberal Party politics by leading a campaign to allow Jews the right to serve in municipal politics in the City of London and later won a parliamentary seat at Greenwich, yet the younger man's interests at the time tended to be in engineering, having promoted the use of electricity, motor cars and improved railway signalling.

Trouble came when the building firm working on his estate dismissed seventeen carpenters for demanding a halfpenny per hour pay rise. The Carpenters and Joiners Union branch had not formally sanctioned the dispute but its supporters quickly printed handbills calling for a boycott of the site. Geer also championed the cause of the men, while he and William Bournes carefully explained that they had no quarrel with the Mayor himself and later highlighted some of the mistakes made by the strikers. Such respect did not last; over the next few decades Sir David's support for protectionism, alignment with the Conservatives and opposition to municipal housing in the vicinity of his estate would draw withering rebukes from the Socialists, in particular those who had previously been members of the Liberal Party.[214]

David Geer's role in the dispute made him an obvious person to run for municipal office in his native East Ward as the official candidate of the Trades Council. However this led to some controversy – the Trades Council itself had earlier in the year been accused of being a 'socialist scheme' and it is clear that some were wary of his membership of the SDF. It seems that heated discussions followed, though these received little press coverage. His nomination, significantly seconded by Councillor Saunders, came in mid-October. As a result, neither *Justice* nor the other socialist papers mentioned his candidacy. A meeting in support, at which William Bournes and others emphasised his work as a trade unionist rather than his socialism, followed.[215]

---

[213] *The Courier 14th June 1895.*
[214] *The Courier 13th September 1895.*
[215] *The Courier October 16th 1895 and October 25th 1895.*

The East Ward election generated much more interest than the others that year. Geer faced two rivals for the seat who had the resources to arrange carriages adorned with their posters to bring supporters to the polling station. They also targeted 'the fairer sex', whom they considered to be more sceptical of socialism. Votes for the other two candidates, Hobart and Foyle, had built up throughout the day, though the tide showed signs of turning in the final hour of polling when 214 working men voted. Geer won 347 votes, his opponents gaining 422 and 421, and despite not winning a seat got much of the applause. Geer's result proved to be one of the two most promising in Kent that year. Arthur Field, who may well have been at the count, reflected that:

> 'At Tunbridge Wells and Dover a socialist ran, in each case backed by a Trade Council, after some hard work to force them into that attitude. At Tunbridge Wells David Geer of the SDF stood for the East Ward and polled 347 votes, against 422 and 421 of his opponents. A year or two ago he put up and polled 30. He hid no facts. In his address after the poll he said that his views had been known for ten or twelve years past. He had been handicapped this time by insufficient means of advertising and organising but with another year of publicity and education he intended to 'get there'. He wound up declaring that those who called themselves the upper classes would bless the day (as much as the workers) that ushered in the reign of socialism...' [216]

This result can be seen as a turning point in the fortunes of the SDF in Kent, persuading its scattered and jaded supporters that the cause could be won. For the moment the Independent Labour Party had fallen into disarray, with Arthur Field very publicly at loggerheads with the Rochester branch. Nationally the party, having failed to win any parliamentary seats, saw its membership slump from 35,000 to 20,000 in twelve months. Some of those who supported both organisations seem to have favoured the Federation. Significantly, both Arthur Hickmott and Arthur Field wrote a letter to *Justice* in May which criticised Keir Hardie's hostility to socialists who opposed, or did not prioritise, the parliamentary route. Hickmott joined both socialist parties. Field now found he had more in common with the Social-Democrats than his erstwhile allies and in 1898 he wrote part of a pamphlet commemorating the life of Eleanor Marx for them. He remained a member of the Federation and its successors, though for health reasons he became less active

---

[216] *The Courier November 1st & 6th & 8th 1895, The Clarion November 16th 1895.*

in 1903 after fifteen years of 'shouting, fighting and starving'. At one point he withdrew from the ILP but re-joined in 1911.[217]

George Lansbury

Perhaps encouraged by the result, the very first copy of *Justice* in 1896 included correspondence from members calling for a SDF campaign in Kent. Dartford was suggested as an obvious starting point. George Lansbury, then the Federation's Organising Secretary (and regarded by Hyndman as the best ever occupant of that role), decided that both Tunbridge Wells – formerly 'a very good centre for Socialist democracy' - and Dartford should be prioritised. He subsequently devoted considerable time to visiting both places, making practical suggestions to the few remaining activists in Tunbridge Wells about how they could organise themselves more effectively.[218]

As well as supporting the branch's reorganisation, a task which seems to have taken from January to April, George Lansbury visited Tunbridge Wells to speak at a public meeting in February. Lansbury is better remembered for his later work as an outspoken supporter of women's suffrage, a pacifist during the First World War and ultimately as a principled Christian Socialist and leader of the Labour Party in the 1930s. In the 1890s he had briefly abandoned his religious faith for secularism and embraced a militant form of socialism. Those gathered in the Oddfellows Hall that late winter's night enjoyed a lecture based on his personal evolution towards socialism, followed by a call for the working men of the town to join the party and 'be done with the cant and cruelty of capitalist-political promises, and work out their own material salvation by active opposition to Liberal, Radical and Tory organisations'. The *Tunbridge Wells Journal* praised his 'excellent address'. Councillor Hickmott also reiterated the call for all those present in the room to join. Other speakers apologised for the fact that things had 'been

---

[217] *Crick, History, p87; letter from Arthur Field to Herbert Bryan March 7th 1937 (Working Class Movement Library, Salford).*
[218] *Justice May 23rd & 29th 1896; Justice January 4th & 25th 1896; also see Shepherd, J. George Lansbury: at the Heart of Old Labour (Oxford University Press 2002).*

quiet lately' and that they would soon 'put the questions of socialism before the people of the town'.[219]

The focus on recruiting soon paid off. It is not always possible to pinpoint exactly when a particular person joined the party, but it seems obvious that quite a number did so in 1896 and 1897. Some, such as Thomas Morris, a carpenter from Pembury, had known David Geer as a colleague and trade unionist, and probably joined the Federation as a result of this personal connection. A few defected from the Liberal Party; Ellis Mann, a 'one-time radical, like most of us', had become disillusioned that, previous rhetoric aside, the Liberal Government had proved timid in government. Mann agreed to take on a succession of jobs in the branch and in August 1901 won election to the Federation's National Executive.

For the first time in some years the party recruited from the middle classes when Frank Colebrook joined the branch. Colebrook, editor of the *Printing Times and Lithographer*, had been well-acquainted with William Morris, who had recently died. A lecture delivered by him in London on Morris' working methods and socialist beliefs had been carried in this paper, which a Tunbridge Wells publisher then turned into a pamphlet, though some of the political content in the original article had been edited out. Colebrook felt it important to argue that Morris' socialism had not primarily been founded on economic theories but instead reflected the aesthetic concerns of John Ruskin. He also recalled Morris' lectures to unemployed workmen and his selling the *Commonweal* on the Strand. Colebrook subsequently wrote to *Justice* several times on education policy in the years ahead. Interestingly he also wrote a guide to the town. The diversity of the new intake reinforced the intellectual energy apparent within the branch from its foundation and in time would enable it to run series of lectures on fields from literature to economics.[220]

Such recruitment and reinvigoration meant that H W Lee, Editor of *Justice*, wrote that the Tunbridge Wells branch had turned the

---

[219] *Justice February 8th,15th & 26th 1896, March 14th 1896; the Tunbridge Wells Journal February 27th 1896.*
[220] *The Courier July 15th 1947; Justice July 12 1902; Justice August 10th 1901; William Morris master-printer : a lecture given on the evening of November 27, 1896, to students of the Printing School, St. Bride Foundation Institute in London by Frank Colebrook; edited with a new introduction by William S. Peterson ; wood engravings by John DePol (see versions published in Council Bluffs, Iowa : Yellow Barn Press, c1989 and Tunbridge Wells: Lewis Hepworth and Co. 1897); Simon, B., Education and the Labour Movement 1870-1920 (London: Lawrence and Wishart 1965) p230.*

corner, was now 'going ahead in a first rate manner and will soon be thoroughly reorganised'. This of course meant a resumption of regular public meetings to supplement the internal organisational meetings which had continued uninterrupted for virtually a decade. The first of these, inspired by those which had taken place in London and other major cities around the world since 1890 and in some provincial towns, including Maidstone and Rochester a few years later, celebrated May Day,

In a classic British compromise this took place on the first Sunday of the month rather than on the actual day, therefore not amounting to a symbolic one-day withdrawal of labour as often happened on the Continent. In Tunbridge Wells that year it also proved a somewhat low-key affair compared to other places; twenty or thirty members and supporters met indoors for tea and speeches, presumably having first decorated the hall with foliage and flowers to mark the season. Although progress had been made, the branch may still have consisted of only a couple of dozen members.[221]

The meetings in June and July, whether indoors or on the Common, drew much larger crowds and often featured home-grown talent. Tom Jarvis addressed an audience at the Cooperative Halls about the need for politics independent of the two main parties. Tunbridge Wells Common on Sunday afternoons in late June now resembled London's Hyde Park, with 'various communities of religious, temperance and socialistic views... promulgating their doctrines to large audiences'. The Battersea branch visited the town for the first time in five years. Clearly impressed by the improved fortunes of socialism at Tunbridge Wells, the *Courier* covered the proceedings in some detail. Visiting speakers addressed audiences near the rocks by the Mount Edgcumbe Hotel, followed by an evening meeting on the 'slopes of Mount Ephraim'. David Geer presided on both occasions. The *Courier* admitted that several hundred men and women had attended the evening meeting, some straight after attending religious services, and that their literature had sold well. Equally significantly, none of the audience challenged the points made by the socialists. Although the branch in Tunbridge Wells had never formally folded, the increased activity led the newspaper to label the branch a new one.[222]

---

[221] *Justice April 18th 1896, May 9th 1896; Aubry, Red Flows the Medway p66, p67.*
[222] *The Courier June 5th 1896, June 26th 1896, July 24th 1896.*

A broader change in culture and leisure gave branches such as Tunbridge Wells a further fillip. The falling cost and greater availability of bicycles liberated adventurous working class men and women from all backgrounds, allowing them to travel more freely. Late Victorian and Edwardian publishers accordingly produced a range of guidebooks suggesting that city-dwellers might wish to explore areas of the countryside within a few hours ride from their homes. The idea spread to smaller places. In 1892 a Labour Cycling Club formed in the Medway Towns and in July 1893 a correspondent to *Justice* suggested the formation of a socialist cycling club which might 'attack the Kent towns'. The *Clarion* newspaper in particular urged the formation of such clubs, though uptake proved faster in the Midlands and the North than in the South.

Despite this, by 1914 seventeen existed in London and four in other parts of the region. The paper also briefly published a journal, *The Scout*, which offered tips on everything from bicycle maintenance through nature notes to public speaking. In early 1895 Tom and Rose Jarvis became the forty-second and forty-third registered members of the Clarion Scouts. The SDF and ILP quickly saw the benefits both for propagandising the countryside and assisting established branches. In July 1895 the ILP visited 25 villages in the triangle between Maidstone, Hadlow and Cranbrook, delivering 1,000 leaflets a day. H W Lee wrote to *Justice* in April 1896 suggesting that 'any of our cycling friends who wish for a day's pleasure and propaganda combined might think of Tunbridge Wells and Dartford. Both places would be very glad of help'.[223]

Although outside assistance may have been vital in April, by late May or early June the branch had grown sufficiently to be able to send activists to assist meetings in other places. Arthur Hickmott and Rose Jarvis both spoke at a Clarion Cycling Club rally at the Angel Corner, Tonbridge, though the *Courier* suggested that few of the locals showed much interest. The SDF's own London cycling group then rode to 'Tunbridge' – whether Tonbridge or the Wells, or both, is not clear - in August. Arthur Hickmott and Tom and Rose Jarvis may also have been involved in organising another rally of

[223] *For an example of such a guidebook, see Hope Moncrieff, A. R {Ed} Black's Guide Books: West Kent (London: Adam and Charles Black) 1909. See also Justice July 1st 1893; Aubry p73; Clarion July 6th 1895; and Pye, D, Fellowship, p25, The Scout March 1895.*

Frontispiece by Herbert Cole from Arthur Hickmott's Songs of a Shopman, his 1910 collection of poetry

the Clarion Scouts at Otford, a village in the Darenth Valley a few miles north of Sevenoaks, in September.[224]

The branch continued to grow rapidly that summer. In late July and early August Rose Jarvis represented it at the meeting of the Second International, formally the Congress of the International Socialist Workers and Trades Union Congress, which met that year in London. Although she lived at Croydon at the time, her husband Tom had a Sevenoaks address. The Tunbridge Wells branch had fifty members on the books, making it one of the biggest branches of either the Federation or the ILP in the region.

Yet, in a reminder of the way in which the labour movement in the south had fallen behind other parts of the country, Tunbridge Wells Trades Council only represented 270 workers from its affiliated unions. The handful of other trades councils in Kent and Sussex were little larger, whereas some towns and cities in the Midlands and North reached the tens of thousands. The Trades Council elected David Geer as its delegate, demonstrating how much respect he had earned from those who were not members of his party. Two days of the congress were dominated by heated arguments over whether anarchists should be admitted while other debates only emphasised the lack of unity between British socialists such as Hyndman and leading figures from the German SPD.[225]

---

[224] *The Clarion June 6th 1896; the Courier June 12th 1896; Justice August 11th 1896; The Clarion September 25th 1896.*
[225] *Anon, Conference Record: A record of the International Socialist Workers and Trades Union Congress (London 1896); Kendall Rogers, H., Before the Revisionist Controversy: Kautsky, Bernstein, and the Meaning of Marxism 1895-1898 (London: Routledge 2015) pp208-214.*

Edith Lanchester

A pair of SDF meetings at Tunbridge Wells in August 1896 looked set to encapsulate some of the wider divisions of late Victorian Britain. Edith Lanchester had been a middle class recruit to the SDF, standing for election to London's School Board in 1894 and had therefore worked with Tom and Rose Jarvis . In October 1895 she announced her decision to move in with her lover, James Sullivan, without first marrying him. In so doing, she had broken taboos about class, race (Sullivan came from a working-class Irish background) and religion. Her refusal to marry stemmed from her belief that by doing so she would become no more than a chattel of her husband. Her family persuaded a Dr Blandford to sign a certificate declaring her to be insane and of committing 'social suicide', thereby allowing her family to have her incarcerated at The Priory, then as now a leading private mental health hospital.

After a very public battle her supporters, who included John Burns, now the MP for Battersea, the SDF, other socialists, secularists and the Legitimation League - an organisation in which Henry Albert Seymour had taken a leading role – obtained her liberty. She later embarked on a tour of branches. However, both open air meetings had to be cancelled after about twenty minutes due to the appalling weather, though she later also addressed a hastily arranged meeting indoors. The impact of the visit seems somewhat muted as a result, although the town's papers gave it some coverage. Public sympathy seems to have been with her, as there seems to have been little opposition from the usual quarters to her visit.[226]

The Fabian Society formed a branch at Tunbridge Wells in 1896. As we have seen, William Willis-Harris, Henry Seymour and Tom and Rose Jarvis all joined this organisation early, although by now they had either left the district or resigned from the Society, leaving only Arthur Hickmott in Sevenoaks. Fabian lecturers had addressed meetings of the SDF, the Tunbridge Wells Cooperative Society and the Women's Liberal Association regularly for the best part of a decade and copies of their publications must have lined many

---

[226] *See Hunt pp 94-106; Rubenstein, D, Before the Suffragettes: Women's Emancipation in the 1890s (New York: St. Martin's Press 1986) especially pp58-63; The Courier August 14th 1896.*

131

Tunbridge Wells bookshelves. Some of this material can be considered as quite innovative, such as a diagram illustrating the distribution of wealth which showed the proportion of the national wealth taken up by rent, income and wages, an idea which sounds similar to 'the Oblong' in the *Ragged Trousered Philanthropists*. Initially the branch had twelve members, and may well have met at members' houses.

As is well-known, the Fabian Society, tended to recruit from middle class circles, in contrast to the SDF and ILP, and this is at least partly borne out in Tunbridge Wells, where tradesmen, doctors, lawyers and university graduates took the leading roles. Rather than trying to rival the Federation, the two tended to complement one another. Indeed a letter written in 1957 by Frank Lawson Dodd, a founding member, suggests that the local society may have been at the heart of a progressive alliance which largely transcended political lines. His claim that they had nine members on Tunbridge Wells Council at the turn of the nineteenth and twentieth centuries initially seems improbable, as only a couple had won election as Fabian Society candidates. However it is possible that the three members of the SDF and a number of left-wing Liberals had also joined the local society by then, although proving it is impossible as the records have not survived. The town's branch of the Fabian Society, like the Cooperative Society, long outlasted the SDF and indeed remains active to this day.[227]

Yet, despite this increase in activity, the 1896 election results proved somewhat disappointing. The Trades and Labour Council only ran candidates in the East Ward. Three candidates contested two seats. Councillor Saunders won re-election with 342 votes, whereas his right-wing rival, Joshua Robert Gower, easily topped the poll with 686. David Geer stood on a joint SDF and Trades and Labour Council platform. He failed to secure as many votes as he had done twelve months ago, although his score of 256 had credibility. Indeed *Justice*, which had ignored his campaign the previous year, noted that he had done well, and the result certainly surpassed that achieved by most of the Federation's other candidates.[228]

---

[227] *The Courier November 16th 1928; Fabian News June 1893; Letter from Frank Lawson Dodd to the Fabian Society, September 29th 1957.*
[228] *Justice November 14th 1896.*

Perhaps chastened by this result, the SDF and its allies turned towards the inadequacies of local housing. This issue had been raised by Rose Jarvis at the start of the decade but had not been a priority for some years. It is possible that this campaign may have also been intended to attract more women to the party, as its recent concentration on trade union matters may have appealed more to men. Crucially, boroughs and urban districts possessed the powers to provide new municipal housing and to improve existing stock under a series of Acts of Parliament starting with the Artisans' and Labourers' Dwellings Improvement Act of 1875. In common with much progressive Victorian legislation these laws permitted (rather than obliged) local authorities to act. Therefore, greater socialist representation on the council could lead to these policies being implemented.

On 16th February 1897 Frank Colebrook and David Geer addressed a crowded meeting at the Friendly Societies Hall to demand that Tunbridge Wells borrow enough money from the Government to construct at least one hundred cottages. Speakers from the floor recounted examples of houses being shared by two families and landlords pocketing exorbitant rents for properties little better than hovels. The points raised gained official confirmation a month later when a report by Dr Stannard, the Borough's Medical Officer, concluded that overcrowding in working class districts meant that the town should immediately build 200 new cottages.[229]

The work of the Fabian Society's new branch complimented the SDF's meetings. The Fabians wanted to make inroads into the South-East and sent J S Hamilton to give a series of lectures, illustrated by lantern slides, at Brighton, Tunbridge Wells, Ashford and St Leonards, the latter being a district described as 'hitherto largely unexplored where arrangements have been made for him with exceptional difficulties'. The Fabians in Tunbridge Wells followed this with what *Fabian News* praised as a very excellent list of lectures for its fortnightly Saturday meetings running from January to April, together with a further course of three lectures by Hamilton on Fridays in the Town Hall on the causes and cures of poverty. These meetings raised the need to construct municipal housing at every opportunity and by June *Fabian News* used the

---

[229] *Kent Times and Chronicle and Maidstone Advertiser* February 18th 1897; *Kent Times* March 18th 1897.

local society's agitation on the subject as an example for other Fabian groups to follow.[230]

Indoor meetings remained key, but the outdoor season in May 1897 started with a procession which can be regarded as a mixture of communal celebration and a demonstration of strength. Perhaps no other single event shows quite how quickly the branch and the wider movement had grown over a period of twelve months. On Labour Sunday a parade of hundreds of trade unionists and others through the working-class areas of the town culminated in a meeting on the Common. Speeches, led by the Secretary of the Trades Council, William Croxon, called for support for engineers locked out in a long-running national dispute and for the Council to provide resources to improve drainage.

Unfortunately the loss of most of the Kent newspapers for 1897 held at the Colindale Library during the Second World War means that there is less information about this parade than those of subsequent years. Enough remains to suggest that trade union organisation had strengthened in the last few months.[231]

The growing power of the town's unions faced a practical test within weeks. 1897 turned out to be something of a year of discontent. Across Kent the various building trades took strike action that summer and autumn. At Tunbridge Wells they paraded through the town in late June collecting donations and 'several dozen' met on the Common. The money thus collected amounted to five shillings for each married man and three for the unwed.

In early July the Federation's cyclists, fresh from a successful meeting at Woking the week before, rode to Tunbridge Wells to support the branch's rally in solidarity with the strikers. Resolution took many months. The Plasterers' Union agreed to return to work for a penny an hour rise in early July. The town's General Labourers demanded a rise of half a penny per hour and the carpenters pressed for a rate of 9d per hour and a maximum nine hour working day from the start of the next year. Even after the plasterers had settled their dispute, 300 other men remained on strike and further parades and collections took place. Other strikers sought work gathering in the hay in the surrounding countryside.

---

[230] *Fabian News February 1897, March 1897, June 1897.*
[231] *Kent Times June 3rd 1897; The Tunbridge Wells Advertiser May 13th 1898.*

134

To add fuel to the fire the Corporation announced that the £10,000 contract for the Corporation Baths had gone to an outside firm who would supply labour from London and elsewhere. The building workers returned to work that autumn. Almost immediately, a further dispute among corporation workmen for a one o'clock finish on Saturdays followed. Details of the strike itself are scarce, though thirty workmen signed a petition and the Ratepayers' and Property Owners' Association, among other bodies, gave their support for the men.[232]

It is hard to imagine a better set of circumstances for the socialist movement to contest the municipal elections. Points about municipal representation and strong unionisation had already been made by the events of the last few months. Again the focus turned to housing. As early as September the Fabian Society detected a change in attitude among sitting councillors and believed that Tunbridge Wells Borough Council had agreed to adopt the Act. This seems to have at least partly been propaganda as later events will show (they also claimed a similar victory in Dublin). The SDF organised a meeting at the Town Hall, with speakers from Brighton and Richmond, as well as local activists and some of the town's clergy. The speakers urged the town to construct municipal dwellings and called on those present to only vote for candidates who supported this demand. Some speakers again cited Dr Stannard's report. Ward meetings followed across the town later than month. The shortage of housing in the area around St Peter's Church meant that twenty people would apply for any cottage, even those in a state of disrepair.[233]

The Trades and Labour Council therefore endorsed two candidates, David Geer in the East Ward and H C Lander in the North. Both candidates campaigned primarily on the issue of municipal housing, Lawson Dodd making a particular pitch to women to support this policy. Others supporting Geer included William Bournes and Ellis Mann, previously another leading figure in local radical liberalism. Amid lively scenes, both candidates won fine victories. The report from *Justice* which appeared a few weeks later is worth quoting at length:

---

[232] *Kent Times June 10th 1897, the Tunbridge Wells Journal July 1st 1897, July 8th 1897, Kent Times October 28th 1897*
[233] *Fabian News September 1897.*

'Comrades here are enthusiastic over the return of Comrade D A Geer to the town council by a vote of 505, of which 395 were plumpers. The above result is largely due to the prominent part Geer has taken in forcing upon the council the adoption of the Housing of the Working Classes Act. His consistent advocacy of social democratic principles for many years past, and conduct generally on all labour questions, has broken down the prejudices of the majority of workmen, and commands the respect of opponents generally. Great credit is due to the many comrades and friends for the valuable work done in canvassing nearly the whole of the working class portion of the ward. It is interesting the note the progress of social democratic ideas, even in this 'strictly proper and respectable' town.'

The election campaign had been something of a reunion as Tom Jarvis and William Willis-Harris had returned to the town to canvas for Geer. *Justice* also noted the links which had been forged with other socialists in the town:

'I am also glad the report that the secretary of the local Fabian Society , H C Lander, has been returned to the top of the poll for the North Ward. Several members of the above society warmly supported and rendered valuable service on behalf of Geer's candidature. The return of two socialists on the council marks a new epoch in our municipal life'.

Lander's victory may in hindsight have been even more significant than Geer's, as no other Trades Council candidate had won in the North Ward, although Geer was certainly the first avowed revolutionary to win a seat in the town. All of the main socialist newspapers recorded the result. Ellis Mann wrote to the *Clarion* to inform its readers of the success of Geer and Lander. *Fabian News* also noted their wins. The SDF celebrated a number of good results that year, with the victory in Tunbridge Wells being one of a net gain of seven seats.[234]

Trebling the representation of the labour movement on Tunbridge Wells Council may initially appear to be more of an opportunity for propaganda than a way to make concrete gains. The town had a total of twenty-four councillors (a third being elected annually) and

---

[234] *Justice November 20th 1897, Kent Times and Chronicle and Maidstone Advertiser November 4th 1897 Justice November 6th 1897, The Clarion 20th November 1897, Fabian News October 1897, December 1897.*

the council then appointed a number of aldermen from its own ranks. Three Trades and Labour councillors could hardly therefore force through change on their own. In this light, it is interesting that most sitting members on the Council viewed the result as a mandate to look seriously at the housing situation. A number of councillors, including Geer, formed a new sub-committee at the start of January 1898. This decided that the Borough should apply for loan from the Local Government Board to buy and develop three and a quarter acres of land. The total cost included £1,200 for the purchase of land, £1,350 for making roads, £14,500 to build the houses and a sum of £1,700 set aside for contingencies. The whole Council held a special session in March and accepted the plan in its entirety. Yet, although not apparent at the time, those who disagreed with the scheme could play for time, hoping that even a slight reduction in the Labour presence on the council could be claimed as public support for its abandonment.[235]

As propaganda the result proved too good to waste. The old tactics of public meetings and letter-writing could now be supplemented by using the council chamber as a soap box. Left-wing policies, from union rates of pay for municipal contracts to raising police salaries could be passed as a resolution at a SDF or Trades Council meeting and moved a few days later in the Council Chamber by Geer, Lander or Saunders. Ellis Mann and Sir Charles Oakley, a leading local businessman, argued for weeks about the rights and wrongs of the engineers' lockout in the pages of the *Advertiser*. A number of public meetings followed. At one, George Lansbury called for utilities to be run by the Council, with any surplus funding the lighting the town's streets and installing electricity or gas in the homes of the working class. Joseph F Green and Frank Lawson Dodd of the town's Fabian Society ran a series of lectures on education, the poor law, and one under the title 'patriotism, true and false', a strong attack on militarism and racism. The series of indoor lectures that spring culminated with a pair by Hyndman and George Bernard Shaw.[236]

Success and hard work brought new recruits. E J Pay (known within the movement as Teddy) moved to Tunbridge Wells from the

235 *The Courier January 4th 1899.*
236 *The Tunbridge Wells Advertiser February 4th 1898; Tonbridge Telegraph March 5th 1898; the Tunbridge Wells Advertiser March 4th 1898; The Courier July 3rd 1901; The Tunbridge Wells Advertiser January 21st 1898 and February 18th 1898; The Tunbridge Wells Advertiser February 18th 1898; The Tunbridge Wells Advertiser March 11th 1898 and April 7th 1898.*

small village of Chartham, near Canterbury, where he had been born in 1874 (some sources suggest that he spent some time in Hastings around 1897). The area to the west of Canterbury had been very active during the Swing Riots, saw an attempted armed insurrection as late as 1838 and had become a stronghold of the Kent and Sussex Labourers' Union in the 1870s. At Tunbridge Wells Pay took a job with the Cooperative Society, rising to become the Departmental Manager at one of its two bakeries. . Within months of joining the Federation he had developed public speaking skills which made him one of the leading socialist activists in Kent and Sussex. Pay's character and oratory led one admirer to question whether many of the Clarion Fellowship would have considered Pay to have been 'tame and respectable enough' for their ranks. He later became a leading activist for the rural trade union movement.[237]

The Labour Sunday parade of May 1898 again demonstrated the strength of the local movement. The day dawned grey and cheerless, as many days in early May can, yet according to the *Tonbridge Telegraph* thousands of people assembled at the fountain at the junction of Calverley, Lansdowne, Pembury, Crescent and Bayhall Roads. The *Courier* less convincingly claimed that only a few hundred turned out. It is not clear whether or not a SDF banner existed at this time but the railwaymen, painters and decorators, plasterers, tailors and gas workers certainly all brought their own.

The procession then made its way through Camden Road, across the bridge at the bottom of Quarry Road, along Upper Grosvenor Road and finished at a meeting at the Lower Cricket Ground on the Common, thus passing through parts of all four of the town's electoral wards. Geer presided over the rally at the end: the Secretaries of the National Association of Plasterers and of Brighton Trades Council supported the local speakers. The speeches lasted some time. Local Tory Members of Parliament and imperialism stood condemned, while demands followed for the payment of Members of Parliament to enable working men to enter it, the provision of old age pensions and legislation for a maximum eight-hour day. At the conclusion those assembled raised £4 to support striking Welsh miners. [238]

---

[237] George Meek, *Bath-Chair Man, The Social Democrat January 1st 1932.*
[238] *The Courier May 13th 1898 and Tonbridge Telegraph May 14th 1898; the Tunbridge Wells Advertiser May 13th 1898.*

The weather seems to have improved enough for a series of successful open-air meetings to take place over the next few months. In June they travelled to Sevenoaks, to be joined by a number of London activists, for an event organised by Councillor Hickmott which combined propagandising with sightseeing. On occasions they were fortunate in their opponents. A local teetotaller harangued some of their speakers that September, claiming that any pay rise won by socialism or trade unionism would immediately be wasted on beer or spirits.

Many in the town, while not necessarily supporting the socialists, seemed to prefer them to the more extreme or unorthodox preachers. The arrival of Mormons in particular seemed to spread a sense of moral panic, as stories emerged about the seduction of working class girls who might find themselves conned into entering polygamous marriages. One paper recounted that on the previous Sunday night, pro- and anti-Mormon speakers, the Salvation Army and the Socialists could all be found. Councillor Geer, surrounded by his many followers grouped around a red flag, attacked a duke for the exploitation of his tenants and argued for the equal rights of man. From the London Road, some distance away from these gatherings, the various speeches merged into one on that hot summer's evening.[239]

As summer came to an end, the Trades and Labour Council turned towards thinking about the municipal elections. Four candidates gained their support: William Bournes of the SDF and three Fabian Society members, Frank Lawson Dodd, Alfred Bishop and H S Roberton. The focus of a series of meetings would be on showing what difference electing socialists could make. Mary Gray, a Poor Law Guardian from Battersea, spoke about the importance of building municipal housing, including at Sevenoaks.

Other issues discussed at ward meetings included whether to supply the town's water from the Ashdown Forest, public concerts and whether the municipality should construct a network of tramways linking the railway stations and town centre with the Recreation Ground, Southborough and Tonbridge. This latter suggestion seems to have been most controversial. The SDF and

---

[239] *Justice June 25th 1898; The Courier September 9th 1898; The Courier August 12th 1898 and Tonbridge Telegraph July 30th 1898; the Tunbridge Wells Advertiser July 29th 1898.*

Fabian Society collaborated in providing a range of speakers across all three wards[240].

Socialism emerged triumphant. *Fabian News* was ecstatic, reporting that:

> '*A great victory has been won in the election of the Tunbridge Wells Town Council. In East Ward two Fabians were returned by large majorities, F Lawson Dodd securing 576 and H S Roberton 510, while the highest unsuccessful candidate only secured 252. In the West Ward, the Tory stronghold of the town, A Bishop was defeated by 225 to 390. He had only lived in the town for eighteen months, the candidates elected being old residents. W Bournes (SDF) was elected in the North Ward, and three other candidates favourable to a housing scheme have also been successful. Progress in Tunbridge Wells should now be rapid'* [241].

Of the three non-socialist progressives, Councillor Abbott, who with his wife Edith had long been active in the Cooperative Society, proved a particularly important ally. Alfred Bishop's result is remarkable, as the West Ward had little working-class housing. The SDF's branch gave particular thanks to Tom Jarvis, William Willis-Harris and Sutton for their hard work during the election campaign. The Fabians too could point to other local successes.

One of the founding members of the Tunbridge Wells society, A Golds, triumphed at the Rotherfield parish elections, while other Fabians won seats at Oxted and the Mallings. Golds also persuaded the School Board to pass a motion in favour of raising the school leaving age to twelve. Again the SDF's branch moved quickly to capitalise on the results. In January Hyndman and George Lansbury addressed separate meetings in the town. Both congratulated the branch for the success, Hyndman called for the eight-hours bill, the nationalisation of railways, an end to child labour and for free school meals while Lansbury called on liberals to join the socialist movement.[242]

---

[240] *The Tunbridge Wells Advertiser September 30th 1898; Fabian News September 1898; The Courier October 25th 189; Tonbridge Telegraph September 3rd 1898.*
[241] *Fabian News December 1899.*
[242] *Justice November 12th 1898; the Tunbridge Wells Advertiser 4th November 1898; Fabian News December 1898, January 1899; The Courier January 18th 1899; Tonbridge Telegraph January 21st 1899.*

Spring 1899 brought two demonstrations of strength. The Gasworkers' and General Labourers' Union held a mass meeting on the Common in mid-April. Its organiser, H Picard, also sat as a councillor at West Ham, the first place in Britain with a labour or socialist majority. Picard expressed his hope that Tunbridge Wells might follow its lead, David Geer and Ellis Mann both subsequently spoke.[243]

The annual May Day parade followed a couple of weeks later. By way of preparation, Tom Jarvis wrote a three column piece for the Advertiser about the significance of this festival, tracing its routes back to the pagan festival of Beltane, through its Christianisation in the Middle Ages to its adoption as an international workers' festival. Even more people than in previous years - two or three thousand - joined the parade. Local union branches – some of whose banners were 'gorgeously emblazoned' – joined other groups, some from places as far away as Fulham. The parade was slightly longer this time, again starting at the fountain and passing through Camden Road, over the Grosvenor Bridge but diverting by way of St John's Road, Grosvenor Road, Mount Pleasant and Vale Road to the Common. William Bournes, as the most recently elected councillor, presided over the meeting. A number of general secretaries and local activists from the various unions also spoke. Reflecting the growing confidence of the movement both locally and nationally, speakers called for the election of socialists to parliament, as well as the council.[244]

These two parades kicked off the summer outdoor meetings that year. One innovation followed, whereby the speeches given by Arthur Hickmott were followed by musical interludes on violins. Yet these may have been somewhat overshadowed by another outbreak of industrial unrest. The SDF's members on the Trades and Labour Council organised support for the strikers and took the opportunity to raise related issues. In July, August and September William Bournes entered into correspondence with the town's Conservative MP, A G Boscowen, to discuss a legal limit to the working day. Boscowen agreed that women and children might benefit from such legislation but considered it inappropriate in the case of adult men,

---

[243] *Tunbridge Wells Advertiser April 21st 1899.*

[244] *The Courier May 12th 1899; Tunbridge Wells Advertiser April 28th 1899; May 12th 1899.*

whereupon Bournes gave evidence that working long hours cut life expectancy.[245]

The first strike came in late May. Building workers belonging to the Gas Workers and General Labourers Union took action in pursuit of a halfpenny increase in pay per hour. They argued that pay had fallen behind other places - they only received 6d per hour, compared to rates of six and a half to seven and a half pence elsewhere. Thirty men working at Strange and Jarvis took the lead. It was reported that the labourers were 'very well organised' and settlement therefore unlikely. However, by mid-June they had won the dispute. A fortnight later it was reported those engaged in action against another firm had also won.[246]

The second significant strike came a few months later and represented a failed attempt at union-busting. The town's branch of the Amalgamated Association of Farriers called for a 1pm finish on Saturdays without loss of pay. On 14th October one employer, Mr Hoadley, gave his men a week's notice to withdraw from their union. Some had worked for the firm for 17, 15 and 9 years. None agreed to his demand. Unable to have his horses re-shoed, Hoadley sent some of them to another blacksmith, Mr Aubin. Here the men also refused to do the work and in retaliation were sacked. The dispute grew to embrace two other forges, belonging to a Mr Roberts and a Mr Pratt. Picket lines followed at the various workplaces, many of them on Camden Road. Aubin's forge managed to recruit non-union members but the others shut down.

Although the *Courier* subsequently tried to portray the strike as not inconveniencing the public, it appears to have been solid. The farriers had held a mass-meeting in Hyde Park in August, and this perhaps had emboldened local activists. The Secretary of the Farriers' Union and William Bournes, on behalf of the Trades and Labour Council, wrote to correct what they regarded as the *Courier's* one-sided account of the dispute The Trades Council also collected significant amounts of money, seeing the actions of Hoadley as an attack on the right to organise. The Farriers' Union eventually claimed victory. This did not entirely end the matter as, emboldened by the farriers' defiance, the conductors of the horse buses which plied the route between Tunbridge Wells and Southborough (and

---

[245] *Tunbridge Wells Advertiser June 16th 1899; The Courier July 14th 1899; Justice July 1st 1899, September 16th 1899.*
[246] *The Courier May 26th 1899, June 16th 1899, June 30th 1899; Tunbridge Wells Advertiser May 26th 1899.*

were owned by some of the same firms) walked out in January 1900.[247]

The Farriers' Union marching from Camden Road into Albion Road. The image post-dates 1903 when the Amalgamated Society of Farriers formed through the merging of predecessor unions but many of the men would have taken part in the strikes of 1898 and 1899. From the collection of Fred Scales and used with permission.

Two deaths in the final months of 1899 would have reminded the pioneers of the branch of the struggles of the mid-1880s. William Willis-Harris, who had done so much to establish and guide the SDF in Tunbridge Wells, died at Park View, his house in Easebourne, on 14th September 1899. His physical and mental health had deteriorated over the last few years. He drank heavily and used opiates. In recent weeks he had been sleeping for up to eighteen hours a day and had not eaten. He had threatened to commit suicide several times and worried that he might end up in the county lunatic asylum, leaving his family to poverty and the workhouse. This was despite the fact that he still had £2,767 13s 8d at the time of his death.

Following his death and based on his last conversation with his wife, the coroner concluded that he had committed suicide from an

---

[247] *The Labour Leader, September 2nd 1899; The Courier October 27th 1899; Tunbridge Wells Advertiser October 27th 1899 and November 3rd 1899;The Courier November 3rd and November 17th 1899; The Courier February 2nd 1900.*

overdose of laudanum whilst in a state of unsound mind. Tom Jarvis wrote a moving obituary in *Justice* which paid tribute to him as 'more than a friend, a brother' and for having met his desire that as a result of his life 'the world should be the better for [his] having lived it', particularly praising his generosity in helping fund the free breakfasts for the children of Tunbridge Wells' unemployed between 1886 and 1888. Despite the challenges brought by William's ill-health and their reduced financial circumstances the coroner noted that Ada remained very attentive to and fond of her husband. His intellectual curiosity, now attracting greater recognition, should also be remembered.[248]

William Willis-Harris died ten days after Toby King, a Hastings secularist who, as discussed previously, had attended meetings of the Tunbridge Wells and Tonbridge Secular Society and later corresponded with Henry Seymour. King, according to various sources, had been the dominant force in secular radicalism in his home town for some decades. Other people maintained the link. Edward Cherill Edwards had recently moved to Hastings with his family, at least one of whom had become a socialist, and E J Pay's brother, H Pay, lived there. Hastings already possessed a handful of people interested in socialist ideas. In 1895 Edward Cruttenden, later to be active in the SDF, called for 'friends of labour' to hold meetings on the beach and so 'set the progressive movement on its legs in the town'.[249]

By 1899 the SDF's successes at Tunbridge Wells persuaded some in the seaside town that the party could fill the gap in Hastings left by King. On 9th September *Justice* carried a short article by John Nunan stating that 'a few of us have banded together for the propaganda of socialism and will hold our first meeting next Sunday at 3 o'clock on the beach (facing the Royal Oak Hotel). Should this meet the eye of other comrades in the neighbourhood, we shall be glad of their support'.[250]

Nunan – who should not be confused with the similarly-named Robert Noonan, : author of the *Ragged Trousered Philanthropists* who had not yet moved to the town - had himself only recently arrived in Hastings. His six year old son, also named John Nunan, had been born in London's St Pancras. The similarity between the

[248] *The Midhurst Times September 15th 1899; Justice November 4th 1899*
[249] *Matthews, M,. Alf Cobb, Mugsborough Rebel (The Hastings Press 200.) p29.*
[250] *Justice September 9th 1899.*

names may explain some of the confusion found when Fred Ball and others attempted to trace Robert Noonan's background some decades later. To make things more confusing, *Nunan* lived at 30 Whitefriars Road while *Robert Noonan* later lived in Plynlimmon Road and Milward Road, all three of which are a few minutes' walk apart. The Tunbridge Wells branch answered his call for help. E J Pay and David Geer both spoke at meetings on the beach in Hastings that September.

For a period the new branch made headway. By the end of the October it claimed to have progressed wonderfully well; new members, including leading trade unionists and co-operators had joined, and regular meetings took place at 12 Russell Street. The branch kept asking for help from visiting activists. However, in common with many other branches of the party and of the ILP, it failed to build a strong base and slowly faded away. Its work, however, had a longer-term impact. Several members transferred their enthusiasm to a new cross-party radical group, the National Democratic League, at whose meetings Nunan appeared, and others later became active again in the SDF when it re-formed its branch there in 1906. It also marks a qualitative change for the Tunbridge Wells branch, which again looked beyond the boundaries of the town to other places in the region.[251]

Events in Tunbridge Wells itself moved fast. Those who opposed municipal housing decided that delaying the scheme would serve their interests best. They picked through the details and questioned whether the plans represented the best value for money. Several contracts, already approved by the council, fell through in June 1899. The Borough Surveyor was asked to re-assess the entire scheme a month later. This meant that the SDF and Fabian Society were forced to re-make the case for municipal housing at the local elections.

The campaign started with a meeting at the Town Hall that September. Geer raised the plight of working class families being driven from Camden Road by rising rents. Councillors Lander, Lawson Dodd, Abbott, King, Forbes, Bournes, Passingham, Gain,

---

[251] *Justice September 23rd 1899, October 7th 1899, October 28th 1899, December 1st 1900; Hopper, T, Robert Tressell's Hastings, The Background to The Ragged Trousered Philanthropists (Brighton: Hopper Books 1999).*

Edwards and Saunders all also spoke in favour of municipal housing.[252]

If the elections can be considered a referendum on the issue, the SDF and Fabian Society won the argument. Councillor Saunders had not sought re-election for personal reasons. He had become close enough to the SDF to write two letters to *Justice* in December that year. The Trades Council and SDF supported James Milstead as their preferred candidate. Perhaps significantly, Councillor Abbott, not a member of the Federation, presided over his meeting. The candidate, adorned with what the *Courier* called 'the red tie of the socialistic order' and Councillors Lawson Dodd, Roberton, Bournes and Geer also addressed those present. Milstead argued in favour of municipal trams and for an end to sub-contracting of council contracts. He won the contest comfortably.[253]

Yet could they have done more? It is odd that they decided against contesting the South Ward, which had a lot of working class housing, in particular to the south of Goods Station Road, around St Peters Church and in the older parts of the town around Mount Sion, where some early lodging-houses had become very crowded. Perhaps Ellis Mann or E J Pay, both of whom were well known in trade union and Cooperative circles, might have run in the East or North Wards. Reflecting this, one correspondent to the *Advertiser* in October 1899 felt that the SDF could win four or five seats if only they had stood in the other wards in the town. Municipal housing to him was a necessity, as for his eleven shillings a week he got a house of six rooms, none of them fit to live in, and Tunbridge Wells properties were far worse than equivalent working class housing in Maidstone. Yet for a working class man or woman, standing for election on a left-wing platform would have implications, ranging from the loss of a few hours pay a week while attending meetings to being dismissed by an unsympathetic employer and blacklisted as a known troublemaker.[254]

As a new century dawned, the Tunbridge Wells branch can be forgiven for congratulating itself on its achievements. In the past fourteen years its fortunes had ebbed and flowed but in the last five they had picked themselves up and grown from being a handful of activists meeting in the front room of a terraced house into one of

---

[252] *The Courier June 2nd 1899, July 21st 1899, September 27th 1899.*
[253] *Justice December 2nd & 16th 1899; The Courier November 3rd 1899.*
[254] *Tunbridge Wells Advertiser October 13th 1899.*

the largest and most electorally successful branches of their party anywhere in the British Isles. Tom Jarvis justifiably declared that his native town had become the most progressive borough in the South of England. A number of liberal-leaning West Kent papers echoed his line. The party's leadership used the branch as an example to others of what might be achieved.[255]

In March 1900 *Justice* argued that the Federation's fight for municipal housing meant that the town had 'straightaway changed its mind and elected our erstwhile rejected comrade Geer its town council, promptly sending five other socialists to keep him company and scandalise further that town of all proprieties'.[256]

The SDF decided to hold a mass meeting at London's Crystal Palace to celebrate the first May Day of the new century. 12,000 people attended, enjoying maypole dancing, cycling, athletics, a banner competition, socialist choirs and six platforms of speakers, followed by fireworks. H M Hyndman asked David Geer, both of whom were on the main platform, 'how goes it in the Wells'. Geer replied that Tunbridge Wells had 'six Socialists on the council and a seventh indistinguishable [from them]'.[257]

Once again, success brought new members. William George Veals, an eighteen-year-old photographer, joined the branch in 1900. Over the next couple of decades he played a leading role within Tunbridge Wells and across the region, before moving to the Luton area. His interests lay in land reform (he wrote extensively about Henry George for *Justice* in 1910) and in building bridges between the various socialist organisations. To this end, he also joined the ILP. His opposition to militarism and war ultimately ended in his imprisonment as a conscientious objector during the First World War, so becoming the oldest and best-known member of the Tunbridge Wells branch to suffer this fate.[258]

[255] *Justice November 4th 1899.*
[256] *Justice March 10th 1900.*
[257] *Justice May 5th 1900; The Courier May 4th 1900. See also the Working Class Movement Library https://www.wcml.org.uk/our-collections/object-of-the-month/objects-of-the-month-2014/may-day-leaflet-1900/*
[258] *Justice February 5th 1910 and February 12th 1910.*

CHAPTER 8 INTERNATIONALISM AGAINST IMPERIALISM: SOCIALISM AND THE BOER WAR

Even as James Milstead campaigned to win his seat in Tunbridge Wells' East Ward and the socialist movement first stirred in Hastings, developments in South Africa came to dominate British politics. War in the Transvaal broke out on 11th October 1899 in what came to be known in Britain as the Second Boer War.

Walter Crane's widely used cartoon against the Boer War. The artist also worked for the SDF, ILP and other left-wing and socialist organisations.

The Social-Democratic Federation, influenced both by Karl Marx and British radicalism, argued that working men and women had more in common with members of their own class from different countries than with the capitalists and landlords in their own nation state. Socialists should therefore refuse to support wars between nations, perhaps even then using vivid aphorisms such as a bayonet being a weapon with a worker at both ends.

British socialists were amongst the most committed internationalists. In 1896 the SDF had brought the issue of colonialism to the Socialist International for the first time and won unanimous support for a motion condemning it. Interestingly this placed them at odds with some in the German movement. Eduard Bernstein felt that nationalism should not be ignored and even that 'the higher culture has rights over the lower', essentially embracing the seizure of land by wealthy nations.[259]

The SDF were not alone in Tunbridge Wells. Joseph Dodd of the town's Fabian Society gave a lecture in January 1899 which concluded that 1898 had been characterised by the 'remarkable development of two opposing forces, socialism and militarism' and attacked 'the new imperialism', although his death in October 1899 at the early age of 36 prevented him from developing his ideas further.[260]

This principled position had some blind spots. In general, the interests of those of white European origin, including the descendants of settlers in such places as North America and Australasia, had more resonance than matters concerning people with darker skins. To its credit, the SDF had campaigned against aspects of British misrule in India from its inception. Reflecting this, in March 1904 J M Parikh, a member of the Indian National Congress, spoke at a meeting organised by the Federation at the Albion Road Congregational Chapel, Tunbridge Wells, to condemn the importation of indentured Chinese labour to South Africa. *Justice* had also as early as 1896 defended the Matabele and Mashona peoples in southern Africa from charges of being rebels and murderers, arguing instead that they were freedom fighters.[261]

A second problem lay in anti-Semitism. Hyndman, in common with many of his fellow socialists, occasionally let slip some disgraceful

---

[259] Kendall Rogers, *Before the Revisionist Controversy* pp174-5;; Baker, B., *The SDF and the Boer War (London: The Communist Party of Great Britain 1974).*
[260] *Fabian News* December 1899 p3; Kendall Rogers, *Before the Revisionist Controversy* pp174-5.
[261] Baker, B., *Boer War*, p5; *The Courier March* 18th 1904. See also George, H., *Progress and Poverty; an inquiry into the cause of industrial depressions and of the increase of want with increase of wealth (London: The Henry George Foundation of Great Britain 1931) p87.*

comments which he then tried to explain, often not entirely convincingly, by claiming that he only opposed wealthy Jewish financiers such as the Rothschilds and had no problem with their working class co-religionists. As early as February 1893 he told a Fabian Society audience that the 'English people take little interest in foreign policy, which was in the hands of the governing classes and the Jews'. Taking their lead from such examples, newspapers such as *Justice, the Clarion* and the Independent Labour Party's *Labour Leader* sometimes carried similarly dubious commentary in their editorials. Few, if any, at least plumbed the depths which the anarchist Henry Albert Seymour had reached in the later 1880s.

Anti-Semitism seems to have been not uncommon across the parties of the Second International. Individuals sometimes changed their views. Michael Rosen has recently pointed to Jean Jaures, a leader of the movement in France during the Dreyfus affair, during which a Jewish army officer had been convicted of treason and espionage and exiled to a penal colony. In December 1894 Jaures wrote that Captain Alfred Dreyfus had only escaped the death penalty as a result of the 'prodigious deployment of Jewish power', yet by February 1895 had revised his opinion and became a great supporter of the campaign to free him. Finally, some socialists, in particular Hyndman and Robert Blatchford, grew increasingly anti-German. Blatchford became the most significant socialist to support the Boer War.[262]

The Boer War proved a turning point for both the SDF and the Fabian Society at Tunbridge Wells. Both struggled to retain the seats which they had won in previous years. Yet both built bridges and strengthened existing alliances. These endured and became even more significant after 1914. The local Fabian Society adopted a position very similar to that of the SDF, whereas the national organisation took a neutral position.

The SDF, composed primarily of atheist or agnostic working class men and women, also found that it had much in common with more radical forms of Christian dissent. In the local context this took in members of the Unitarians, Quakers and Primitive Methodists. The leading figures from the congregations of the first two of these groups were generally from middle-class backgrounds whereas the latter had its base in the working class Camden Road.

---

[262] *Fabian News February 1893;* Crick p159; Rosen, M., *The Disappearance of Emile Zola (London: Faber and Faber 2017) pp156-8.*

Many conservative Christians actively supported the war. Several vicars and ministers put their name to a letter to the *Courier* in November 1899, and the Reverend J Mountain even accused the Boers, with no evidence, of murdering British civilians,[263]

Frank Lawson Dodd, active in the Unitarian Church, exemplifies these threads. In February 1900 he won election to the Fabian Society's Executive on an anti-war platform. A month later he compiled a list of eight other candidates for the Executive who shared his beliefs about the conflict. To improve their chances of winning, he asked his relatives, including Charles Tattershall Dodd, who appears to have been the son of the locally celebrated artist of that name, to join the Society. Lawson Dodd also played a leading role in a new organisation, the South African Conciliation Committee. His fellow Fabian, H C Lander, also proposed three friends or acquaintances as new members. It is interesting that he specifically set out to influence 'the more advanced section of the Fabian Executive so as to bring the Society into closer touch with the General Socialist Movement'.[264]

Spearheaded by the members of the SDF and the Fabian Society a broader anti-war movement grew up in the town which soon found allies in the Liberal Party and Cooperative Society, in particular the Women's Cooperative Guild. Liberal women from Tunbridge Wells collected signatures for a petition opposing annexation during their annual outing in July 1900[265].

None of these developments could have been predicted at the start of 1899. The differences within the movement were exposed when the Russian Tsar, Nicholas II, announced that he would lead a Peace Crusade. This soon gained support from the great and the good, including the Mayor and the Member of Parliament for the Tonbridge Division. Most clergymen also supported it although its half-filled meeting rooms suggested a degree of cynicism from the rest of Tunbridge Wells.

---

[263] *The Courier November 3rd 1899, February 7th 1900.*
[264] *Fabian Society archives - Letter from Frank Lawson Dodd to Mr Blake-Caarten March 26th 1900; Fabian News February 1900, April 1900, June 1900; Liddington, J., The Long Road to Greenham: Feminism and Anti-militarism in Britain since 1820 (London: Virago 1989).*
[265] *Riedi, L., 'The women pro-Boers: gender, peace and the critique of empire in the South African War' Historical Research, vol. 86, no. 231 (February 2013) p103.*

151

The SDF refused to join the party, highlighting the Tsar's record in respect of minorities, organised labour and perhaps disliking the religious overtones of the initiative. The International Socialist Congress had also condemned the initiative. At a meeting in March, James Milstead heckled one speaker who had praised the Tsar, highlighting instead the Russian occupation of Finland. A cleric, Father Staples, joined in and others followed.

A member of the SDF then attempted to move a motion from the floor condemning the proposed increased expenditure on British armaments as being not conducive to peace. Uproar followed. The chair refused to allow David Geer the chance to second the motion. A few days later, the Secretary of the Peace Crusade's branch, Joseph Green, wrote an open letter condemning the behaviour of the Federation. By way of retaliation, venues including the parish rooms in St James and St Barnabas and the schoolrooms in Albion Road refused to host socialist meetings.

The difficulties did not last long. James Milstead admitted to having twice interrupted the meeting, but had not encouraged the other people present who had done the same. Joseph Green, then apologised to the branch, declaring his sympathy for the provisions concerning peace in the Federation's programme and their compatibility with his Quaker faith. After the Tsar's crusade crumbled with the outbreak of hostilities, Green and his co-religionists worked closely with the Federation on campaigns against imperialism and war. He also presided over a meeting at the Friends Meeting House on 1st January 1900 which agreed that a close reading of the scriptures in 'this era of social and political unrest' proved that war, whatever the cause, could never be justified. The meeting decided to publish a pamphlet addressed to the other Christian denominations in the town.[266]

Despite the best efforts of Lander and Lawson Dodd, the Fabian Society nationally refused to take a position on the war. In April 1900 Arthur Hickmott resigned at the organisation's failure to adhere to internationalist principles. Both Arthur and Ellen Hickmott subsequently worked tirelessly for peace. Across Great Britain another sixteen members also resigned the same month and it is interesting that the group included such familiar names as

---

[266] *The Courier February 24th 1899, March 24th 1899, April 7th 1899; Tunbridge Wells Advertiser March 24th 1899, March 30th 1899 and April 7th 1899; Green, J., A Few Serious Thoughts on the Subject of War addressed to the Society of Friends, Tunbridge Wells to their fellow Christians of other denominations (Tunbridge Wells 1900).*

Ramsay and Margaret Macdonald, Walter Crane, Pete Curran and Emmeline Pankhurst.[267]

Others wished to reform the Fabian Society from within. Joseph Gundry Alexander, another leading local Quaker, proved to be a particularly important ally due to his standing in the community. His views on international relations held weight through his being the Secretary of the International Law Association. In the first few decades he had been active as a member of the Tunbridge Wells Higher Education Committee, the Committee of the Homeopathic Hospital and served as a magistrate for the County of Kent. He also played a leading role in expanding the Adult School movement at the Friends Meeting House near the town centre and at High Brooms.[268]

Opposition to the fighting did not quite turn the socialists of Tunbridge Wells into a single issue pressure group, but in a way that will be familiar to anyone involved in left-wing politics at the time of the Second Gulf War, it overshadowed the rest of their activities. The SDF published and distributed a manifesto, *War in South Africa*, in January 1900. This immediately hit a nerve, with the war's supporters in Tunbridge Wells writing to *Justice* to complain at its failure to tow the patriotic line. Two rants from the town appeared in the paper in February and March. The first, from a man who had claimed to have been in South Africa for twenty years, told the Federation to 'go to hell with [their] damned rubbish', that the war was just and that the Federation knew nothing about it. The second, in rather more threatening terms, declared that the 'author of the 'manifesto' and 'all members of the SDF ought to be where Cronje has been just lately', asking whether they were in 'collaboration with Dr Leyds', that the Federation were among our enemies and that the sooner they drop out of existence the better for 'Old England'. The branch responded by strongly denouncing the war during the May Day parade of 1900 and distributing 2,000 copies of the manifesto house to house in the summer.[269]

---

[267] *Fabian News April 1900; Riedi, pro-Boer p95, p108*
[268] *Tunbridge Wells Advertiser 7th July 1916, September 15th 1916; The Courier September 15th 1916, January 19th 1917. See also Alexander, H.G, Joseph Gundry Alexander (London: The Swathmore Press Ltd 1920) pp171-4.*
[269] *Justice, February 24th 1900, March 10th 1900. Cronje at this stage had been captured after the battle of Paardeburg and was to be exiled to St Helena, and Leyds had served as a diplomat, The Courier May 11th 1900.*

Colonel Blimpish responses may have been expected, but the SDF and other opponents of the war, whether Liberal or Labour, also faced an onslaught of violence. At Tunbridge Wells the branch had enough members for its meetings to be left unmolested, though in many other places the supporters of the war succeeded in breaking up their meetings and attacking speakers, as well as organising boycotts of public halls. A large number of councillors opposed the conflict, though the Borough Council raised the Union Flag over the Town Hall and held a dinner to celebrate the return of volunteers.

Frank Lawson Dodd (British Library, used with permission)

The historian can be grateful for a remarkable little book by Samuel Conwright Schreiner, who made a careful note of the intimidation experienced by the anti-war movement. Frank Lawson Dodd organised a meeting at home to form a branch of the South African Conciliation Committee on 20th April. J A Hobson and Conwright Schreiner spoke, sixty attended, and a Mr Shillito elected Chair. Some Social-Democrats must have attended though none are named. Exactly a week later the Liberal *Advertiser* carried a report of this 'Pro-Boer' meeting. The paper advised Conwright Schreiner to give Tunbridge Wells a wide berth. The Tory press stirred things up further.[270]

Things deteriorated after the relief of Mafeking on 17th May 1900, followed by the fall of Pretoria on Tuesday 5th June. . That evening, a group of 'roughs, mostly young and well-organised, armed with pail, brush and newspapers', made their way to Frank Lawson Dodd's house, followed by a large crowd. This group attached posters from a London evening journal – not freely available in the town – to the front door and side wall of the building. The growing mob sang patriotic songs, such as *Soldiers of the Queen*, booed and hissed. Reverend Mountain, whose church lay at the top of the

---

[270] See the *Courier* March 2nd 1900; Conwright Schreiner, *The Land of Free Speech: Record of a Campaign for peace in England and Scotland in 1900* (London: The New Age Press 1906) pp253-4.

street, attended. Mountain led the crowd in singing the National Anthem and declared the war to be just. Probably embarrassed by what happened later, he subsequently claimed to have tried to get the crowd to disperse, claiming that others had incited them to commit violent acts. By 11 o'clock the pubs had emptied, swelling the crowds. Shortly afterwards the lights went out.[271]

For the first time in Tunbridge Wells since the 1860s a night of serious rioting ensued. . Frank Lawson Dodd's house became the target for a sustained assault. Stones and half-bricks rained down on the property, breaking windows and destroying the conservatory and plants in the garden. Lawson Dodd himself was at a Unitarian Church conference in London but his wife was at home and lucky to avoid injury. His sister lay ill in one of the upstairs rooms. The police, who had done far more to prevent disorder than their equivalents in many other places, then came under attack. Chief Constable Prior, Inspector Greenwood and Police Constables Blackford, Gooding and Hodges all suffered injuries, and several passers-by were also wounded. The stand-off continued until 1:30 when the police charged the crowds.

A day later, even larger crowds assembled but the police, marching shoulder to shoulder to disperse the mob and placing cordons across Grosvenor Park, contained the situation. . The fire brigade, carrying axes, also mobilised to reinforce the police. The lights remained on all night. A cab owner from Southborough attempted to charge the police lines but Inspector Marriner and PC Blackford stopped the horse before it reached the cordon.

Unrest that night covered a wider area. . Mobs from Southborough joined in on the St John's Road, where William Bournes lived, and a mile or so away William and Kathleen Veals' home on Mountfield Road and another house on Sutherland Road received a visit. One woman suffered a broken arm. After this, despite attempts to whip it up again, the unrest subsided, with a shower dispersing the crowds on Thursday. These events in Tunbridge Wells received coverage in the Paris papers although one correspondent to the *Courier* tried to minimise their seriousness.[272]

Although the town's labour movement claimed some successes in other fields, such as a well-attended mass-meeting of the Gas

---

[271] *Conwright Schreiner pp254-6; The Courier May 23rd 1900.*
[272] *The Courier May 23rd 1900, June 8th 1900 and June 15th 1900; Tunbridge Wells Journal June 14th 1900; Conwright Schreiner, Record.*

Workers and General Labourers Union on the Common in July and two strikes which raised the pay of bricklayers to 9d from 8d by late August 1900, the war dominated politics.

The town's first two socialist councillors, David Geer and H C Lander, faced re-election that autumn. Both campaigned on a variety of issues, including measures to improve sanitation, build tramways and provide facilities for public recreation. Their opponents wrapped themselves firmly in the Union Flag. Geer lost by 160 votes and Lander by 202. At the count, Geer received a mixture of cheers and hisses, and Lander suffered heckles of 'pro-Boer'. *Justice* concluded that the result stemmed from the 'usual imperialist balderdash' and *Fabian News* likewise put it down to 'an absurd prejudice caused by their attitude to the South African war'. The *Courier*, in contrast, claimed that the candidates had lost due to their support for municipal housing.

Jingoism had taken its toll but many voters stood by the socialists. Geer won 380 votes – more than he had got in 1895 and 1896 - and Lander secured 309. The reactionary element on the council immediately forced through the abandonment of the municipal housing scheme and sold the land. This reversal would later be calculated to have wasted £814. Conservative working men, blinded by nationalism, had thrown away the chance to improve their lot.[273]

Attitudes hardened on each side as the war entered its second year. *Justice* carried articles about the burning of farms and of a new British invention, the concentration camp. A correspondent to the *Courier* claimed that the incarcerated Boers were better fed than they had been in their own farms and defended house-burning as militarily necessary. In response others, one of whom wrote under the name 'Justice', quoted a Government White Paper which itself had concluded that such a scorched earth policy had no justification and described the poor hygiene and mouldy food in the camps. Pro-peace opinion increasingly cited such atrocities. In November the Tunbridge Wells Peace Union attacked the conditions in the camps and *Justice* in January 1902 carried reports of the deaths of children in them. The Stop the War Committee stated that the war had degenerated into a campaign of extermination. 20,000

---

[273] *Justice November 24th 1900; Fabian News December 1900, The Courier June 1st 1900, July 13th 1900, August 24th 1900; Tunbridge Wells Journal, May 15th 1902.*

had died by the end of the conflict in the camps while child mortality was fourteen times that of British cities.[274]

Although generally less spectacular than the events which followed the Relief of Mafeking, simmering anger and occasional violence against those opposed to the war marked the year 1901. The council organised a reception for local volunteers in May at the Town Hall; the crowd which assembled demanded that Councillor Lawson Dodd turn up, then, on his failure to do so, hooted and derided him as a pro-Boer.[275]

Two months later, Arthur Hickmott became embroiled in disturbances which scarred his native Sevenoaks. Members of the National Democratic League (figures range from 1,200 to 7,000 or 8,000) visited the town in July, many of them from London. Hickmott started the proceedings peacefully with a short lecture on the town's history at the Oddfellows Hall. Others, including the trade unionist Ben Tillett and London County Councillors Will Crooks and Will Steadman then spoke. A 'hooting mob' whipped up by well-known Tory activists duly assembled outside. They repeatedly sang *Rule Britannia* and *God Save the King*. A member of the League responded that you couldn't 'go on to the Common without meeting asses'. A fight for the National Democratic League's flag ensued, the League's stewards moved to protect its members and the police moved in to try and separate the two factions. Outnumbered, the officers then forced the National Democratic League's supporters to retreat to the railway station towards the bottom of Tubs Hill. As the situation deteriorated members of the League decided to use some large pieces of flint with which the railway company had decorated the station area as missiles. Keir Hardie had declined an invitation to attend and was thus spared the wrath of the crowds, and it can perhaps be speculated that Will Crooks' memories of this and similar incidents led him to support the First World War – by which time he sat in Parliament as a Labour MP - so wholeheartedly.[276]

The Socialists gave as good as they got at their 1901 May Day rally on Tunbridge Wells Common. The bitter tone of many of the contributions is clear. One local speaker, whom the *Courier* described as a 'gentleman we need not name', declared his

---

[274] *Liddington, Greenham, p52- 53.*
[275] *The Courier May 3rd 1901.*
[276] *The Courier July 19th & 26th 1901; Tunbridge Wells Advertiser June 19th 1901; the Labour Leader July 20th 1901.*

solidarity with his 'friends, the Boers', blaming the war on capitalist greed, and talked about educating people in Marxist economics. Another speaker, A C Burns, a member of the Executive of the Gas Workers and General Labourers Union, having noted a group of military volunteers heading into a church that day, argued that they were going to ask God to 'forgive them for their wicked ways', before going on to declare that 'our land had been robbed and the people who had robbed us of it charged us for living on it. Now we had sent our soldiers to rob another people of their country'. Representatives of the Plasterers and Farriers unions also spoke.

The *Advertiser* condemned many of these speeches for being 'of a Pro-Boer and somewhat abusive character' and suggested that turnout had fallen since the previous year. International relations rather obscured the domestic concerns also mentioned in the various speeches. William Bournes and A W Ireland presided over the ritual passing of resolutions in favour of greater labour representation and to improve the law in relation to municipal housing and expressed his support for the Penrhyn quarrymen then on strike. A collection for the latter cause received £1 3s in solidarity. Sir David Lionel Salomons had recently endorsed the popular Conservative cause of protectionism, so William Bournes took the opportunity to deride his recent paper, *British Commercial Superiority*, claming that a schoolboy could do better. [277]

Identity politics and xenophobia reached their apogee in the municipal elections that autumn. In October the Conservative *Courier* printed a letter, purportedly from 'an English Working Man', which asked that others of his class should refuse to 'give your votes to pro-Boers, Socialists and other enemies of your country', singled out the SDF for not supporting the 'Liberal Imperialist' candidate at the last General Election and for 'their red flags and outrageous utterances [which] disgrace our beautiful Common'. In the days before the vote, men paraded the streets of the North and East wards waving Union Jacks and placards calling on voters to support 'Loyal and True Englishmen'.[278]

---

[277] *The Courier May 8th & 24th 1901, Tunbridge Wells Advertiser May 10th 1901.*
[278] *The Courier October 18th 1901, November 8th 1901.*

Despite such cheap tactics from the right, the result proved no disaster. In the East Ward, the winners Wesley Smith and Carpenter beat Frank Lawson Dodd and David Alfred Geer, the first two gaining 536 and 499, the latter 473 and 429. Lawson Dodd therefore lost his seat, but the relatively small margin of defeat perhaps suggested that the fortunes of the socialists might soon turn. In the North Ward, William Bournes won 455 votes on behalf of the SDF and Trades and Labour Council, easily securing victory over a right-wing candidate who trailed with 296.[279]

A protectionist meeting at Tunbridge Wells.
The Conservatives, using the idea of Britain as a great imperial power, tried to promote the notion of national superiority, while calling for 'Fair Trade' i.e. protectionist policies against Britain's rivals.
The rear of the card calls on consumers to buy 'Imperial' produce, such as freshly-laid Kent and Sussex eggs and (perhaps less fresh) New Zealand butter.
Postcard by Lankester for Hughes Stores, 'Ye Pantiles'

---

[279] *Justice November 16th 1901; The Courier November 8th 1901.*

The electricity works in Tunbridge Wells, photographed in the 1950s / 1960s.
St. Barnabas' Church in background on right.
Local politics in Tunbridge Wells between 1902 and 1906
was dominated by the argument over whether such undertakings
should be owned by the municipality, or by private enterprises.

CHAPTER 9 YEARS OF FRUSTRATION AND ACHIEVEMENT

The Social-Democrats and Fabians of Tunbridge Wells struggled to regain their former level of popular support in the period between the end of the Boer War and the election of a Liberal Government in 1906. They continued to recruit new activists and used innovative new methods to try to make the socialist case. Their internationalism became even stronger. Yet, at election after election, socialist candidates failed to win seats, often by very small margins.

National politics were in flux during these years, something which has rather been overshadowed by the war in South Africa. A short description of some of these developments will help the reader to understand the next few chapters. These changes need to be borne in mind when considering the course of events locally.

On the left, the Labour Representation Committee had formed in 1900. This aimed to bring together trade unions, socialist societies and the cooperative movement to win representation at Westminster. As it is generally regarded as the forerunner of the Parliamentary Labour Party it has been accorded a significance which was not apparent at the time. In many ways it merely developed the work that various local Trades and Labour Councils had been carrying out locally in the 1890s, including at Tunbridge Wells.

One implication is that it gave the socialist societies – the SDF, ILP and, even more dramatically, the Fabian Society – far greater representation in the new body when compared to the trade unions than their relatively small membership would seemingly merit. Despite this, by the end of 1901 the SDF had withdrawn from the LRC, as it refused to commit itself to recognising the class war. Many on the left of the ILP regretted this step as weakening their position, while *Fabian News* mocked the SDF as the 'Fifth Monarchy men of Labour', a reference to an extreme religious cult in the 17th century English Civil War. Some in the party felt that merely having joined the LRC in the first place had undermined its claim to be a revolutionary organisation, and several groups seceded, including those who formed the Socialist Labour Party in 1903 and the Socialist Party of Great Britain a year later. [280]

Secondly, although every cooperative society in Great Britain and Ireland had the opportunity to join the new LRC, only the Tunbridge Wells society decided to take this step - something which suggests that a majority within it now regarded themselves as politically 'labour' in one form or another. In 1906 it voted to join the newly-formed Labour Party for the sum of one and a half pence per member a year, again being the only such society to do so. [281]

The formation of the LRC undoubtedly helped the cause of working class representation. Socialists and trade unionists took a handful of seats in Parliament and a significant number of council wards across the country. This focussed minds among Conservatives and their Liberal Unionist allies (the latter a group of Liberal MPs who broke with Gladstone over his Irish policies in 1886 and formed a governing coalition with the Tories in 1895). The London Municipal Society, formed in 1894, became the model for this fightback. Better funded than its left-wing rivals, this organisation held 500 public meetings and distributed four and a half million pamphlets before the municipal election in 1895 and repeated this work year after year.

The national press led many of the attacks on the left. From November 1901 *the Times* published a series of letters and 17 articles critical of municipal trading over a period of twelve months. Some of these arguments alleged instances of extravagant spending while others concentrated on the threat to small businessmen and independent traders (the cooperative movement also came under attack for this). More effective measures against the trade unions emerged at the same time. William Collison's Free Labour Association, which supplied strike-breakers, formed following a conference in London in August 1893. The Primrose League also stepped up its anti-socialist campaigning. [282]

---

[280] *Crick, History, p148; Miliband, R., Parliamentary Socialism: A study in the politics of Labour (London: Merlin Press 1987) p21; Fabian News November 1902.*
[281] *The Courier April 28th 1905; The Courier October 19th 1906; The Tunbridge Wells Advertiser August 10th 1906.*
[282] *Young, K, Local Politics and the Rise of Party: the London Municipal Society and the Conservative intervention in local elections, 1894-1963 (Leicester University Press 1975) pp67-69, p86; Collison, W, The Apostle of Free Labour: The Life Story of William Collison, Founder and General Secretary of the National Free Labour Association, Told By Himself (London: Hurst and Blackett 1913) pp92-93.*

If the socialists of Tunbridge Wells had organised themselves more effectively than their equivalents in most other towns, their opponents did likewise. The principal backer of the Free Labour Association, Sir George Livesey, lived in Tunbridge Wells. He had successfully broken the strike in the South Metropolitan Gas Works in 1890 and the presence of men supplied by a 'London contractor' during a dispute at Rusthall in the same month that the Free Labour Association emerged, may have been a result of these contacts.

This experiment seems not to have been repeated, no doubt as a result of the fights which broke out on the picket lines and the embarrassment caused by importing labour at a time of high unemployment. In the first decade of the twentieth century a grisly array of new anti-socialist and anti-Liberal groups formed, including the Imperial Sunday Alliance, the British Constitutional Association (1905) and the Middle-Class Defence League (1906).[283]

A local organisation openly set up to fight socialism, the Ratepayer's League first became active in 1902. Like its London forerunner, this carefully distanced itself from the Conservative Party. It claimed, not always convincingly, that its funding came from 'private' (i.e. wealthy) residents rather than any industrial or political association. Leading activists included a Mr Hicks of Culverden Castle and two retired colonels, Newnham-Smith of Woodbury Park Road and Trevenen Holland of Mount Ephraim House.

The subsequent history of anti-socialism in the town will be discussed later, but it enough to note that Sir Robert Filmer, prospective Conservative candidate for the Tonbridge Division in 1907, and Herbert Spender-Clay, the Member of Parliament after 1910, both served on the steering committee of a new national body, the Anti-Socialist Union, in the years after its formation in 1908. The *Courier* also regularly gave column space to a variety of anti-municipal trading opinion pieces.[284]

How did this impact on the SDF and the Fabian Society? The formation of the Labour Representation Committee seems to have been greeted as a positive step by both. The socialist movement in the town, and in the Tonbridge Constituency, had never been so

---

[283] Berger, S., *British Labour Party* pp56-7.
[284] Raw, L., *Striking a Light* p169; Brown, K. D., *The Anti-Socialist Union in Essays in Anti-Labour History: Responses to the rise of Labour in Britain* Brown, K. D,. [ed.] (Macmillan 1984) p241.

united, and this seems to have been a spur to becoming increasingly active. The Social-Democrats and Fabian Society organised an impressive schedule of public meetings, some of them organised jointly through a new organisation, the Sunday Social Gathering Committee.[285]

James Keir Hardie

This unity probably lay behind the decision of Keir Hardie - probably the most impressive orator among the Labour Representation Committee's handful of Members of Parliament - to lecture twice in the early months of 1901. Unlike many a later leading parliamentarian, it seems that he took time out to explore the town and meet some of its inhabitants, concluding that 'far from a place to retire to away from the cares of the world, Tunbridge Wells and its people were very like those of other places'. Herbert Burrows of the SDF spoke around the same time. All these meetings drew what the *Advertiser* called 'capital audiences'.[286]

Keir Hardie and Herbert Burrows were unusual within the socialist and labour movements in the importance they attached to winning women the vote. Their speeches may have helped the Tunbridge Wells branch address what had become something of a gender imbalance following the departure of early recruits such as Constance Howell and Rose Jarvis. Two younger women, Maud Ward and Kathleen Kough, joined in 1901 or 1902 and almost immediately played an important role. Maud Ward, who had grown up in a country rectory and having been denied the education offered to her brothers, took a two-year course in cookery and moved to Tunbridge Wells to teach the subject. Kathleen Kough had been active in the National Secular Society in London before moving

---

[285] *The Tunbridge Wells Advertiser February 22nd 1901 and March 15th 1901; Justice January 25th 1902.*
[286] *The Tunbridge .Wells Advertiser February 22nd 1901; The Courier May 24th 1901.*

to Kent. They lived together from around 1902 at 46 Dorset Road, Hawkenbury, and from 1905 at 149 Stephen's Road.

Maud Ward, clearly a good speaker and energetic organiser, turned politics into a career, later lecturing from 1908 until 1912 for the Adult Suffrage Society, a socialist-inspired campaigning organisation which aimed to win the vote for all men and women irrespective of means, as well as for the SDF. Her later relationship with Margaret Bondfield, the first woman to serve in a British cabinet, has attracted some attention. Whether or not Kathleen Kough and Maud Ward were lovers is not clear – the former's only known comment on relationships, that secular women should not marry Christian men and that 'bachelors should not espouse women who were not free thinkers' revolved around heterosexual partnerships, if a little eccentric. If they were romantically linked, there seems to have been little if any prejudice against them in the branch.[287]

The work ethic of some members, however, left quite a lot to be desired. In August 1901, George Hewitt, who had succeeded George Lansbury as organiser, felt that William Bournes and James Milstead had worked tirelessly as councillors. However, he felt that others could do more, arguing that Tunbridge Wells should be 'a stronghold for social democracy' with a little more commitment. This may have spurred it to launch a drive for new members. Over the next twelve or so months, Messrs Godbold, Brown, Martin, Reeves and Davy joined the branch and most of them became active, whether as writers of letters to the newspapers, canvassers or otherwise.

Unlike Kathleen Kough and Maud Ward, most of the new male recruits came from working class backgrounds. Despite the electoral setbacks, Tunbridge Wells still had a high profile in the party and seems to have been one of the largest and strongest branches. Ellis Mann won election to the Federation's National Executive in August 1901 as a result of a single vacant seat, open to all provincial branches, and retained it in April 1902.[288]

What was the attitude of the Tunbridge Wells branch of the SDF to its party having disaffiliated from the LRC? Many activists found

[287] See Kelly's and Pelton's Directories 1902-1906; Bondfield, M., A Life's Work (London: Hartman & Co 1948) p75-76; Hunt, Equivocal, p270, p273.
[288] Justice August 3rd 1901, June 29th 1901 August 10th 1901, April 5th 1902, July 5th 1902.

themselves in an odd position. A handful of members, such as William Veals, held membership of both the SDF and the ILP. A much larger number of men and women in the branch, as trade unionists or as members of the Tunbridge Wells Cooperative Society, retained at least nominal representation, in a more diluted form, within the LRC. It appears that quite a number within the branch felt that disaffiliation had been a mistake, though none seem to have resigned from the SDF as a result. Many continued to regard themselves as part of a broad labour and socialist movement which transcended organisational structures.

The first test came with a flurry of parliamentary by-elections in early 1902 which led the branch to raise funds and hold public meetings to pass supportive resolutions. Harry Quelch of the SDF stood at Dewsbury and Philip Snowden of the ILP stood at Wakefield. In neither case did these candidates win their target seat, though both scored reasonably well, Snowden taking about forty percent of the vote. The reports of the meetings suggest that the Tunbridge Wells branch show strong backing for both candidates. They also purchased LRC material from time to time. Thus, in November 1903, E J Pay wrote to Ramsay MacDonald to for samples of the LRC's leaflets, which the branch intended to distribute door to door. This effectively refutes the stereotype of the SDF as a narrow and sectarian party.[289]

These differences also failed to divide the town's Trades and Labour Council. Here the key development lay in the unionisation of groups of previously unorganised workers, an echo of the new unionism of the early 1890s. The enthusiasm these showed rather put their longer-established fellow organisations to shame. The National Amalgamated Union of Shop Assistants, Warehousemen and Clerks formed a branch in the town in 1901, with fortnightly members' meetings from June that year. Likewise, the National Union of Gasworkers and General Labourers established a local presence in May 1902. David Geer joined the latter, while remaining a member of the Carpenters and Joiners, while William Bournes worked hard to build the shop assistants' union. Some of the town's women's organisations also built links with this union, which unusually aimed to recruit from both sexes equally, and perhaps found it easier to harness middle-class guilt about the abuses of the 'living-in system', poor conditions and long hours of work than their male-

---

[289] *Crick, History*, p148; *Justice February 15th 1902 and March 15th 1902; Letter from E J Pay to Ramsay MacDonald, November 8th 1903. LRC11/365.*

dominated equivalents. The *London Trades and Labour Gazette*, produced by the London Trades Council, joined *Justice* at SDF meetings and carried reports from the town and other nearby trades councils, including Chatham.[290]

These new unions would have had their first outing at the May Day parade and rally of 1902. The Trades Council again organised this in fine style. London and local speakers representing the National Union of Gasworkers and General Labourers, the Tailors' Union and the Farriers' Union addressed the 'large, supportive crowds' on the Common's Lower Cricket Ground. Rather than the *Red Flag* or *Marseillaise*, the band played an American tune, the *Washington Post*. Republicanism received its first airing for several years; William Bournes declared that 'we have no quarrel with the King... but he happened to know that the King was the head of that class which depended on the labour of the masses'. Shortly afterwards, on May 18th, the SDF re-started their Common meetings, distributing a quire of pamphlets each week along with *Justice*. A significant blow came when Ellis Mann left Tunbridge Wells for Dublin that July, though others stepped in to cover his work.[291]

In 1902 the Ratepayers' League alighted on what they considered to be the least popular of public services, municipal telephones, as a precursor to a much broader attack on the public provision of any service. Only a handful of middle- and upper-class households, together with some businesses, then owned such devices. Thus money spent on them could easily be portrayed as a waste which would only benefit a minority. The Ratepayers' League utilised all the propaganda at their disposal to blame the Social-Democrats, Fabians and any other 'progressive' for the situation.

In retrospect these allegations hold little water. The town had voted to establish its own telephone system in January 1897, almost a year before any socialist had been elected to the council. The scheme then had cross-party support. The Conservative Member of Parliament for the Tonbridge Division, Sir Arthur Griffith-Boscawen, had done all he could to ensure that Central Government supplied the appropriate loans. Socialist support for them was at best lukewarm. Councillor Bournes went on the record in April 1902 to condemn the amount of effort allotted to the scheme, arguing that

290 *The Tunbridge Wells Advertiser May 31st 1901; The Courier June 21st 1901,May 2nd 1902; Hamilton, M.A., Margaret Bondfield (London: L. Parsons 1924) p43-44, p53.*
291 *The Courier May 7th 1902; the Tunbridge Wells Advertiser May 9th 1902; Justice July 12th 1902.*

the recent death of three children from a preventable contagious disease meant that the money should be used for housing instead. He also attacked the £500 spent, without a word of opposition, on celebrating the Coronation.

Ironically the telephone system immediately proved highly profitable, with an initial surplus of £130, something expected to grow to a thousand annually in a few years. Rather than being a burden on the rates, the system subsidised them. It is little surprise that the whole affair seemed somewhat bemusing to later generations. In 1946 a guide published by the *Courier* to celebrate the congress of the South-Eastern Union of Scientific Societies labelled the scheme an unqualified success. The town had more telephones per head than any other in Britain, as well as the lowest charges, and had linked up the neighbouring towns and villages.[292]

Post-truth politics, however, are not a recent invention. The issue of whether Tunbridge Wells should own its own telephones generated articles in national newspapers and questions in Parliament. Both sides recognised that the issues raised would have national implications. A sympathetic Member of Parliament and councillors from London and Manchester joined a delegation from the town to Austin Chamberlain, the Tory Postmaster General, to secure his support for the scheme.[293]

The Ratepayers' League had an overwhelming problem. Tunbridge Wells had shown how municipal socialism could be far better at providing goods and services than private companies. Demand for electricity meant that the works soon needed to be expanded. The praise frequently given to the town in left-wing newspapers may have irked the right. The ILP's *Labour Leader* highlighted the Corporation's success in using surplus land for agricultural purposes in December 1901. The town grew hops, soft fruit and livestock on the North Farm, near the sewage works. Some of this livestock had won prizes at the region's agricultural shows, while in

---

[292] *Tunbridge Wells Journal January 14th 1897, March 28th 1901; The Tunbridge Wells Advertiser October 4th 1901, February 14th 1902 and July 25th 1902; The Courier April 4th 1902, August 1st 1902; Griffith-Boscowen A.S.T, Fourteen Years in Parliament (London: John Murray 1907); Given, J.C.M, Royal Tunbridge Wells Past and Present (Tunbridge Wells: The Courier Publishing and Printing Company 1945).*
[293] *The Courier November 21st 1902; Tunbridge Wells Journal November 13th 1902.*

November 1902 the socialists and the Liberal *Tunbridge Wells Advertiser* claimed a profit from the hops of £500.[294]

The speakers at the 1902 May Day Rally addressed these themes. The Conservative turn towards protectionism came under attack, as speakers feared that this would enrich landowners and larger farmers at great cost to working families. Sir Arthur Griffith-Boscowen had previously weighed into the debate, labelling free trade 'a radical bogey'. Yet the strongest attacks targeted the cartels and trusts which had become embedded in industries in Britain, Europe and, most powerfully, the United States. The example of the cement cartel, with its works on the Lower Medway and Thames Estuary, showed the dangers. In 1900 they imposed wage cuts of up to forty percent, something which the unions could not stop. The company most strongly denounced, because it had shown an interest in buying Tunbridge Wells' municipal system, was the National Telephones Company.

Another theme which resonates today came when a trade unionist denounced the shallow patriotism of those who 'vaunt their pride in the Empire [but] were quite willing to put that pride in their pockets with American dollars'. So that their motives could not be misconstrued, they also declared their 'fraternal greetings to the workers of all countries'.[295]

In July the Ratepayers' League announced that they wished to contest the forthcoming municipal elections in every ward where the other candidates failed to support privatising the town's telephones. A ferocious attack on both the principal of municipalisation and on the character of those who supported it ensued. They particularly singled out James Milstead for abuse and promised to use all means at their disposal to unseat him if he wished to stand for re-election.   Colonel Holland, the leading propagandist behind the organisation, wrote almost weekly to the *Courier* and *Advertiser* to attack the SDF and ILP. In September he combed *Justice* for useful material, concluding that socialism 'owed as large a debt of gratitude to the law-breaker as the law-maker' and had at its core the aim of educating people to become revolutionaries. Another contributor declared that socialism, communism, anarchism and

---

[294] *The Labour Leader December 21st 1901; Tunbridge Wells Municipal Post November 1st 1902; The Courier November 7th 1902; Tunbridge Wells Advertiser October 17th 1902.*
[295] *The Courier April 25th 1902, May 2nd 1902 and May 7th 1902; The Tunbridge Wells Advertiser May 9th 1902, July 17th 1903; Aubry, Red, pp95-98.*

nihilism are synonymous terms, while a Christian minister attacked the socialists for the desecration of the Sabbath with their 'secular political revolutionary speeches and addresses on the Common', and hoped that the police would intervene.[296]

At the same time these newspapers, in particular the *Courier*, received a deluge of letters written anonymously. Most claimed to be from working class men. An early example, from 'a working bricklayer', attacked Bournes and stated that he was watching Milstead 'very closely'. Something very similar later came from 'a Southborough boy'. Another, from someone who claimed to be 'a practical socialist', clearly tried to sow discord in the movement. In response, William Bournes noted that the author had got the name of the Trades and Labour Council wrong and suggested that a member of the Ratepayers' League had written it. E. J. Pay denounced it as the work of 'a freak, if not a fake'. A presumably more middle-class correspondent, who also claimed to be a socialist, attacked Lander and Lawson Dodd of the Fabian Society for having failed to rise for the National Anthem when news of a victory in the Boer War was announced on stage during a London theatre performance some months earlier, showing that the old jingoistic themes could be rehashed. Perhaps the most entertaining of the genre, allegedly from 'a poor working man', came in the first week of 1903:

> *'Me and my mates has been talking about them gents as have lately subscribed there money... not a penny from the SDF, or Fabian Society, or labour union... We does not see even an odd six pennies payed to us by Bournes, Lander, Strange, Geer, T. Marsh, Edwards, Grover, Pink, Putland, Lawson Dodd, Fletcher Dodd'.*

One suspects that this gem came from a man whose knowledge of the way in which working people expressed themselves was rather limited.[297]

The socialists tended to counter every allegation made in detail. Little else appeared in the letter columns for some months. This at least allowed the Social-Democrats and Fabians to fully air their views, though it may have had the disadvantage of allowing the Ratepayers' League to set the agenda.

---

[296] *The Courier July 4th 1902, September 15th 1902, October 17th 1902; The Tunbridge Wells Advertiser July 4th 1902, September 5th 1902.*
[297] *The Courier July 11th 1902, August 1st 1902, August 15th 1902, October 29th 1902, January 9th 1903, January 16th 1903.*

On the positive side, *Justice* noted that 'never was socialism more to the fore in Tunbridge Wells than today'. David Geer addressed some of the attacks on his revolutionary creed head on, agreeing that working people should manage and control their own industrial and social concerns and calling for 'revolution or complete change, which socialists are striving for'. W J Tubbs and David Geer argued that the much-vaunted 'independence' of the Ratepayers' League was a scam, identifying a right-wing pressure group, the Industrial Freedom League, as the source of its propaganda and finance.

Another tactic of the League was to suggest that members of the SDF were standing under other names or as independents. E J Pay refuted this allegation with reference to the party's rules, which banned such tactics. Councillor Abbott, who may have been a target of this smear, and Walter Godbold, a socialist councillor in West Ham, also wrote several times to support municipal trading in principal. A handful of other working men wrote anonymously to support the socialist position, such as 'Jack Plane' – a carpenter – who may have feared for his job had his name been published.[298]

The branch also turned their attention to a series of public meetings which supplemented the usual gatherings on the Common. E J Pay and David Geer challenged Colonel Holland repeatedly to a debate under the title *'Private Enterprise or Socialism: what would benefit the British people?'*, yet the League's representatives refused this invitation on each occasion. James Milstead took up the role of lecture secretary and immediately arranged for a series of outside speakers. George Bernard Shaw and Sidney Webb both addressed large audiences at public meetings which set out the case for municipal services.

In September a march along a similar route to the annual May Day procession ended with a rally on the Common. Will Thorne had to pull out but Alderman Hayday and Councillor Steadman stepped into his shoes. The socialists also made a pitch for the support of the growing number of municipal workers with reference to their recent pay rise. As well as these one-off events, the branch started holding open-air meetings at the corner of Wood Street and Camden

[298] *Justice September 27ᵗʰ 1902; The Courier September 17ᵗʰ 1902, January 16ᵗʰ 1903; The Tunbridge Wells Advertiser August 22ⁿᵈ 1902, October 31ˢᵗ 1902.*

Road, outside the house in which Henry Seymour had hosted secularist meetings about twenty years earlier.[299]

The SDF, having taken the lead in putting the case for municipalisation, decided not to stand a candidate themselves. The branch instead campaigned vigorously on behalf of their Fabian Society allies who had lost their seats as a result of the Boer War. The Ratepayers' League, clearly well resourced, deluged the electors with letters and pamphlets, from which the reader learned that socialists, rather than deciding for themselves, merely follow the instructions of 'socialist committees'.

The contest proved extremely close, but the Fabians fell just short on each occasion. Lawson Dodd gained 539, losing by 39 votes and H C Lander took 364 votes, losing by 72. Even more galling, a few weeks later Lawson Dodd lost a by-election by a mere eighteen votes. The pattern continued in March 1903, when H C Lander, supported by the Trades and Labour Council, lost to Colonel Newnham-Smith.[300]

The SDF and Fabian Society also decided that they needed a fortnightly half-penny fortnightly paper to defend the principle of municipal ownership and make the case for socialism. This used the rather uninspiring title of the *Municipal Post* and, more cheekily the town's motto, *Do Well, Doubt Not*, as a masthead. E.J Pay, now living at 55 Garden Street, acted as advertising and wholesale agent and it was printed at 86 Camden Road. Two or three other Social-Democrats joined Pay on the committee. The *Courier* immediately denounced its new rival as a scurrilous socialist rag and sought to undermine it at every opportunity.

The *Municipal Post* first hit the streets on September 20th 1902. Unsurprisingly, its core aim was to win support for progressive candidates at the forthcoming municipal elections. It condemned the Ratepayers' League as part of a nationwide movement against 'progress', defended those councillors who had worked hard for municipal housing in the town, and highlighted the neglect of this cause with the money lavished on the Coronation celebrations, the

---

[299] *The Tunbridge Wells Advertiser September 26th 1902; Tunbridge Wells Journal October 23rd 1902.*

[300] *Justice November 29th 1902;, The Courier November 7th 1902, December 12th 1902, November 5th 1902; Tunbridge Wells Journal December 25th 1902; Fabian News November 1902; The Tunbridge Wells Advertiser November 28th 1902, March 27th 1903; The Courier March 27th 1903.*

proposed construction of a new courthouse and the expansion of the electricity works. It also sought to expose the workings of trusts and cartels and argued that a vote for the Ratepayers' League is a vote given to the National Telephones Company. Interestingly it also addressed head-on the conflation of socialism and atheism: socialists had a range of views on religion, but pointing out that H C Lander was a Quaker and Frank Lawson Dodd the President of the Tunbridge Wells Free Church.[301]

As the newspaper developed, it carried longer articles and more analytical pieces. In December it continued the religious theme with an article on the pagan roots of Christmas and looked back at the South African War. In January it discussed the economic ideas of Hyndman and Marx. Maud Ward also contributed a lengthy piece on the implications of the Taff Vale Case, which had made it impossible for trade unions to take strike action without being sued, and on the related need to have workers' representatives in Parliament to challenge the domination of it by the wealthy.[302]

The success of this newspaper is hard to judge. In January 1903 it claimed a guaranteed circulation of 4,000. It attracted advertisements from some of the town's larger firms, as well as for David Geer's business. Circulation figures tended to be questionable: one of the town's leading papers claimed a figure in Tunbridge Wells equal to the whole of the other local and district papers while its chief rival advertised itself as having ten times the circulation of any other newspaper within 20 miles of the town. The *Municipal Post*'s figures may have been no more accurate. The edition published on February 7th 1903 was possibly the most varied to date, with reports on the Penrhyn quarrymen's strike, a review of Kropotkin's *Mutual Aid*, and even poetry, together with other articles written by leading members of the Federation and the Fabian Society branches. However, the next issue, advertised as being due on February 21st, did not appear.

The failure of the paper almost certainly stemmed from the amount of work which had to be put into it. Had such efforts been diverted into canvassing, the Fabians and SDF might have prevailed and begun to turn the tide in favour of socialism. On the other hand, it

---

[301] *Justice September 27th 1902; The Tunbridge Wells Municipal Post September 20th 1902, October 4th 1902 and November 1st 1902; The Courier October 10th 1902 and October 24th 1902.*
[302] *The Tunbridge Wells Municipal Post December 13th 1902 and January 10th 1903.*

should be remembered as a brave attempt to reframe the terms of debate.[303]

The Ratepayers' League lost no time in pressing home their advantage on the Council. Within days of the November 1902 election they had organised and won a vote to sell the municipal telephones to the National Telephone Company. Separate delegations from the Council and the League immediately lobbied the Postmaster General to gain permission for the sale. Councillors Bournes and Strange did their best to call for a re-think, but to no avail. Their allies in the press again tried to undermine the case for the sale.

The *Labour Leader*, noting the national significance of the fight in Tunbridge Wells, calculated that municipal enterprises there had made a total of £12,950 in profit over the past five years. In similar fashion, the *Tunbridge Wells Advertiser* reproduced articles from national newspapers, including the *Morning Leader* and the *Daily Chronicle*, which had opposed the decision. Yet the speed at which events moved made resistance futile. The *Courier* carried full details of the terms of the sale a mere two days into 1903.[304]

Demobilisation following the South African War meant that unemployment rose again. The Social-Democrats took up the cause. A local slump in the building trade, which had already gone on for than a year, made matters worse. The Trades and Labour Council set up a Labour Bureau at the Friendly Societies Hall to try to quantify the problem. In December 1902 David Geer led a delegation of trade unionists to demand public works. 609 men at the time had no jobs. The Board of Guardians at Pembury funded enough work for 50 of them and the Council employed the same number, a figure which rose to 70 or 80 by the end of January, though only married men with children could apply. Their friends in the Adult School movement provided free breakfasts for the unemployed the same month and allowed progressive politicians, including Ashby Wood, H C Lander, Fletcher Dodd and David Geer, to talk to them about the causes and remedies of unemployment. The town had some pockets in which lack of work had become particularly prevalent. At High Brooms, still dominated by the

---

[303] *Mitchell's Newspaper Press Directory for 1903 (London: C. Mitchell and Co.)* p 332 and p312; *The Tunbridge Wells Municipal Post February 7th 1903.*
[304] *The Tunbridge Wells Advertiser November 28th 1902; the Labour Leader November 15th 1902; The Courier January 2nd 1903.*

brickworks and gasworks, a soup kitchen fed 150 children twice a week. David Geer, who had years of experience of fighting for the cause of the unemployed, attended as a delegate at the conference at London's Mansion House, a meeting which has been credited with changing opinion about the legitimate role of the state in alleviating distress.[305]

In March Tom Jarvis died at Croydon of typhoid. 150 mourners attended his funeral, many from Tunbridge Wells. *Justice* praised his work as a founding member of the branch alongside William Willis-Harris, David Geer and James Sutton. It also noted that he had made himself known throughout both England and much of the Continent. Reflecting this, Italian and German socialists had joined the mourners. Although he had left the town, his continuing relationship with the Tunbridge Wells branch had been cemented both by his sister's marriage to James Milstead and by his willingness to return to the town to canvass for the party. *Fabian News* also recorded his hard work in Tunbridge Wells, London and Croydon. The most remarkable tribute came in the pages of the Conservative *Courier*:

> 'It is with regret that we have to record the death of Mr Tom Jarvis who died at Croydon last week. Mr Jarvis will be remembered as one of the founders of the local branch of the Social-Democratic Federation in the early Eighties and it must have been peculiarly gratifying to him, before he died at the comparatively early age of 42, to see that his spade-work had not been in vain, and that the propagation of socialists, with which he had thrown his energy, had succeeded to such an extent that our local municipal elections are fought on socialistic lines. The funeral took place at Mitcham Road Cemetery last Thursday afternoon, attended by a large gathering of friends, including Mr H Burrows and Mr H Quelch (Editor of Justice) and members of the Croydon, Battersea, Norwood, Tunbridge Wells and other branches of the SDF. Very touching were the tributes paid to the energy he had thrown into the cause by Messrs Burrows, Quelch and Muggeridge. During the simple ceremony at the grave three of his favourite songs were sung, 'The Fatherland', 'Men whose boast it is that ye' and 'England Arise!'.

---

[305] See Crick, *History*, p172; *The Tunbridge Wells Advertiser* October 18th 1901, December 19th 1902, December 24th 1902, March 13th 1903; *Justice* January 17th 1903; *The Courier* December 19th 1902, January 2nd 1903; *The Tunbridge Wells Advertiser* January 9th 1903, March 6th 1903.

The playing of the hymn *'Men whose boast it is that ye'* at his funeral may suggest that his youthful atheism had softened by this point. His widow Rose Jarvis soon moved to Northampton but remained in touch with members from Tunbridge Wells.[306]

By the spring of 1903 it is clear that the fight seems to have taken a toll on both the SDF and their Fabian allies. There are some parallels to the downturn in the fortunes of the Social-Democrats in the early 1890s, although this should not be overplayed. Membership remained healthy, recruitment continued and the growth of the labour movement nationally had positive effects for the branch. William Veals wrote to *Justice* to admit that they needed more active members at the end of 1902, a call repeated by E J Pay eight months later. The Fabian Society had also cancelled a series of lectures to fight these election campaigns – although the Social-Democrats had at least run a few - and announced that it would no longer be able to run those planned for the spring.[307]

Once again, the SDF and the Trades and Labour Council stepped in to ensure that Tunbridge Wells remained suffused with socialist ideas. Growing dislike of the Conservative Government – which ultimately led to the Liberal landslide of 1906 – increased the effectiveness of their work. The branch frequently tried to link the decisions of right-wing borough councillors with the Tories at Westminster. They invited Will Reason MA and Charlotte Despard to speak that spring, the latter on Saint Francis of Assisi.

For the first time, the 1903 May Day parade had to be cancelled due to the weather, something which had disappointed the significant numbers who had assembled for it. A meeting at the Friendly Societies Hall took place instead, although at most a few hundred would have been able to cram into the available space. Councillors Bournes and Abbot invited the Labour MP for Derby, Richard Bell, to address a meeting at the Pump House, close to the West Station, in June. This meeting, an effort to reach out to local members of the railway unions, allowed the speakers to again condemn the Taff Vale decision and attack conditions on the railways, where more shunters died each year than officers had during the entire Boer War. The plight of those widowed and orphaned by an explosion at

---

[306] *The Courier* April 3rd 1903; *Fabian News* June 1903; *Justice* March 27th 1903 and April 4th 1903.
[307] *Justice* November 29th 1902, July 18th 1903; *Fabian News* November 1902, December 1902.

Woolwich Armaments Factory also gave the branch a topic for a meeting in July.

On several occasions, Councillor Bournes attacked the pay and conditions of workers at the Municipal Electricity Works, 'the worst sweatshop in the town': Alderman Robb intemperately retaliated by calling him a 'member of the agitator class'. Such a response only heightened the sense that working men and women needed elected representatives from their own background.[308]

For a few weeks the branch looked overseas. A resolution passed at a meeting in late May or early June 1903 condemned:

> 'The brutal massacres of the Jewish population of Kishinieff in South West Russia and express our sincere sympathy with those Russian citizens who rendered protection to the victims of the maddened crowd.'

Joseph Green attended the meeting to collect money to support the victims. The murders had taken place on 19th and 20th April although the Socialist International's resolution only passed in mid-July. The *Labour Leader* and other papers carried reports of what had happened that May. The Social-Democrats of Tunbridge Wells followed events in Russia very closely for many years.[309]

The SDF and Fabian Society decided, perhaps in light of new activists coming forward, to improve the skills of their members. In October 1903 a correspondent to the *Courier* noted that Frank Lawson-Dodd had started a series of elocution classes at the Technical Institute. The letter writer disliked this, arguing that the townspeople were already 'deafened by tub orators on the Common'.[310]

In February 1904 Maud Ward who, her comrades noted, had a splendid grasp of the teachings of Marx, ran a series of classes on economics. Karen Hunt has rightly recognised the significance of the way in which her lectures would have helped break down gender stereotypes within the organisation. This can perhaps be

---

[308] *The Courier April 10th 1903, June 2nd 1903; The Tunbridge Wells Advertiser; Justice May 30th 1903, July 3rd 1903, July 17th 1903, October 9th 1903, and October 16th 1903; The Tunbridge Wells Advertiser May 8th 1903, June 12th 1903; Crick, History, p97.*
[309] *The Tunbridge Wells Advertiser June 3rd 1903. See the Labour Leader May 23rd 1903 and July 25th 1903.*
[310] *The Courier October 2nd 1903; Justice December 12th 1903.*

slightly qualified by noting that she and Kathleen Kough organised a social evening the same month at which 80 were present, something which many contemporaries might have considered to be women's work. The economic classes continued for several years and by May 1906 David Geer had taken charge. The branch also carried out a door-to-door distribution of leaflets in the areas of the town in which they had most support – presumably the East and North Wards - to try and win new converts to the cause.[311]

The election of J W Boulter as secretary of the Tunbridge Wells branch in March 1904 marked a return to prioritising public activities. Before the month ended, a 'labour social and tea' showed the strength of socialism in the district. A C Burns joined local speakers Arthur Hickmott, Frank Lawson-Dodd, David Geer, Edward Baker and E J Pay. For the first time in a few years concerted work outside the town followed, as Arthur Hickmott requested support for a campaign, ultimately successful, to get Fred Hooker returned as a second socialist councillor at Sevenoaks.[312]

The issue of the importation of indentured Chinese labour into South Africa gave the town's socialists a platform for their views on economics, international relations and empire. The Social-Democratic Federation ran a series of meeting which perhaps brought out both the best and the worst in the local movement. The view of J Mason of the Plasterers' Union that 'the whole of the races' of South Africa, including the black majority, would suffer, is most credible, as is the genuine horror at the exploitation of the Chinese expressed by several speakers. Socialism thus embraced the world, not only its white men and women.

By contrast, the Amalgamated Carpenters' Union branch's attack on a policy which benefitted 'the cosmopolitan money-grabbers' has more than a taint of anti-Semitism, and those present would have understood it in these terms. No similar comments from the town's Social-Democrats can be found, though as explained earlier, newspapers such as *Justice* and *Labour Leader* had published some fairly unpleasant material. The two aspects of the immigration debate put Sir Arthur Griffith-Boscowen and the rest of the Conservative Party in the rather contradictory position of

---

[311] *Justice February 20th 1904; Hunt, K., Equivocal Feminists p210; Justice May 6th 1906.*
[312] *Labour Leader January 6th 1905; Justice February 20th 1904, March 12th 1904; The Courier April 1st 1904.*

supporting the movement of cheap labour in South Africa while at the same time prioritising restrictions against the movement of subjects of the Russian Empire, many of them Jewish, into Britain.[313]

In April 1904 the Social-Democrats and wider labour movement prioritised the elections for Poor Law Guardians. Councillor William Bournes led the call for the election of three female Guardians, including Amelia Scott, something which put the wider issue of women's political rights on the agenda. The plight of children arriving at school too hungry to learn also focussed minds. The branch passed a resolution in favour of state funds being used to provide free food for children and forwarded it to the two local Members of Parliament. Griffith-Boscowen remained neutral but Charles Frederick Hutchinson, the Liberal Member of Parliament for Rye, which included the most southerly suburbs of Tunbridge Wells, supported the proposal.[314]

By that summer the work to equip the branch with the skills to advance the socialist cause had done it a lot of good. The meeting on the Common on 19th June ended with a collection, excluding sales of papers and pamphlets, of 17s 6d, the best since the branch had formed eighteen years ago. By September they could claim that their summer series of meetings had set a new record. Recruitment remained strong, and new members, including William E Doust and Miss Chatfield, threw themselves into activity. The branch even took inspiration from the Salvation Army and similar religious bodies: a self-denial week raised 11s 10d in September.[315]

Despite this, the SDF and Fabians still struggled to find election candidates. The Trades and Labour Council therefore approached James Richards, one of the most interesting characters in the town at the time, to run in the East Ward. Richards had opened a shop at 85 Camden Road – opposite the printers of the *Municipal Post* – as a lending library, newsagents and to sell his photographic postcards. Although the negatives from the latter have not survived, the remaining images form a unique record of working class life in the town, in particular the East Ward, and a handful cover political subjects, including parades of the Cooperative Society and the women's suffrage movement.

---

313 *The Courier March 11th 1904, April 1st 1904, March 18th 1904.*
314 *The Courier April 1st 1904; Justice April 30th 1904; The Courier April 22nd 1904; Hunt p226.*
315 *Justice June 25th 1904, September 3rd 1904 and September 24th 1904.*

It is possible that his strong religious views – he presided as a lay reader over Methodist services in the chapels of the district – dissuaded him from joining the SDF, though he had worked with the labour movement since 1902 and clearly identified with socialism. His opponents made much of his long hair. Councillor Bournes led his campaign. On this occasion Richards lost. William Bournes stood unopposed in the North Ward and therefore automatically retained his seat. In recognition of his length of service he became the first working class magistrate appointed in Tunbridge Wells, something supported by both the Trades Council and Arthur Griffith-Boscowen. [316]

In December 1904 the branch moved their meetings to Emma Wilshere's Dining Rooms at 27 Camden Road, a venue which may have seemed more comfortable and modern than the halls normally hired for this purpose. E J Pay and Joseph Green addressed a meeting on the international socialist movement that month while Herbert Burrows gave a wide-ranging speech under the title 'Some objections to socialism' which considered the Marxist idea of historical materialism and argued that socialists, although extreme individualists, maintained common fundamental principles. He concluded by saying that the Liberal Party would do nothing for the working classes. The 'unusually large audience' at this meeting meant that the branch had to find a new venue in February 1905 for the remainder of the series of lectures. The last of the series in

The Byng Hall today

February and March addressed the relationship between socialism and modern science and the ways in which both could transform home life. The Social-Democrats also reprised their call for work for local men. George Lansbury and William Bournes addressed a public meeting at the Byng Hall using the example that there were only

[316] The Courier December 16th 1904 and January 18th 1905; Labour Leader December 9th 1904

two local men among the eighteen employed on a scheme to improve nearby Culverden Down.[317]

Events hundreds of miles away soon caught the imagination. 1905 began with strikes in Russian factories. Leon Trotsky's later account remains a very good guide to the course of events. 140,000 men and women had walked out by 7th January. Two days later the army massacred several hundred demonstrators in St Petersburg and injured thousands more.

This sparked a much larger wave of industrial action which spread across the country. Hyndman addressed a crowded meeting in Tunbridge Wells Town Hall on the *'Social Revolution at Home and Abroad'* in mid-January. Unsurprisingly Russia took centre stage. A series of open-air meetings followed throughout the rest of the year. On 30th July the branch collected a pound in solidarity for the victims on the Common. A few weeks later, Zelda Kahan, herself from a Russian Jewish background and after 1920 one of the most prominent figures in the early CPGB, addressed a meeting on the same spot. Remarkably the *Tunbridge Wells Advertiser* recorded that the branch announced openly that the money collected would go to buy guns to enable Jewish and socialist groups in Russia to defend themselves. It is almost certain that the funds were used for their intended purpose: the SDF spent more than a year smuggling such weapons to Russia from small harbours in the north-east of England and the east coast of Scotland until the authorities decided to clamp down on the shipments.

By November Russia entered a period of revolutionary struggle which ended with a mixture of extreme state repression and a few short-lived democratic concessions. The branch later drew significant conclusions from the course of events, which appeared to mark a further stage in the great revolutionary movement that would free 'not only their own country, but Europe at large, from the largest and most powerful mainstay of despotism'.[318]

The other great campaign of 1905 related to emigration. As already discussed, the SDF had long rejected this as a cure for

---

[317] *The Courier December 4th 1904, January 4th 1905; Tunbridge Wells Advertiser January 6th 1905, March 3rd 1905; Justice December 10th & 24th 1904, January 14th 1905*

[318] *Trotsky, L, 1905 (Harmondsworth: Penguin 1971), pp89-99; The Courier January 27th 1905; the Tunbridge Wells Advertiser January 27th 1905; Justice August 5th 1905, August 26th 1905; Lee and Archibold pp148-154.*

unemployment and this had differentiated the party from other radicals, including Charles Bradlaugh, and a number of trade unionists. The idea that Britain could export its surplus workers saw a revival during this period and, reflecting this, a group of men described - in a tongue-in-cheek way - by *Justice* as 'gentleman of the highest patriotism' formed the Tunbridge Wells Colonisation Society. This new body organised a meeting in February at the Town Hall which intended to take names of local workers who might be willing to go abroad.

Seeing this as a threat, the Social-Democrats invited one of their key national speakers, Jack Williams, who joined Teddy Pay and Edward Baker in the audience. One socialist refuted the idea that Britain had too many people living in it, arguing instead that the country had millions of acres of unused land, much of it used by 'the idle rich' for shooting and deer parks. Uproar followed, and the Mayor agreed to attend the Federation's own meeting and not to take down any names of prospective emigrants at this stage.[319]

The large audience assembled for the Social-Democrats' own meeting the following week heard from a range of speakers, including H C Lander of the Fabian Society and Harry Quelch. Perhaps the most insightful perspective came from Edward Baker who described his own experiences in Canada. A motion, passed almost unanimously, concluded the meeting; emigration amounted to transportation for life in the interests of the capitalist class. Those present instead demanded the common ownership of industry and the land to enable Britain to feed itself.

Both Baker and W G Veals wrote to the *Advertiser* in early March to give further arguments against signing up to leave the country. The SDF and the Trades and Labour Council also suggested more short-term ways to alleviate unemployment, holding a meeting in May to support legislative solutions and, with an election pending at the end of the year, writing to the Liberal and Conservative candidates for the Tonbridge Division to see whether they would support them.[320]

Agitation against emigration combined naturally with opposition to protectionism, the other great Conservative cause. Again the Tories

---

[319] Crick, History, p33-34; Justice February 11th 1905.
[320] The Courier February 24th 1905; Justice February 11th 1905; The Tunbridge Wells Advertiser March 3rd 1905; Justice April 15th 1905; The Courier December 29th 1905 and January 5th 1906.

hoped the policy would win working class support. Their public meeting in August, with a paid speaker who may once have been a trade unionist, fell flat. The socialists in attendance 'literally pulverised' his arguments, allowing the Liberal-supporting *Advertiser* to crow that tariff reform would not win any support from the 'Labour party' in Tunbridge Wells. E J Pay noted the high levels of unemployment in countries which had protectionist policies, Bournes argued that British workers received better wages than them, while Edward Baker said that he had found a lot of poverty in the United States. W G Veals and Baker attacked the wealth and the power of trusts in that country, demanding socialism as the better alternative.

In November Harry Quelch debated the same question with a Mr Hicks, the protectionist Mayor of Tunbridge Wells. The *Advertiser* again sided with the socialists, though it recognised the Mayor's 'temerity' in debating with the 'great socialist, Mr Quelch. The *Courier* felt that Hicks had done better. Each side accused the other of not answering the question. Hicks alienated much of the audience by claiming that 'the workman was of no use without the capitalist', 'socialism has failed, free trade has failed and trade unions have failed'. Quelch concentrated on the rising cost of living that protectionism would bring and won applause by arguing that socialism and trade unions wanted protection, but rather than against foreign workmen they wanted it against the world's capitalists.[321]

Public meetings enabled a significant part of the town's population to be exposed to socialist ideas, but the branch perhaps realised that adult males tended to form the bulk of the audience. By late 1905 the Social-Democrats may have feared losing ground among more radical women. The Tunbridge Wells branch responded by forming a Women's Socialist Circle. Relatively few branches set these up, and of those that did they tended to concentrate on social rather than political questions. Women such as Kathleen Kough and Maud Ward ensured that this did not happen at Tunbridge Wells: members read from Robert Blatchford's *Britain for the British* and the hope seemed to be that those attracted to the Circles would also become active in the party.[322]

[321] *The Tunbridge Wells Advertiser September 1ˢᵗ 1905.*
[322] *Hunt, pp226-250.*

The creation of the Women's Socialist Circle attracted little interest from the town's press. The Social-Democrats' next move, however, proved more controversial. The branch formed a Socialist Sunday School which initially, like many of the Circles, met in the front room of a member. On January 21st 1906 nine children and two adults attended. At this time it seems to have been the smallest such school of the 41 in the British Isles, though it was also the only one in the south-east outside London. Numbers enrolled soon grew and in February 1906 the need for more space led it to rent a large room above the Cooperative Society's Kensington Street shops. The *Advertiser* gave a vivid, if not altogether flattering description. One man addressed the fourteen children present, as much as possible in words of one syllable, on socialist ideas which came in the form of fables about 'pussy cats and puppy dogs'. The five girls all wore red dresses. The session concluded with the singing of the Red Flag, the high treble voices of the young socialists being assisted by two burly, good natured looking socialist men of maturer years in their 'blood red' ties. *Justice* suggests these men may have been James Milstead and H W Roberts.

Reactions in Tunbridge Wells proved more muted than elsewhere. A couple of years later the town's Socialist Sunday School visited Hastings. One newspaper in that town purchased a copy of the *Red Catechism* and expressed its anger at the contents - the working classes are represented in the depths of poverty and misery while every employer of labour is a bigoted, merciless monster, whose only desire is to suck the blood of the working man who is robbed and tossed from the frying pan into the fire and back again. Little of this appears in the movement's own journal, *Young Socialist*, which instead emphasised solidarity, compassion, the love for and appreciation of the natural world, the traditions of the English, Scottish, Welsh and Irish countryside and the questioning of all forms of arbitrary authority. These values should be favourably contrasted with the diet of deference to God, King, Empire and the rich, together with militarism and racism, found in mainstream education at the time.[323]

---

[323] *The Courier February 2nd 1906; The Tunbridge Wells Advertiser February 2nd 1906; Simon, B., Education p27, p39; Matthews, M., Alf Cobb, p35; Justice May 5th 1906; The Young Socialist February 1906.*

Herbert Burrows

1905 ended on a positive note for the branch. Herbert Burrows, who had spoken several times in the town over the last twenty years, praised the wonderful progress made in the town and argued that socialists acted both as the doctors of present society' and as prophets of the future. The attempt by the Ratepayers' League to privatise the electric power station failed when the Town Council overwhelmingly voted to keep it in public hands that October. David Geer, Frank Colebrook, E J Pay, H C Lander and Frank Lawson Dodd lobbied councillors, addressed public meetings and written letters to outline just how much the town's ratepayers had saved by municipal ownership – as early as 1903 it had already made a gross profit of £19,262 and net of £6,154 after paying off interest at 6% a year. The *Clarion*, using words which today sound rather Soviet, reported in July 1905 that:

> 'The enemies of the people at Tunbridge Wells, having succeeded in transferring the municipal telephones to private enterprise, have now turned their attention to the electricity department'

The article noted the £1,000 annual profit from the works and attacked the 'representative of the dividend-hunters on the council' who had proposed the privatisation.[324]

A few weeks later the Ratepayers' League suffered another stinging defeat. In the East Ward, James Richards, standing as an 'advanced progressive and labour' candidate with the support of the Trades and Labour Council, topped the poll with 464 votes. An independent, Mr Collyer, took the other seat, leaving the Ratepayers' League candidate trailing in last place with 295 votes. Although William Bournes, Frank Lawson Dodd and David Geer, along with Councillor Edwards all worked hard on Richards'

---

[324] *The Courier October 27th 1905; The Labour Leader June 24th 1903; The Clarion July 14th 1905; The Courier September 29th 1905; The Tunbridge Wells Advertiser September 28th 1905; The Tunbridge Wells Advertiser October 6th 1905.*

campaign, no Social-Democrat was in a position to contest a seat that year. In hindsight this may be considered a lost opportunity. Had one of their number, perhaps E J Pay or W G Veals, won that year in the North Ward, it is probable that schemes such as municipal housing could have been resurrected.[325]

Scenes from the 1906 General Election:
outside the Town Hall at Tunbridge Wells; and at Tonbridge.

[325] *The Courier November 10th 1905; The Tunbridge Wells Advertiser November 5th 1905; the Clarion November 10th 1905.*

PART C   KENT AND SUSSEX FOR SOCIALISM

CHAPTER 10   THE SOUTH EASTERN COUNTIES FEDERATION OF SOCIALIST SOCIETIES

In August 1905 the Social-Democratic Federation forwarded a cutting from a local newspaper, the *Tunbridge Wells Argus* –one which has unusually not survived in the British Library archive - to *Justice*. The editor of the latter decided to reproduce it in full:

> *'Just now controversial oratory is in full swing on Tunbridge Wells Common. The four competitive parties seem to be the Baptists, the YMCA, the Salvation Army and the Social-Democratic Federation. The last-named, of late, seeing the largest crowds, talk politics with fluent audacity of feeling and statement. These followers of the now familiar crimson flag, planted near the 'liberty-tree' on the slopes of Mount Ephraim, are often interrupted in their arguments by less advanced thinkers, as the latter pass over the Common after the hours of church and chapel services. But scores of working men who surround the Socialists seem to relish the iconoclastic attacks on the 'classes' and capitalists. Indeed the hold these advanced politicians are now getting over the industrial classes in the Borough almost gives a shudder to complacent, orthodox Tunbridge Wells. Scores of women now applaud the Social-Democratic Federation speakers'.*[326]

Tunbridge Wells, however, was extremely unusual among southern towns. One Labour Member of Parliament, James Parker, believed that the Independent Labour Party hardly existed in the Home Counties before 1906. The SDF had even less support. Small nuclei of activists gathered in pubs, halls or front rooms in many of the market towns in Kent and Sussex and often agreed to form a branch, whether of the SDF, ILP, Fabian Society or Clarion Fellowship, yet these tended to be only slightly more successful than their equivalents of the 1890s. Stronger party organisations with deeper roots existed in the outer suburbs of London, the Medway Towns, Maidstone and Brighton, but these can be considered the exceptions that prove the rule. Few held public meetings. However, all parts of the labour and socialist movement entered a period of growth from 1905: the Social-Democrats added

---

[326] *The Tunbridge Wells Argus, quoted in Justice August 19th 1905.*

one hundred new branches across Britain between 1906 and 1908, reaching a membership of 12,000.[327]

The Tunbridge Wells SDF had a number of speakers with a sufficiently high reputation to be in demand in other places. E J Pay spoke two or three times at the briefly resuscitated Brighton branch in late 1904, though the relative weakness of the movement even there can be shown by the fact that, except to distribute *Justice*, it had ceased to function by early 1906.

The Social-Democrats next turned their attention to neighbouring Tonbridge and Sevenoaks. In April 1905 they placed a notice in *Justice* asking for supporters in those towns to contact them to assist in running a series of meetings. Weekly meetings every Sunday at 'industrial'[328] Tonbridge followed from June to October. David Geer, Baker and Kathleen Kough addressed what the branch considered to be fair sized audiences. This demonstrated the success of the branch in training speakers, as they simultaneously ran two meetings on Tunbridge Wells Common on the same dates, although when their former fellow branch member W T Kenward visited from Southampton they were very grateful for his assistance. Once again, however, no separate branch of the SDF formed in either Sevenoaks or Tonbridge, though their work may have given a boost to the small ILP group in the latter town.[329]

Counter-intuitive it may be, but the General Election of January and February 1906 seems to have accelerated the growth of the socialist movement in the South-East. Perhaps the breaking down of the old order gave some the idea that change could happen, while the limited nature of the Liberal Party's radicalism made a smaller number believe that society needed far more extensive alterations. Not only did the Liberals win by a landslide, with 400 seats to the Tories' 157, but for the first time a significant number of Labour Members of Parliament entered the Commons.

The Tonbridge Division of Kent, with Tunbridge Wells its primary town, threw out Sir Arthur Griffith-Boscowen and replaced him with the Liberal candidate, Alfred Paget Hedges, a member of the cigarette manufacturing family who lived at Leigh. His ecstatic supporters pulled his carriage from Tunbridge Wells to Tonbridge,

---

[327] *Labour Leader April 20th 1906; Crick, History, p176'*
[328] *According to Frank Colebrook in Justice September 23rd 1905.*
[329] *Justice October 8th 1904, March 24th 1906, April 15th 1905, June 3rd 1905, June 10th 1905, August 5th 1905, August 26th 1905.*

where thousands of Liberals held a torchlight procession. Oddly enough, the semi-rural Sussex constituency of Rye (in which a small proportion of Tunbridge Wells residents lived), together with its more urban neighbour Hastings, bucked the national trend and elected Conservatives in place of Liberals.[330]

The SDF expressed no real enthusiasm for the contest. Hedges came from the moderate wing of his party. SDF policy at this stage was only to support Liberal parliamentary candidates if they were strongly anti-imperialist. A correspondent to the Liberal *Advertiser* had attacked the 'impossible socialist attitude' on unemployment, and David Geer had clashed with the Liberal candidate on the subject. Geer called on his fellow Social-Democrats to spoil their ballot by writing the word 'labour' across it. As only 'nine or a dozen' actually did so, it seems that a majority of those in the party who had the right to vote – all women, lower-income men and anyone who had received poor relief had no such opportunity - either abstained or, one would assume, voted Liberal.[331]

David Geer persisted in his criticisms, arguing that, although he opposed protectionism, if as the Liberals contended, free trade could be a panacea for the nation's problems, then thirteen million people would not be in poverty, a figure taken directly from the new Prime Minister, Campbell-Bannerman. Yet other members of the Federation reached out to their opponents and in some cases won converts. For one young Liberal sub-agent at Rusthall, the most memorable encounter of the election period came when he met a member of the SDF:

> 'He was the driver of a traction engine, a giant of a man – thick black hair, deep voice – red tie. When I called on him to get his vote he poured scorn on the Liberals as no better than Tories; both were the Capitalist enemy. He was indifferent about the Tariff and Education issues, and, as for the Chinese slaves, 'what are we, comrade, but wage-slaves'. I enjoyed the rough debate with him and when his huge hand covered mine to say good-bye he exclaimed, 'Comrade, go on thinking and reading and you'll be a Socialist within twelve months.' I laughed denial, but he turned out to be right'.

---

[330] Brockway, F., *Inside the Left: Thirty years of Platform, Press, Prison and Parliament*, (London: New Leader Ltd 1947) p13.
[331] *The Tunbridge Wells Advertiser* December 8th 1905; Crick, *History*, p94; Beer, M., *History* p270.

Thus Fenner Brockway, not long out of public school, started on the path which would see him join the SDF's branch in London's St Pancras – which impressed him much less than its Tunbridge Wells equivalent – and then become one of the leading figures of the ILP.[332]

The election of the Liberal Government of 1906 also put the issue of women's suffrage back on the agenda. As we have seen, the Social-Democratic Federation's position, in common with much of the left, was in favour of universal adult suffrage. Maud Ward had explained her reasons for this in May 1905: there should be no reason why everybody should not be sufficiently educated to take an intelligent interest in current affairs. A proposed bill that year was insufficient as it would still deny married women the vote.

Unfortunately this principled position suffered from two weaknesses. Firstly the labour and socialist movement devoted relatively little time to the cause. Secondly quite a number of men within found that they could get away with belittling women. The bizarre views of Ernest Belfort Bax, who seriously seems to have considered both that men suffered oppression from women and that females could not take part in public life as periods or the menopause rendered them periodically insane, together with the snarky remarks of Quelch, did the SDF no favours.[333]

Within months it became apparent that many Liberal MPs were reneging on promises to support extending the vote to women. Members of the National Union of Women's Suffrage Societies held activities in Tunbridge Wells that year, including a conference in October which was later credited by Millicent Garrett Fawcett with turning the tide in favour of the cause. Amelia Scott, whom the labour movement had supported, played a leading role locally. Yet as Anne Carwardine has noted, the suffrage movement in Tunbridge Wells was exclusively middle class.[334]

In hindsight it is clear that both movements had a problem at the point at which gender intersected with class. Selina Cooper, a working-class Lancashire suffragist and socialist, attended a meeting at Tunbridge Wells during 1906 and was admonished by Susan Power, a middle-class member of the local movement, 'not to

---

[332] *The Tunbridge Wells Advertiser February 2nd 1906; Brockway, Inside p13, p19; Coxall and Griggs p175.*
[333] *The Courier May 12th 1905; Bondfield, Life's Work p76.*
[334] *Carwardine, A., pxiii, p73-5.*

let that class-hatred and bitterness come into your heart again... none of us can help society being broken up into classes, and therefore why hate each other for it'? She had previously won the endorsement of both the SDF and ILP in her campaign to be elected a Poor Law Guardian and might have felt more at home at a socialist meeting in the town. The local women's suffrage campaign accordingly struggled to attract working class support, while the SDF, Fabian Society and Trades and Labour Council seem not to have attracted as many women as they had done in previous years.[335]

In May the Tunbridge Wells branch organised a social to celebrate International Workers' Day. William Bournes turned on his previous party, arguing that no real differences existed between the Tories and the Liberals, while welcoming the new era brought about by the Labour Party's presence in Parliament. Councillor Hickmott spoke about the growth of the labour movement in the town and the country, while Maud Ward called for action on high railway fares and the ownership of the press by the 'plutocracy at the present time'. They particularly welcomed Keir Hardie's *John Bull and His Unemployed*, presenting a copy of this to each of the town's councillors and handed out 2,000 copies of the Federation's *Right to Work Manifesto*.[336]

Other socialists in the south-eastern counties, many of them unattached to branches or parties, took heart from the General Election result. As with their equivalents in Tonbridge the year before, a few wrote to the Secretary of the Tunbridge Wells branch to ask for speakers or asked for a notice to be placed in *Justice* or the *Labour Leader*. The socialists of Strood agreed arrangements first. This industrial district, dominated by a series of complex railway junctions, the large works of Aveling and Porter - one of Britain's leading manufacturers of traction and ploughing engines - and several barge-builders, lay across the River Medway from the historic city of Rochester.

In 1906 the new Member of Parliament for Chatham, John Hogan Jenkins, had taken the Labour Party whip and his Rochester neighbour, Ernest Lamb, though formally a Liberal, had Labour sympathies. William George Veals and E J Pay visited the town in

---

[335] See Liddington, J., *The Life and Times of a Respectable Rebel: Selina Cooper 1864 – 1946* (London: Virago 1984) p99, p159, p186; and Hunt, *Equivocal Feminists*.
[336] *The Courier* February 16th 1906, April 13th 1906 and May 11th 1906; *Justice* May 5th 1906; *The Tunbridge Wells Advertiser* May 11th 1906.

May. For all this, though, Strood SDF did not prosper and only one active member remained by autumn 1907. In July E J Pay travelled to the very different town of Eastbourne, perhaps the most select of all southern resorts, to address a meeting of the Clarion Fellowship.[337]

The Social-Democrats of Tunbridge Wells had by this stage a particular incentive to try to take the lead in building the movement in the region. In April the branch had moved a motion at the party's annual conference – defeated following a powerful speech by Harry Quelch – to commit the party to unification with the ILP. In this they had the support of Robert Blatchford of the Clarion Fellowship, partly as it would prevent the Labour Party from being a mere appendage of the Liberal Party. George Meek, who had organised the meeting at Eastbourne, also saw the logic in building a strong unified socialist organisation. E J Pay, whom Meek called 'the gifted pioneer', joined the Labour MP T F Richards at another rally in Eastbourne in August. Teddy Pay and William Veals spoke there again in September and October. By this stage the Social-Democrats of Brighton had also rebuilt their branch, though primarily through their own resources rather than outside assistance.[338]

As explained previously, the Hastings branch of the SDF had faded in the early years of the century. The links between the radicals there and the socialists of Tunbridge Wells remained: the Hastings branch of the National Democratic League had held fifteen open-air meetings by August and thanked the Social-Democrats of Tunbridge Wells branch for sending a series of speakers including W G Veals and H W Roberts. Much as the members of the Hastings SDF had earlier decided that their future lay within the broader NDL, a faction within the latter now decided that the time was right for reinstating a branch of the SDF. This met on 14th October 1906.[339]

George Meek, while enthusiastically welcoming these developments in newspapers like the *Labour Leader*, felt that it had been a bit piecemeal. He had, ever since 1897, harboured grander plans. In August 1906 he organised a meeting of 50 activists to the cause, which agreed to his plan to form a cross-party alliance, the South

---

[337] *Justice May 19th 1906; Aurbry, Red, pp110-114.*
[338] *Justice April 21st 1906, September 8th 1906, September 29th 1906 and October 6th 1906; Coxall and Griggs p120; Labour Leader July 27th 1906.*
[339] *The Hastings Mail August 18th 1906, October 20th 1906.*

Eastern Counties Federation of Socialist Societies. This agreed to write to every branch of SDF, Clarion Fellowship and ILP in the counties of Kent, Sussex, Surrey and Hampshire (those in Surrey and Hampshire did not get involved much). Towns with a strong socialist presence would adopt one where the movement was weaker or non-existent. Sidcup had responsibility for rebuilding the Sevenoaks branch and Tunbridge Wells would do the same in Maidstone. Speakers and visiting activists would also assist at Ashford, Dover, Hastings, Eastbourne and Brighton. Although the organisation intended to address the 'deep, terrible, cruel poverty' in the region, its attention first turned to the towns rather than the often even worse situation found in the countryside. Branches at Sidcup, Tunbridge Wells, Ashford, Dover, Hastings, Eastbourne and Brighton affiliated immediately, though Croydon ILP refused to do so. Erith, Hook and Southampton joined the following month [340]

The project assigned to Tunbridge Wells, Maidstone's branch of the ILP, soon took root, with 20 members in September and 43 in November. This, with Hastings, showed that George Meek's approach worked. Through the pages of the socialist press, he asked sympathisers at Reigate, Epsom, Thornton Heath, Bexleyheath, Erith, Rochester, Sheerness, Tonbridge, Chatham, Dartford and Portsmouth to contact him to build the SECFSS further. E J Pay delivered two 'rousing speeches' at the market town and railway junction of Ashford that September. Although Meek, the originator of the scheme, took on the role of secretary, the level of demand for speakers from Tunbridge Wells, the way in which the largest branches had the most delegates (one for every twenty-five members), and their friendship with activists like Arthur Hickmott at Sevenoaks and Mr Cripps at Maidstone ensured that Tunbridge Wells had more influence on the direction of the SECFSS than would otherwise have been the case.[341]

What, though, of work in Tunbridge Wells that summer and autumn? One meeting in particular stands out. A novel by Upton Sinclair, *the Jungle*, which charted the exploitation of workers and adulteration of tinned food in Chicago's meatpacking district, rapidly made a great impact on the public following its publication in February 1906. Copies soon made their way to Britain. Paget

---

[340] *Justice August 4th & 25th 1906; Coxall and Griggs Meek, pp116-118.*
[341] *Coxall and Griggs, Meek p119-12; the Clarion September 7th 1906, November 16th 1906, March 22nd 1907; Labour Leader August 24th 1906, September 14th 1906; Justice October 13th 1906.*

Hedges highlighted his opposition to such practices in his successful election campaign, though this may have been slightly before the appearance of the book. The SDF asked an American comrade who had worked in the industry to tour some of their British branches. His performance on Tunbridge Wells Common in June drew large crowds, many of them not members of the party. The speaker left little to the imagination: the finished product used all parts of the animal as well as 'deceased cats, ancient cows, dogs etc.', together with a liberal sprinkling of human limbs. Some, however, left at the point he declared that 'cannibalism was not yet extinct in England'. The meeting concluded with an attack on the power of America's trusts and poor food hygiene standards in Britain.[342]

The Liberal Party headquarters, Tunbridge Wells, in 1906. The large banner or sign makes reference to the adulteration of food, something the SDF also took up that year.

The tedious old attitudes remained. In July a speaker discussed the Social-Democrats' call for secular education, quoting from one of the party's more surprising recruits, the Countess of Warwick. A religious crank, reciting a great many scriptural passages, left by declaiming that he would oppose socialism 'to his dying day'. This drew heckles from the crowd and the meeting only concluded at

---

[342] *Justice June 23rd 1906, July 21st 1906; The Courier June 22nd 1906; The Tunbridge Wells Advertiser June 22nd 1906.*

9pm, presumably as the light had faded. As the weather turned, the Federation, ILP and Fabian Society organised other lectures under the Sunday Social Gathering Committee. Keir Hardie and Herbert Burrows both agreed to speak that November. Hardie's meeting, presided over by Lawson Dodd, gave the audience an 'inspiring exposition of socialist principles', concluding with an uncompromising declaration against the Tories and Liberals alike. At the close, E J Pay, on behalf of both the Tunbridge Wells SDF and the Tunbridge Wells ILP, thanked him for the brave stand he had made for years past in the House of Commons, and expressed his hope that a united socialist party would soon come into being. This is one of very few references to a Tunbridge Wells branch of the ILP before its revival in the 1920s, and it is likely that it only lasted for a relatively short period of time.[343]

The lectures by Herbert Burrows and Keir Hardie may have helped David Geer's attempts at re-election in his native East Ward. Once again he stood as a Social-Democrat and Trades and Labour candidate, being nominated by Cllr James Richards and by a Mr Rogers. Yet his opponents had themselves agreed an alliance. The Conservatives and Liberals had each put up a single candidate for the two seats. He fought hard, supporting a proposal that the town purchase the chalybeate springs on which its fame as a spa town had arisen. However, the electorate preferred the older parties and he took a mere 372 votes, the Liberal winning 641 and the Tory 626. Geer reflected on the result in his concession speech, arguing that 'the red flag has just as good a colour in defeat as victory', that the 'moderates' had won – probably a reference to the right-wing in London municipal elections - and that he would fight on for the interests of his fellow workers. *Justice* concluded that many working men did not support him as he had refused to vote for the 'capitalist radical candidate', Hedges, at the General Election, and that the Liberals had worked with the Tories to deny him the seat in revenge.[344]

Cold and wet weather means that the winter months are not great for open-air rallies, although E J Pay spoke in Brighton in January 1907. The SDF again turned their attention to demanding the right to work for those unemployed in Tunbridge Wells. The economy had

---

[343] *Justice December 1st 1906; The Courier November 23rd 1906,The Tunbridge Wells Advertiser November 30th 1906, July 20th 1906; Labour Leader November 23rd 1906*
[344] *The Courier October 26th 1906, November 2nd 1906; Justice October 6th 1.906, November 10th 1906 and December 15th 1906; The Tunbridge Wells Advertiser November 2nd 1906; Justice November 18th 1905 and November 25th 1905.*

taken a downward trajectory. From November 1906 the branch lobbied the Council and the Guardians for public works and organised a public meeting at the Pump Room in December. The Unemployed Workmen's Act of the previous year allowed local authorities with a population of fewer than fifty thousand, such as Tunbridge Wells, to request the formation of a distress committee to register those out of work and to provide jobs. A register duly opened, with 452 men being recorded in February (women, boys and girls seem to have been ignored, as would those men working for fewer than their normal hours).

The sole SDF MP, Will Thorne, demanded much more radical measures; the fact that Hedges had voted against him gave the branch an excuse to challenge him in the pages of the *Advertiser* and at public meetings. Two delegations, both led by David Geer, walked to the Pembury Guardians and the Town Hall, the latter being formally welcomed by Councillor William Bournes. Some relief work followed, but that provided by the workhouse paid only half of much as the average agricultural labourer's hourly rate, a level itself little better than subsistence wages. Many had to wait until the spring for work.[345]

By April or May 1907 it had become clear that some of the differences within the socialist and labour movement which had arisen during the Boer War had become more pressing. Henry Mayers Hyndman's distrust of Germany led him to call for an increase in the size of the Navy, Harry Quelch wrote about becoming 'an armed nation' and that war might solve the problems of over-production and unemployment. Robert Blatchford, unsurprisingly, went much further.

It is clear that members of the Tunbridge Wells branch and their allies grew increasing concerned at these trends. Arthur Hickmott wrote a well-argued response at the end of April, suggesting that ending child labour, limiting hours of work and redistributing wealth would be a more appropriate answer to economic difficulties. Mediation between nations, open diplomacy, home rule for those within the British Empire, a mandatory referendum on declaring war would preserve peace. If conflict should break out all men should be given the right to register as conscientious objectors. At almost exactly the same time as the edition of the *Social-Democrat*

---

[345] *Justice January 19th 1907; Harris, J., Employment pp157-180; Justice February 9th 1907; The Courier February 8th 1907 , March 15th 1907; Justice March 23rd 1907.*

containing Hickmott's article reached the public, the socialists of Tunbridge Wells purchased and distributed 2,000 copies of their anti-imperialist manifesto.[346]

The SDF also organised a party. James Andrew Seddon, Labour Member of Parliament for Newton, Lancashire, arrived as guest of honour at the May Day celebration in the Friendly Societies Hall. David Geer's work organising the unemployed and in running for election, so 'raising the ire of the Liberals', won him praise. Significantly Sam Noble, Secretary of the Tunbridge Wells branch of the National Amalgamated Union of Shop Assistants, presided over the meeting. Days later the railwaymen of Tunbridge Wells and Tonbridge organised a joint meeting to call on the two local railway companies, the London Brighton and South Coast and the South Eastern and Chatham, to give official recognition to their union. Both industries had much in common, with endemic low pay and long hours, and in each case there was a large and growing pool of potential recruits.[347]

Yet, even as they prepared to mark May Day, the Tunbridge Wells branch carefully prepared for the year's work beyond the confines of the town. They discussed their priorities in mid-April and the *Clarion* called on any socialists visiting the south coast that summer to help build the movement. George Meek welcomed the growth of socialism in Maidstone yet asked why nothing had yet happened in Ramsgate, Margate, Faversham and Whitstable. Hastings praised the assistance they had received: 'with the help of our Tunbridge Wells comrades we have planted a healthy little branch of the SDF in this old Cinque Port' and in return Tunbridge Wells sent speakers to it and Eastbourne regularly throughout the summer.[348]

Events in late summer only boosted the branch's confidence. A pair of by-elections that month returned two socialists to Parliament. Pete Curran, a trade unionist who had joined the SDF, Fabian Society and ILP, won at Jarrow, and Victor Grayson, an avowed revolutionary on the left of the latter organisation, took the Colne

---

[346] *Social Democrat, 5th May 1907 (http://www.marxists.org/history/international/ social-democracy/social-democrat/1907/05/hickmott.htm). See Kennedy, T.C. The Hound of Conscience: A History of the No-Conscription Fellowship 1914-1919, (Fayetteville 1981) p13; Justice May 11th 1907.*
[347] *The Courier May 10th & 17th 1907; The Tunbridge Wells Advertiser May 10th 1907.*
[348] *The Clarion April 12th & 26th 1907 and May 10th 1907; Justice April 13th 1907, April 20th 1907, May 11th 1907, June 8th 1907, August 3rd 1907.*

Valley seat. For the first time, the branch mused about whether a Labour candidate could be found for the Tonbridge Division. The town hosted two major labour movement conferences. The region's cooperative societies met first. Councillor Bournes, representing the Trades and Labour Council, attacked those who proclaimed themselves Christians yet did 'not practice the teachings of Christ', while a Mr Sheward for the town's Social-Democrats rounded on the Liberals for allowing thirteen million to be on the breadline.[349]

The other meeting, the Second Annual Conference of the SECFSS, followed a few days later on 4th August. Progress had been rapid. Twenty-four organisations attended, including ten branches of the ILP, six of the SDF and one of the Fabian Society. The indoor section took place in Clarendon's Dining Rooms, immediately opposite the Central Railway Station. Quite a number of high-profile speakers showed some interest in attending. The organisers approached H G Wells, who did not come, and Peter Kropotkin, who cancelled at the last minute due to ill-heath. Arthur Hickmott chaired the sessions and Herbert Burrows spoke several times. His public speeches on

Clarendon's Dining Rooms in the Great Hall. From Peter MacLeod's collection and used with permission.

the Common to large crowds reached out across the movement-Jesus Christ had founded socialism - and concentrated on indictments of contemporary society, such as the children in London's schools fainting through malnutrition. Burrows concluded by noting that socialism had progressed well in perhaps the most bigoted town in England, composed as it was of half-pay colonels and retired missionaries. It should now do the same in other places across the South-East. The meetings terminated by singing the *Red*

---

[349] *The Courier July 11th & 25th 1907, The Tunbridge Wells Advertiser July 12th 1907.*

Flag, which had by now replaced the *Internationale* and *England, Arise* as the movement's most popular song.[350]

Difficulties, however, lay behind the scenes. For all of the rhetoric of unity, brotherhood and sisterhood, the socialist and labour movements have never been immune to personal ambition. As mentioned, Ramsay MacDonald harboured a particular dislike of the SDF and began to put pressure on branches of the ILP in Kent and Sussex to cease co-operating with it. Under his influence, the *Labour Leader* increasingly criticised joint organisations. Tunbridge Wells, however, had furnished speakers and activists to build branches across the region and he faced an uphill struggle. The Dover branch of the ILP unanimously passed a motion to condemn MacDonald's negative approach to the Social-Democrats and forwarded a copy to him. The branches of the same organisation in Tonbridge, Sidcup and Deptford soon followed suit. Gillingham Labour Party, by contrast, supported MacDonald, though his most vocal ally, Paul Campbell, came from as far away as Walthamstow. Campbell, the son of a Scottish minister, had tried to establish a Labour Church in London in the 1890s, and represented a very different approach to socialism than that of the SDF.[351]

At this moment, Ramsay MacDonald must have felt that he had found a source of information close to the centre of the enemy's camp. Shortly before the conference he received a remarkable letter from Edward Baker, living in Silverdale Road in the High Brooms district of Tunbridge Wells. Baker declared that he previously had supported socialist unity but could no longer work with the Social-Democrats. His letter came with useful material:

'I am sending you Agenda of Conference [and] also proposals of new rules which were drawn up by the S.D.F. With regard to the issue of the summonses to the Conference it has been done entirely by the local S.D.F in Tun. Wells who have invited all socialist bodies in Kent, Sussex and East of Hampshire. Webster lives near Folkestone and comes as a delegate. Fallon comes by the invitation of the local S.D.F. to speak at the mass meeting on the Common on the evening. Burrows invited himself and you see

[350] *The Courier August 9th 1907; Justice August 10th 1907; Coxall and Griggs, Meek, pp156-161; The Tunbridge Wells Advertiser August 9th 1907; The Clarion August 9th 1907.*
[351] *Ramsay MacDonald Papers (University of Manchester) RMD 1/2/23; Coxall and Griggs p177; Thompson, P., Socialists, Liberals and Labour, The Struggle for London 1885-1914 (London: Routledge 1967) p158.*

by the Agenda is going to give the closing address to the Conference'.

Baker then outlined the rules for representation at the conference and suggested that a carefully-worded amendment be put which the SDF would be unable to support, thus undermining their claimed support for socialist unity. He criticised those members of the ILP who had supported motions of censure against MacDonald as the 'catspaws of the S.D.F. in trying to bring discredit on their leaders'. Ultimately he claimed to have acted in the interests of the wider movement, as many in his town admire the Labour Party but cannot stand the S.D.F. He stated that 'candidly I want to see this Federation smashed' and that, having done so, the I.L.P. could establish a strong branch in its place.[352]

Could there be more to this letter than meets the eye? Edward Baker had spoken on SDF platforms several times in previous years. Much of the information apparently came from William Veals, who always seems to have prioritised his membership of the Federation over his activities for the ILP. The Tonbridge branch of the ILP, as already explained, strongly supported the South-Eastern Counties Federation. Quite how Baker came by some of the documents is not clear. He also rather overdoes the vitriol. Perhaps MacDonald fell victim to an elaborate plot?

Ramsay MacDonald used much of the material in a letter to the *Labour Leader* which appeared two days before the conference. He argued that the Social-Democrats had more representation than can have been merited and had drafted many of the proposed rule changes and resolutions. *Justice,* however, obtained what MacDonald's supporters claimed had been a private letter from him to an unnamed member of the ILP – perhaps Baker - who had passed it to the Federation. This again suggests some skulduggery. The South-Eastern Federation passed a motion of censure against MacDonald by the significant majority of 22 to 14, though this was based on correspondence received by one of the branches rather than this private letter.

Whatever the truth, MacDonald's tactics had backfired. Supporters and opponents of the South-Eastern Federation flooded the *Labour Leader* with letters for some weeks. Paul Campbell called the meeting 'farcical', attacked what he felt had been a 'carefully

---

[352] *MacDonald correspondence RMD 1/2/30.*

engineered attack on the chairman of the ILP' and bemoaned the way in which the private letter had ended up in the hands of a 'member of the SDF in the South of England'. He also accused the Social-Democrats of sectarianism for failing to invite members of the Socialist Labour Party and Socialist Party of Great Britain to the meeting, although neither organisation had branches in the region. Further, the SPGB have not ever joined an organisation along the lines of the South-Eastern Federation.

It is doubtful that there were any members of these parties in the district at the time. Meek and Hickmott came under fire. One if the delegates from Sidcup rebuked Campbell for 'doing an injury both to himself and the honourable reputation he has won in socialist propaganda' while Arthur Hickmott regretted the tone of the letters from Campbell and Davidson, declared the SECFSS's committee 'a thoroughly competent one' and noted that there was no rule against any organisation joining, concluding by hoping that 'sweet reasonableness will grow as our members increase'. The SDF in Tunbridge Wells had cemented their leading position in the region's movement. Two of the seven elected to the South-Eastern Counties Federation management committee – E J Pay and W G Veals – came from the town. [353]

The SDF next turned its attention to the Seventh Congress of the Second International which took place in Stuttgart in Germany. Charles Baker represented the Tunbridge Wells branch, one of 123 British delegates to attend from the Federation, ILP, Fabian Society and other organisations. Few, if any, others came from the southern counties outside London. Arrangements for delegates are not that clear, although it is likely that the branch would have had to raise the money for travel and other costs.

That Tunbridge Wells did so re-affirms the importance of internationalism within the local SDF. The conference condemned militarism and colonialism as products of the capitalism system which all socialists should oppose. The SDF strongly supported both resolutions, Harry Quelch's intemperate language leading to his dramatic expulsion from Germany.

The other major debate related to women's suffrage. Kathleen Kough, formerly of Tunbridge Wells but now representing South-

---

[353] *Labour Leader August 2nd & 16th & 23rd 1907. Also see Coxall and Griggs, Meek for a good account (including the notes to p177).*

West Manchester, was elected as one of a handful of delegates from Britain to address the question, drew up a resolution and played a very full role in the debate. The Second International committed itself to universal suffrage and formally repudiated any alliance with those who supported the extension of the vote to women on the basis of a property qualification or marital status.[354]

[354] *Secretariat of the Second Socialist International: Report of the 7th Socialist International Congress in Stuttgart (1907); Hunt pp170-173.*

CHAPTER 11   AN ANTI-SOCIALIST CRUSADE
AND THE RIGHT TO WORK

As we have seen, the socialist and labour movements had established a foothold in many of the larger towns in Kent, Sussex, Surrey and Hampshire in the years after the 1906 General Election. Unsurprisingly this provoked a strong reaction in Conservative circles. This played itself out in different ways. Right-wing and religious organisations sent speakers to challenge Social-Democratic Federation and Independent Labour Party speakers in towns where branches existed and a series of debates took place between ambitious young Tories and their opponents. In the countryside, however, the squirearchy tended to use physical force to deny socialists a platform. In a few cases, the Conservatives made a specific pitch for proletarian support. In Tunbridge Wells they opened an association specifically for working class men at 141 Camden Road. Those who were politically reliable would be first in line for work as footmen, gardeners or butlers.[355]

The various factions in south-eastern left-wing politics soon stopped bickering. Ramsay MacDonald told his members that his party should be organised into county federations: the ILP's Kent branches, including Maidstone, Ashford, Dover, Tonbridge, Gillingham and Bexleyheath, thus met in Maidstone in the early autumn. The supporters and opponents of MacDonald reached a compromise. The Kent Federated Union would 'lead, simplify and direct the work of the ILP in the county, necessitating terms of friendship and, where necessary, co-operation with similar local movements'.

Almost immediately members of the ILP and the Fabian Society joined forces to run open-air meetings at Canterbury. The *Labour Leader* soon resumed reporting the work of the South-Eastern Counties Federation in some detail, and Tunbridge Wells agitators again appeared on platforms across the region. By November, Phillip Snowden, one of the ILP's leading figures, agreed to appear as the main speaker at a meeting of the South-Eastern Counties Federation in Maidstone, accompanied by those from 'neighbouring branches, other socialist societies, local labour organisations and

---

355 *The Courier February 21st 1908.*

trade unionists'. The Social-Democrats of Tunbridge Wells, I assume, were prominent amongst them[356]

An Anti-Socialist Union badge

Tunbridge Wells, High Brooms and Tonbridge first received anti-socialist speakers in August, September and October 1907, something which reflected the fact that the Conservatives now funded twenty such itinerant lecturers by the end of that year. At least three made extended visits to the Tunbridge Wells area, suggesting that they had real concerns regarding the district. Like their socialist opponents they came from a variety of backgrounds. A Mr MacCartney from Lancashire emphasised his working class credentials, Mr Hutson's speeches on behalf of the Constitutional League may have been aimed at more middle-class people, while the background of T Enfield is less clear. The socialists also raised their game, bringing down John Scurr and Victor Fisher from the SDF and a Mr Montagu from the ILP to assist. Meetings and debates took place almost every night. Three Conservative speakers attended the Federation's meetings on the Common, the arguments being witnessed by 'enormous crowds'. Between one and two hundred watched MacCartney and Montagu at the Angel Corner, Tonbridge, while a debate between the former and the Social-Democrats at High Brooms lasted until ten in the evening.[357]

What impact these debates had on the local population is hard to quantify. Much of it seems crude today. MacCartney's attacks on the Liberal Party, Labour Party and the spectrum of socialist organisations, including the ILP, SDF, Fabian Society and the Socialist Party (I assume this is the Socialist Party of Great Britain), all of whom had shared sinister aims, seems desperate. Hutson's attacks on socialism as a 'foreign import' that 'breaks up family life' and led to 'free love' seem little better. The religious and xenophobic may have agreed with him. By contrast, Scurr's lecture in High Brooms outlining the Marxist theory of historical materialism may have been harder for a general audience to understand. Yet, in a

---

[356] *The Clarion September 6th & 20th 1907, Labour Leader November 15th 1907.*
[357] *Brown, K. The Anti-Socialist Union, p235-6..*

move that would have delighted the audience, a precocious teenager could prick the pomposity of some of the Tories. Although the exchange probably dates from 1908 or 1909, Alf Killick later reminisced about an Anti-Socialist Union speaker holding forth in the Lime Hill Road. The speaker declaimed that a socialist government would mean that the capitalists would take their wealth out of the country. Killick then asked whether they would take all of the land, factories and railways with them. His answer 'Sonny, you'd better go back to school' was countered, amid roars of laughter, with 'Mister, I should guess you've never been to school'. This exchange secured Killick's place as one of the youngest members of the Tunbridge Wells branch. Killick had also won a debate on socialism at the Young Man's Fraternal, a debating club hosted by the Congregational Chapel. Interestingly his Scout Troop had asked him to speak for socialism in a debate against a much older man, illustrating the party's success at winning support from the youth.[358]

One meeting in October suggests that the anti-Socialists felt that things had not gone their way. This had been advertised as a debate on 'tariff reform versus socialism' and also a lecture on 'unemployment and its remedies'. However, not only did this 'debate' allow only one point of view - Tory protectionism - but Robert Vaughan Gower, the Chair, claimed it to be non-political. After some heckling, David Geer asked to speak. Gower refused, as his meeting would not become a 'platform to be used by socialist agitators'. The SDF, joined by a few Liberals, left in protest. *Justice* later claimed that the number of socialists alone who had walked out numbered 100, and the room ended up being pretty empty.[359]

Enthusiastic cyclists among the Social-Democrats in Tunbridge Wells now had an auxiliary organisation, the Cycling Scouts. Gordon Bretherton took the lead in organising this group, though I suspect that other enthusiastic riders such as David Geer joined in. This held its first recorded meeting in the 'small village' of Crowborough, seven miles away, in September. The *Clarion* welcomed this initiative to reach places still 'untouched by the agitator'. This meeting proved trouble-free, though Tory tactics in often involved thuggery rather than reasoned debate. At Lindfield, a village near Haywards Heath, a 'patriotic mob', including the

---

[358] *The Courier October 4th 1907; Justice October 12th 1907; the Clarion October 4th 1907; Killick, Mutiny! p4.*
[359] *The Courier October 18th 1907 and October 11th 1907; Justice October 19th 1907.*

205

Church Lads Brigade, pelted the ILP's speaker with rotten eggs and threatened a dunking in the village pond. The socialists left the village under a police escort. Similar scenes took place in other villages and small towns. Perhaps the best description of such events, drawn from a number of incidents, comes from the *Ragged Trousered Philanthropists*. : The socialists arrive at their assembly point where their notably well-dressed opponent give a speech ignoring 'the Distress Committee or the Soup Kitchen or the children who went to school without proper clothes or food' yet said 'a great deal about the Glorious Empire! And the Flag! And the Royal Family!' The audience responds with rapturous applause and sings the National Anthem. Stones and fists soon start to fly. Such a description is all too plausible. A correspondent to the *Labour Leader* summed it up well: the 'ill-treatment of our socialist speakers in Sussex disgraced the south of England... Most people present wanted to hear the meetings yet the audiences were broken up by organised bands of young ruffians, incited to molest us by local publicans and others.'[360]

1907 concluded as usual with some right-to–work agitation and the municipal elections. By the following January, the Borough had employed four hundred to sweep snow from the streets. More elaborate schemes failed due to concerns over their cost. William Bournes in the North Ward again stood unopposed. In the East Ward, as always the most strongly contested, David Geer came third of five candidates, again just missing out. His opponents had used their motor cars and carriages to bring the electors to the polling station, something the socialists had no means of doing. Even a well-attended public meeting, with speeches by Sam Noble, James Richards and E J Pay, failed to redress the balance in resources. Once again is clear that the local labour movement struggled to find candidates with the time and money to stand in winnable seats.[361]

The winter months of 1907 and 1908 gave the branch the opportunity to run a course of lectures in the Albion Road Schoolrooms. Rather than the efforts of the past years, when Maud Ward and David Geer ran classes on Marxist economics, these took

---

[360] *Justice September 14th 1907; The Clarion September 13th 1907; The Clarion October 18th 1907; Ball, F. C One of the Damned: the life and times of Robert Tressell, author of the Ragged Trousered Philanthropists (London: Lawrence and Wishart 1979) p111-112, Labour Leader October 18th & 25th 1907.*
[361] *The Courier October 25th 1907, November 3rd & 8th 1907; Justice October 19th 1907 and November 9th 1907;Tunbridge Wells Advertiser November 8th 1907.*

the form of one-off discussions by a member concerning a subject that interested them. This set the pattern for the next few years. E J Pay lectured on the rather broad subject of the economic and social history of England, G J Harris tackled a work by an Italian journalist and criminologist, Enrico Ferri's *Socialism and Positive Science*, G A Price considered Kropotkin's *Fields, Factories and Workshops* and W G Veals analysed the ideas of August Bebel. Again the choice of Italian, Russian and German thinkers underlines the internationalism of the branch. Over the next few weeks, Gordon Bretherton spoke about the Workman's Compensation Act, part of the Liberal Party's package of reforms, while Arthur Hickmott addressed the branch on how he became a socialist (sadly for posterity the notes have not survived). In complete contrast to these often rather heavy topics, the branch organised a tea for the children of members of the Cooperative Society in March. Tunbridge Wells remained one of the strongest provincial branches, something which secured the election of J G Webster to the party's Executive.[362]

Perhaps the most significant of all the set-piece public debates between a member of the branch and an opponent came in April 1908. The Federation had challenged the Conservatives to such a confrontation as long ago as the previous August. They decided that their agent for the Tonbridge Division, Sir Robert Filmer, might be the appropriate champion of their cause. The Social-Democrats chose E J Pay, perhaps their best local speaker. The exchanges were carried at length by the *Advertiser* and the *Courier*, and the latter decided to publish the whole thing as a pamphlet. It is not clear from the printed accounts who won, though the sources agreed that both made strong points. *Justice* considered that Pay had 'fought with his gloves off in his usual militant fashion while the *Courier* felt that the Tory had done better overall. The socialists also showed enough confidence in their man's performance by writing afterwards to Paget Hedges to challenge him to debate the question 'should the working class support the Liberal Party'. Hedges declined.

The terms of the debate are worth recording in depth. Pay gave a Marxist account of history from the Romans to the present, arguing that the land had been robbed by the Tories and Whigs, who, 'having stolen our land in exchange gave us a debt, the national

362 *Justice February* 7*th* & 15*th* 1908, *March* 14*th* 1908, *April* 4*th* 1908; *Labour Leader April* 24*th* 1908.

debt', and argued for collective ownership, free school meals, afforestation and the cultivation of waste lands. In response Filmer attacked the Federation and the ILP. Significantly he singled out the programme of the Tunbridge Wells branch for supporting a socialist economy, equality between the sexes, abolition of the monarchy and repudiation of the national debt. Filmer particularly disliked the idea that those of different ability should be paid the same, and tried to win friends among the working men and women by claiming that members of cooperatives and friendly societies would lose their property under socialism. Pay defended his view of the national debt, accrued largely from fighting useless wars, though admitted that questions of compensation to landowners would need to be considered. Filmer then proceeded to claim that working for government bosses would be more repressive than those from private firms. Both then had ten minutes each to respond to the points made by the other.[363]

Although it is clear that younger activists such as Pay, Veals, Doust, Webster and Bretherton had taken the lead in moving the branch forward, the pioneers of eighties and nineties still played their part. On May Day 1908 the Trades and Labour Council marked David Geer's long service to trade unionism. Sam Noble of the Shop Assistants' Union presided. Councillor William Bournes, E J Pay and Councillor James Richards also spoke on his behalf. The Friendly Societies Hall displayed a framed testimonial in his honour. In June the branch unveiled a new flag on the Common, something made necessary by the SDF having changed its name to the Social Democratic Party.

A less palatable reminder of the challenged faced by the branch in its first years soon followed. In July the Women's Freedom League's Suffrage Caravan visiting the town for what they hoped would be a four day visit. Although the SDF, as explained previously, opposed limited women's suffrage on the basis of a property qualification, David Geer led a delegation of local trade unionists and socialists to listen and perhaps try to defuse any difficulties. However, his call for 'fair play' from the Caravan's opponents went unheeded. A crowd of several thousand of the town's more thuggish elements, consisting largely of over-excited boys and youths, jeered and hissed the speakers and deluged them with potatoes and banana skins. The suffragettes and their supporters soon had to leave early

[363] Reports from the Courier and from Justice April 4th 1908, The Tunbridge Wells Advertiser August 23rd 1907, May 1st 1908

under police escort. Even though a suffrage meeting the following Wednesday night took place relatively peacefully, the mob violence and the similar scenes faced by socialists in nearby villages over the past few months must have reminded the branch that only the size of their support base prevented their own meetings from being broken up.[364]

The Tunbridge Wells branch's work within the South-Eastern Federation during 1908 started as early as February, when E J Pay travelled to Ashford to speak at an ILP meeting on combines and trusts. He returned to preside over a meeting of the SDP in the summer. Some places proved less hospitable. Mobs destroyed the hats of three of the six socialists who had attempted to hold a meeting in Chichester, punched one of the activists and then sprayed them with a foul-smelling liquid. In more enlightened places the exchange of speakers worked well and allowed audiences a variety of voices and perspectives. In June a member of the Brighton branch, F Ingham, spoke at Tunbridge Wells while E J Pay and W G Veals visited Hastings. However the most significant move came at the end of the month or in early July when the Tunbridge Wells SDP organised a joint meeting with Tonbridge's ILP, which they announced as the first of several such events. The line-up of speakers, drawn from across Kent and Sussex, included J Grimes, Walter Speed and E J Pay, and they drew a crowd estimated at between 1,000 and 1,500 on the Common. This cooperation again put the possibility of running a joint Labour candidate in the constituency on the agenda. The Conservatives, perhaps alerted to the threat, sent MacCartney to speak in Rusthall and on the St John's Road against socialism, a campaign which culminated in a debate with a socialist speaker from Woolwich.[365]

The branch had two hundred members at the time of the publication of the *Who's Who of Tunbridge Wells* for 1908, which I assume to have been published at the start of the year. In the ensuing months a number of new recruits joined. One of them, Sam Noble, soon took a leading role. He had long acted as one of the town's principal trade unionists and in August 1906 achieved the highest score in a competition to write an essay on the history and

---

[364] *The Courier June 26th 1908 and July 3rd 1908; Tunbridge Wells Advertiser May 15th 1908, July 3rd 1908;, Justice June 20th & 27th 1908.*

[365] *Tunbridge Wells Advertiser February 7th 1908; Justice June 20th & 27th 1908, July 4th & 11th 1908; The Courier July 16th 1908, August 7th 1908; the Clarion July 10th 1908; Labour Leader July 17th 1908; Thomas, D., Socialism in West Sussex: A History of the Chichester Labour Party (Chichester 1983).*

principals of co-operation. The intellectual calibre of the branch can also be seen clearly in a debate about the future of agriculture under socialism. Arthur Hickmott favoured the creation of smallholdings, while E J Pay supported larger-scale farms which could be run more scientifically. This debate played out in the South-Eastern Counties conference in Maidstone in August, when Hickmott's motion prevailed, and led to correspondence in *Justice* and the *Labour Leader*. The Independent Labour Party's Kent Federation decided to support the nationalisation of the land as their priority while the veteran socialist Edward Carpenter proposed a mixture of state farms and smallholdings. Many of the socialists who attended the Maidstone conference did so by bicycle and their experiences on the road led to a motion opposing the proliferation of motor cars.[366]

The countryside, however, remained overwhelmingly Tory. In Tonbridge a massive demonstration calling for protection against foreign hops drew thousands from the surrounding countryside.

Protectionist demonstration in Tonbridge against foreign hops

London readers of the *Labour Leader* decided that this needed a response. They liaised with local socialists and agreed to hold an 'invasion of the Kent hopfields' on 13th September. London branches of the SDP, ILP and Clarion Scouts all agreed to assist. However,

---

[366] *The Tunbridge Wells Advertiser August 10th 1906; Justice July 25th 1908 and October 10th 1908.*
[366] *The Tunbridge Wells Advertiser August 7th 1907; Labour Leader July 17th & July 24th 1908.*

they lacked local knowledge, something supplied by the activists in the county. The Tunbridge Wells branch organised a meeting in Horsmonden, Three or four hundred people heard speeches by E J Pay, W G Veals and Dora Montefiore, one of the Federation's leading national speakers. Dora Montefiore had earlier led a march in support of the hop pickers through London and addressed a crowd at Tower Hill, at which point a group of hunger marchers joined the procession. Demonstrations also took place the same day in East Farleigh, Wateringbury, Offham Green, Five Oak Green and Selling. The authorities feared unrest, and the Metropolitan Police had a large presence at Charing Cross Station. Groups of policemen were also posted to all the meeting points in Kent before people began arriving, though no trouble is recorded.[367]

Within weeks of these meetings in the hop gardens, Dora Montefiore's other great cause – women's suffrage – gained further ground at Tunbridge Wells. Branches of both the NUWSS, which campaigned using constitutional means, and of the Women's Freedom League, which supported some methods of direct action but not attacks on property, and which opposed the increasingly undemocratic trajectory of the Women's Social and Political Union, both formed at Tunbridge Wells in Autumn 1908 (Dora Montefiore had herself resigned from the latter organisation in 1907 as a result of such concerns). The work of Dorothy Le Lacheur of the Women's Freedom League is reminiscent of the early days of the Social-Democrats: she organised open-air meetings, chalked the pavements and constantly pushed the cause. Perhaps the Social-Democrats suffered from the competition. Relatively few women came forward to play leading roles in the branch at this time.[368]

The success of the invasion of the hopfields and the regular meetings and conferences of the South-Eastern Counties Federation of Socialist Societies led naturally to a region-wide campaign for those out of work. Unemployment ran at 8.5% that year. This raised a question of tactics. The SDF at Tunbridge Wells had organised processions of the unemployed from its foundation. By contrast, the Hastings branch of the same party refused to support such demonstrations as they considered that they amounted to no more than a form of charity. Their fears may have been compounded by

---

[367] *Justice September 19th 1908; Labour Leader August 7th & 21st 1908, September 4th & 18th 1908; Montefiore, D.B., From a Victorian to a Modern (London, E. Archer 1927) p123.*

[368] *Carwardine,. A., Disgusted Ladies, pp109-116, 133; Hunt, K., Equivocal pp172-3.*

protestors in the Sussex town singing the National Anthem, something which contrasted with the red and black banners and the *Marseillaise* of their Tunbridge Wells equivalents. However, the economic downturn meant action had to be taken, Brighton's socialists had formed a 'Right to Work' committee as early as May. The SECFSS agreed to establish a regional committee in August and two months later the SDP asked all socialists to demand work organised on cooperative principles.[369]

Tunbridge Wells may have been slightly behind Brighton but it soon caught up. A Right to Work Committee, including trade unionists and members of various organisations, formed that October. Its resolution bears the mark of a member of the SDP:

> *'This meeting of workers of Tunbridge Wells and district, employed and unemployed, declares that while unemployment is the inevitable result of the present system of production for profit, the central and local authorities have the power to mitigate the worst effects of the evil and should be compelled to do so.*

> *'This meeting therefore condemns the inaction of the Government in not having amended the Unemployed Workmen's Act of 1905 in a practical manner, and demands that the Government shall, immediately on the re-assembly of Parliament, introduce legislation for the organisation of labour, the reduction of the working day, the expenditure of public money either directly by the government departments or by the subsidising of local authorities on works of public utility and necessity, instead of their having to rely on charity for that purpose.*

> *'This meeting also demands for the workers not only the right to work but the right to live, and declares that if these be not soon made possible, it will be left to hungry men to ignore the rules of a society which has no regard for them.'*[370]

The conclusion of this letter strikingly resembles the one sent by Tom Jarvis to the Tunbridge Wells Commissioners as long ago as November 1887. The similarities did not end there. A few weeks earlier, Robert Vaughan Gower, slum landlord and ambitious Tory councillor, received a postcard warning him that his properties would be at risk. In the last days of September, 48 High Brooms

---

[369] See Matthews, M., Cobb, pp21-22; *Labour Leader* May 8th 1908; Crick, *History*, p177; *The Clarion* October 23rd 1908.
[370] *The Courier* October 16th 1908; *Justice* October 17th 1908.

Road caught fire. Shortly afterward, another card arrived, explaining why he had been targeted. As with the waves of arson in 1886 and 1887, the socialists used the incident to give their demand greater weight. This does not mean that they had any involvement in it. *Justice* that October informed its readers that the unemployed would institute a reign of terror [and] make the governing classes howl with affright at the danger to their skins and stolen wealth. This arson attack did nothing to stop Gower's through Tory ranks to become Mayor and later the Member of Parliament for London's Hackney Central and then Gillingham.[371]

'Not only the Right to Work but the Right to Leisure' This is thought to be the Tunbridge Wells SDP flag unveiled in 1908. The lack of females suggests that the branch faced competition from the women's suffrage movement at the time. From Michael Walker's collection.

The campaign had new ideas. It opened a Committee Room at 83 Camden Road. This was both an office and a place for the

[371] *The Courier* October 2nd 1908; *The Tunbridge Wells Advertiser* October 2nd 1908; Crick, *History*, p18.0

unemployed to come and socialise. It had a register to quantify the problem. 195 men signed immediately. 47 of these had a total of 478 dependents – wives, children, incapacitated siblings or elderly relatives. A week later this had grown to 353, representing 858 dependents. It included men from Southborough as well as Tunbridge Wells, while meeting after meeting followed in Tonbridge and Sevenoaks, as well as on the Common and Lime Hill Road. Herbert Heskett, almost certainly by this stage a member of the SDP, won election as Secretary. David Geer and John Bullen, an unemployed joiner of 27 Great Brooms Road in Southborough, joined the Committee.

The Borough Council found some work for the unemployed at the Sewage Farm. This relief only scratched the surface. Herbert Heskett wrote that the men working here could not still afford proper food and shoes, and accused the council of a dereliction of duty for failing to feed the children of the poor.[372]

The Right to Work campaign lasted for five months in Tunbridge Wells and its neighbourhood. Meetings took place at the Angel Corner, Tonbridge, where the unemployed carried their own banners, and in Southborough. Five thousand copies of the SDP's 'Right to Work' manifesto had been distributed by March 1909. The campaign drew its largest crowds in the Lime Hill Road. On one occasion, Bullen condemned the Borough, the Guardians, and the churches for doing nothing to alleviate unemployment. Heskett violently denounced the 'Government, the Royal Family and the existing order of things generally', while Geer followed by attacking the Government and Church. Finally, E J Pay declared that those assembled must strike fear and terror into the hearts of their oppressors.

Modern communications allowed the participants to feel that the Right to Work campaign had become a national movement: activists at one open-air meeting in Tunbridge Wells relayed details to its equivalent in London's Trafalgar Square by telephone. The visit of a group of hunger marchers from Birmingham reinforced this link.[373]

---

[372] *The Tunbridge Wells Advertiser October 23rd 1908, January 8th 1909; The Courier October 23rd & 30th 1908.*
[373] *The Tunbridge Wells Advertiser October 16th 1908, November 27th 1908; The Tunbridge Wells Advertiser February 26th 1909; Justice March 6th 1909.*

Rev W Potter who joined the SDP in 1908/09

These attacks on organised religion should be placed in context. The SDF and its successors always insisted that they welcomed those of all faiths and none. The early militant atheism of the members in Tunbridge Wells had softened by then. One local minister, Reverend W Potter of the Camden Road Primitive Methodist Church, had even joined the Federation by early 1909 and wrote to *Justice* to explain his decision. Potter had broad radical sympathies, later allowing the Women's Social and Political Union to use his church for a jumble sale.

Thus some of the town's churches and chapels began to take a more positive approach to the socialists, much as the Quakers and Unitarians had done since the Boer War. St John's Free Church Hall organised a free meal of roast beef, mutton, potatoes, cake, tea and coffee for 175 or 180 of the town's unemployed and their dependents in January 1909. Reverend Potter and David Geer spoke at the dinner while Julian Taylor, one of the branch's most active new recruits, recited a poem called 'if Jesus came to London'. Following the meal the unemployed paraded the town's streets. The collection amounted to 9d per participant, the money being distributed at the Primitive Methodist Church. In the weeks that followed the campaign organised more free meals, including breakfasts for the wives and children of the unemployed.[374]

---

[374] *Justice March 6th 1909; The Courier October 18th 1912.*

The culmination of the agitation came in early February. Heskett and Bullen led a large march to the workhouse in Pembury to lobby the Poor Law Guardians. Accounts differ. The *Courier,* which played it down, reported that one man kicked a workhouse official, but that the police prevented serious unrest. The *Advertiser,* in an over-excited manner, reported an 'attempted raid' leading to a:

> '*Scuffle with the Police and porters [which] was of a somewhat lively nature and for a few minutes the position was a critical one, the would-be invaders kicking and pushing desperately'.*

The authorities took no chances. A large body from the Kent County Constabulary from Tonbridge under the command of Superintendent Styles accompanied the march back to the border with Tunbridge Wells, at which point the Borough force led them back into the town centre by way of Sandown Park. Yet the Borough Council proved unwilling to make further provision. Councillors Berwick and Bournes led calls for a rise in the rates of a penny to provide for more public works, but were rebuffed.[375]

Sympathy for the unemployed remained high. By mid-February they had purchased collecting boxes, raising £22-15s one week and £17-8s-6½d a couple of weeks later. Yet in Mid-March the campaign faced embarrassment. The police in Sevenoaks arrested a man who carried papers, purportedly from Herbert Heskett, which apparently allowed him to collect money, and jailed him. This came too late to cause serious damage, as the warmer weather meant unemployment had eased somewhat and the campaign wound down. The coordinated regional campaign had succeeded. Kent, according to the *Kent Messenger,* perambulated with such hunger marches, Chatham's unemployed walked as far as Woolwich and marched on the Medway Workhouse. Other demonstrations took place in Rochester and Maidstone. As late as July the Tunbridge Wells branch sent a copy of the *Social Democrat* newspaper containing an article on unemployment by Hunter Watts to Arthur Hedges, the Liberal MP for the Tonbridge Division, who apparently read it with pleasure. The government took a notably more interventionist position regarding the question, passing the Labour Exchanges Act the same year and the National Insurance Act in 1911.[376]

---

[375] *The Tunbridge Wells Advertiser February 5th 1909; The Courier February 5th 1909.*
[376]*The Courier February 12th , 19th & 26th 1909, March 19th 1909; The Tunbridge Wells Advertiser July 2nd 1909.*

Although the Right to Work Campaign took up most of the branch's time, they also twice repeated the format of the debate between E J Pay and Sir Robert Filmer. In December 1908 Herbert Burrows of the Social-Democrats took on Benjamin Woollan, recently the Mayor, at the Great Hall. Burrows argued for an end to the hunger and starvation caused by capitalism, and both speakers were loudly cheered by their supporters. According to the report carried in *Justice,* Burrows received a 'splendid ovation' from the crowd.[377]

In late February 1909 Julian Taylor debated with F L Goldsmid, a prominent local Tory, at the Town Hall. This followed a lengthy exchange of letters between the two and a meeting in High Brooms that January during which Goldsmid had attacked the socialists. He had initially tried to wriggle out of a formal debate but the Social-Democrats had distributed handbills throughout the town challenging him to attend. Cllr Richards, Geer and E J Pay all supported Taylor. Goldsmid attacked the Federation' proposals to repudiate the national debt, nationalise the land and abolish the monarchy, asking the audience whether they would prefer to have King Edward VII as leader, or Keir Hardie, Victor Grayson, Harry Quelch, Henry Hyndman or John Burns. These points seem to have been taken from Conservative and Anti-Socialist Union propaganda, such as the example on the next page.

E J Pay very effectively refuted these attacks, as well as Goldsmid's understanding of free love, which Pay felt he had 'confused with lust'. This is one of the few occasions on which members of the branch acknowledged the existence of any form of relationship other than the nuclear family. Pay won applause with his closing point; he wished to see the 'international social democratic commonwealth of the human race'.

Julian Taylor capitalised on this debate, writing an open letter to Goldsmid to thank him for:

> '*A most successful meeting, Sir, and one to which the use of your name doubtlessly contributed. The immediate result is several prospective new members to our branch*'.[378]

---

[377] *The Courier December 4th 1908; The Tunbridge Wells Advertiser December 4th 1908; Justice December 12th 1908.*
[378] *Justice March 6th 1909; The Courier January 8th 1909 and February 26th 1909; The Tunbridge Wells Advertiser March 5th 1909.*

SOCIALISM EXPOSED!

1 State Socialism is an Abstraction. It is impossible as a Social System.

2 Socialism is opposed to Monarchical and Parliamentary Government, and therefore leads to Anarchy.

3 Socialism denies the existence of God and the truth of all religions. It is therefore Atheistic.

4 Socialism is against the Marriage Tie and advocates Free Love. It is therefore immoral..

5 Socialism is against the Family Life. It says your Wife and Children should belong to the State. Comment is needless.

6 Socialism unsettles security for Investments of Capital, and is therefore the cause, of Bad Trade.

7 Municipal Socialism has been a financial failure, and has always resulted in increased rates.

8 Socialists are against Civil Liberty. They would rob you of your household furniture, and even your kit of tools. All property will be claimed by the State.

9 Socialists persecute Trade Unionists, but use their votes and money as levers to hoist themselves into representative and paying positions.

10 Socialism is utterly impracticable. It is a sham, a delusion, and a snare.

WORKING MEN !

SHUN THE DEMAGOGUE SOCIALIST. HE CAN ONLY MAKE HIS LIVING IF HE CAN GULL YOU. DON'T YOU BE GULLED BY HIM.

Where did the branch stand in early 1909? Work within the SECFSS had worked wonders, with thirty-one branches affiliated and a programme of five joint demonstrations planned. Tom Kennedy, a parliamentary candidate for the SDF and one of its leading voices, felt that cooperation between the two socialist parties in the region had eliminated much of the bitterness and strife found elsewhere in the country. Tunbridge Wells had played a great role in this. Julian Taylor, the branch organiser, head of its trading department and its delegate to the annual conference somehow found the time to write a proposed general election address, for which he won the first prize of one guinea. However this extremely gifted activist soon had to move away from the town to Coventry. His new branch quickly decided that he would be the best-placed person to run for Member of Parliament at the next General Election.[379]

Although the socialists of the south-eastern counties stood united, the deterioration in international relations began to divide the grassroots movement from its national leadership. The multi-layered Bosnian Crisis of 1908 to 1909 threatened to unleash a Europe-wide war. Robert Blatchford, unsurprisingly, pushed extremely xenophobic propaganda in his newspaper. More worryingly for the Tunbridge Wells branch, Henry Mayers Hyndman, who had long advocated a larger navy, now predicted a war with Germany. The town's Social-Democrats began to seriously consider how to prevent the workers of Europe from slaughtering

---

[379] *The Clarion December 11th 1908; Justice March 6th 1909, March 13th 1909 and May 1st 1909; Justice December 10th 1910*

each other. In August 1909 they wrote to *Justice* asking the newspaper to publish articles on the following points:

1. The immediate abolition of secret diplomacy;

2. No war to be declared without a two-thirds vote of the electorate;

3. All expenditure of more than £1,000 on arms to be disclosed to the public;

4. The convening of a conference between European governments for arms limitation;

5. The immediate convening of a conference of the International Socialist Bureau to discuss the present position and to demonstrate international workers' solidarity'

6. To get the King, as head of state, to issue a proclamation opposing anti-German sentiment.

Several of these positions would have won support from across the left of the political spectrum. The first and fourth were closely echoed by President Woodrow Wilson when he set out his Fourteen Points at the end of the First Wold War, though the idea of a two-thirds referendum majority and the disclosure of arms expenditure would even today be regarded as dangerously radical.

At no point, however, did they propose any way to actually stop a war, such as organising a general strike or encouraging mutiny within the armed forces, once it was underway.[380]

The spring and summer of 1909 saw the first deployment of a Clarion Van to the region. Similar horse-drawn vehicles, which had living accommodation, room to store literature and a platform to speak from, had been used by the Liberal Party, women's suffrage movement and socialists for several years, in particular to reach remote areas. The tour of the south-east both visited new places and gave existing branches support. Thomas Kennedy spoke at the Angel Corner, Tonbridge, in April.

---

[380] *Justice August 21st 1909.*

One of the Clarion Vans, photographed by Frank Kehrhahn, a socialist from Bexleyheath (within the area covered by the SECFSS).

In August he made a longer tour of the region. The van appeared at three and six open-air meetings in Tunbridge Wells, at least one in Southborough and another four in Tonbridge. F Ingham from Brighton and E J Pay spoke extensively, and there was a 'much needed general revival of interest locally' and the last four meetings, including the one at Southborough, proved 'from every point of view, excellent'. Once again, they were fortunate in their opponents, as the 'questioners of the cock-sure Daily Express variety have helped us to drive our points home'. At Lime Hill Road in Tunbridge Wells 'a small knot of people' gathered to hear speeches from the van criticising both the Tories and Liberals. The Tunbridge Wells Advertiser reported on an encounter on the Common between a 'fiery young man from London' representing the socialist cause and a Conservative, reporting that the socialist personally abused newspaper editors and leading politicians and the Tory responded with as much 'if not more, personal epithets', concluding that attendees 'listed in vain for an argument for or against socialism'.

The return of the van to Tonbridge, where the tour had started, saw very successful meetings at the Angel Corner, far better than those in April had been. As a result, more members joined the local branch of the Independent Labour Party, which was previously in a

220

poor financial position. Opposition proved stronger in smaller towns. At Uckfield the Tories evicted it before a meeting could take place and at Sevenoaks a 'hot-bed of Toryism and respectability' – fewer attended and those who did ran the gauntlet of the 'stupid behaviour of bad-mannered youth'. Things there got even worse, and despite the efforts of W G Veals and E J Pay to assist, the sales and collections remained poor, the correspondent hoped that the lack of support was due to any local socialists being on holiday. He expressed no regrets about leaving that inhospitable region.[381]

Branches sprung up or re-formed across the region that summer. Socialism re-emerged in Sheerness and a branch formed in the small Kent town of Hythe. Speakers from Tunbridge Wells addressed meetings in Maidstone, Hastings and Eastbourne. E J Pay and Julian Taylor spoke alongside W E Speed of Canterbury and Councillor Jack Jones from West Ham at a united socialist meeting at Faversham. The strongest links remained with Hastings. J W Herd of the Tunbridge Wells branch proposed a resolution at the National Labour and Socialist Conference on our Food Supply that July, this being seconded by G Herd of the Hastings branch. I assume the two were related.[382]

One of the surprising aspects of the branch is that they had not had a clubhouse or meeting rooms since relinquishing their first hall in about 1890. Other, less established branches had done so quickly, for example in November 1908 E J Pay had the honour of opening the Federation's hall in Hastings. This can partly be explained by the opposition of leading branch members to serving alcohol in socialist premises, something which would have given a regular source of income. In 1902 Arthur Hickmott called in the *Labour Leader* for the regulation of the drink trade as a step towards its abolition Three years later, Maud Ward had written to *Justice* to ask that the Federation's clubs be alcohol-free, a position supported by Rose Jarvis, by now in Northampton. Other branches rejected this positon as a 'fad'. The branch subsequently passed a resolution that members should 'deprecate in every way possible the abuse of alcoholic stimulants on all occasions'. As an alternative, the branch established a committee during the summer of 1909, agreed to introduce a small levy on members and in late September opened a

[381] *The Courier April 16th 1909, August 6th 1909; Justice August 28th 1909; The Courier, The Clarion August 13th & 27th 1909, The Tunbridge Wells Advertiser August 6th 1909, September 3rd 1909.*
[382] *See reports in Justice and Labour Leader July and August 1909.*

clubroom at 60 Grosvenor Road, at the junction with Grosvenor Park. These rooms were open daily to members and supporters and received a selection of daily and weekly newspapers and had games tables. A library soon followed.[383]

The branch reorganised itself in the autumn. *Justice* declared it to be in 'very good condition right now' as it efficiently collected the members' subscriptions. Ordinary meetings took place every Thursday evening and the branch ran lectures each Sunday. They also introduced a monthly social evening with vocal and instrumental recitals. James King took on the role of running the branch's trading department, something which Julian Taylor had previously done, and something which must have become more important with the new headquarters.

Public work seems to have been more limited. In October the branch passed a motion condemning the execution of the Catalan anarchist Francesc Ferrer during a period of martial law in Spain. It also helped to ensure the re-election of SECFSS Pothe Trades and Labour candidate for the East Ward, Henry Thomas Berwick, but were unable to put any of their own members forward as candidate. Few public meetings took place that winter, although the Social-Democrats organised one at

« A »

DEMONSTRATION

OF THE

SOUTH-EASTERN COUNTIES'
FEDERATION of SOCIALIST SOCIETIES

In conjunction with the Horsham
Branch of the Social Democratic Party

WILL BE HELD IN THE

CARFAX,
ON

SUNDAY, SEPT. 12

1909, at 3 p.m., *when the Speakers will be the
Secretary of the Federation,*

Wm. G. VEALS,
S.D.P. and I.L.P. Tunbridge Wells,

ISAAC STEVENS,
Eastbourne Clarion Fellowship,

JOE YOUNG,
Brighton S.D.P., and others.

QUESTIONS AND DISCUSSION INVITED.

A CORDIAL WELCOME TO ALL.

The Southern Publishing Co., Ltd., 61 West Street, Horsham.—81,976.

Poster for Horsham, with Veals as main speaker. Used with permission from Horsham Museum / Horsham DC

---

[383] *Justice* November 28th 1908; *Labour Leader* August 23rd 1902; *Justice* September 23rd & 31st 1905, *Justice* June 19th 1909, September 25th 1909 and October 16th 1909.

the Town Hall in March 1910, when Joseph Frederick Green spoke on behalf of the International Arbitration and Peace Association.[384]

May Day 1910 fell on a Sunday. Rather than holding separate celebrations, the Social-Democrats of Tunbridge Wells, Hastings and Eastbourne decided to travel to London to join the May Day procession there. However the Hastings SDP had to pull out.

Once again the branches in Kent and Sussex exchanged speakers. W J Bourne of Maidstone ILP and Alf Cobb of Hastings SDP lectured at the Party's meetings on Tunbridge Wells Common and W G Veals spoke in return at Hastings. Other speakers came from further afield. Frank Edwards of Birkenhead gave six lectures to attentive audiences at Tunbridge Wells on Sunday 5th June, assisted by Val McEntee and T Glossop, before lecturing for a week in Hastings. In July the Tunbridge Wells branch, after an 'excellent' meeting, made the best collection of the season.

The most remarkable breakthrough for the movement came in the small Sussex villages of Dane Hill and Cuckfield. The Independent Labour Party established a following in each. At Dane Hill the village blacksmith forged a sign for his chimney which informed passers-by that 'socialism was the only hope of the workers' and the Dane Hill and Horsted Keynes branch of the party followed soon after.

The Social-Democrats also built a base at Horsham at around the same time. Delegates to the SECFSS's regional meeting in Tunbridge Wells that July enjoyed a tea could be purchased at sixpence a head from the clubroom. Representatives came from Erith, Cray Valley, Penge, Beckenham, Dover, Hythe, Herne Bay, Tonbridge, Tunbridge Wells, Hastings, Eastbourne, Brighton, Horsham and Dane Hill. The discussions were mainly practical in nature. They voted to call a two-day conference to attract any 'unattached' socialists in the region. Another regional rally followed at Haywards Heath, Sussex, with activists attending from Brighton, Eastbourne, Dane Hill, Cuckfield and Tunbridge Wells.[385]

Heartened by the success of radicalising at least a little of the countryside, the Clarion Van again toured the district in September.

---

[384] *The Tunbridge Wells Advertiser October 22nd 1909; The Courier November 5th 1909, December 10th 1909.*
[385] *Justice June 18th 1910, July 2nd & 16th 1910; the Tunbridge Wells Advertiser August 6th 1910; The Clarion September 9th 1910.*

The Clarion's correspondent wrote that *'In Tunbridge Wells, where I have spent the whole of the past week, there is one socialist party, the SDP. Whether it is the SDP or the ILP, my experience is that where the work of a socialist branch is done the right way, there is no need for two branches. Two meetings were on the Common without the van, all others at Lime Hill Road. The crowd were most helpful, as objectors and as listeners'.*

Audiences at Tunbridge Wells were also unusually willing to put their hands in their pockets, while in Tonbridge and Maidstone, despite good crowds and selling many papers and pamphlets, the collected very little money. At Tunbridge Wells the literature sales far exceeded the average. Herbert Heskett, W E Doust Junior and Katherine Veals did much of the work. At Maidstone W G Veals and E J Pay joined the Clarion speakers for the eight meetings held there. Nine new members joined the ILP branch there the week. Anti-socialist speakers fielded in Tonbridge that October included MacCartney and Robert Vaughan Gower. Some Tunbridge Wells activists turned up put their side of the argument.[386]

The series of outdoor meetings in Tunbridge Wells and further afield ended in late October when E J Pay, William George Veals and James Milstead addressed an audience of 1,500 to 2,000 as part of an ultimately unsuccessful campaign to try and get Alf Cobb elected at Hastings. Arthur Hickmott gave the first indoors lecture of the winter series. Katherine Veals lectured on 'a socialist woman's view of the home' while E J Pay spoke on one of his favourite themes, repudiating the national debt.[387]

The Social Democratic Party and British Socialist Party made a determined effort to try and recruit young men and women to the cause after about 1910, although they had no specific youth wing. The Socialist Sunday School and Tunbridge Wells Cooperative Society also attracted younger participants. George Dutch (left) worked for the Society before joining the party. His

George Dutch
(by permission of the Bishopsgate Institute)

---

[386] *Justice September 17th 1910; The Tunbridge Wells Advertiser September 16th 1910; The Clarion September 16th & 23rd & 30th 1910 and October 30th 1910; The Courier October 28th 1910.*
[387] *Justice October 15th 1910, November 5th & 12th & 19th 1910 and December 17th 1910.*

sister Daisy and a close friend joined around the same time, as did the similarly-aged Alf Killick.

The Tunbridge Wells Cooperative Society's Children's Procession on 12th August 1911 which proceeded along St. John's Road, is shown below.

Cooperative Society Children's Procession August 1911

CHAPTER 12   THE BRITISH SOCIALIST PARTY

1911 is a difficult year for the historian of Tunbridge Wells as most of the local newspapers have been lost. We are therefore largely reliant on the labour movement's own publications, something which makes an objective analysis of the course of events far more difficult. We also lack the extended reports of meetings which the *Advertiser* and *Courier* carried. Yet it was clearly an eventful year. The Social Democratic Party dissolved itself and a new organisation, the British Socialist Party, emerged. Generally this has been regarded as of little importance, though I will suggest that, in the south-east at least, it demonstrated that a party which had much in common with Continental Marxist traditions could in fact establish itself on English soil. The year also marked a significant upsurge in trade union activism. Industrial syndicalism influenced some labour leaders, including Tom Mann, formerly of the SDF and ILP, but now heading towards an outright rejection of the idea of a parliamentary road to socialism. George Dangerfield, writing in the 1930s, noted that, although the period appeared prosperous on the surface, falling real wages, the investment sent overseas to the detriment of domestic industry, the increased concentration of capital in trusts and combines and the disappearance of the small entrepreneur had changed things. The result, for workers, was a massive increase in strikes and a new militancy 'from every factory, every workshop, mine, wharf and slum throughout the length and breadth of England'.[388]

The year began with the branch running a campaign against the dumping of the town's refuse in old clay pits in the working class district of High Brooms, something that had been an issue since at least June 1905. Victor Grayson addressed the largest ever indoor socialist meeting at Tunbridge Wells that March, even though the branch charged for admission. George Lansbury returned to the town to speak at the Cooperative Society's Hall the same month on unemployment and the need for the state maintenance of children. At the latter he denounced the responsibility of 'capitalism and liberalism' for the premature deaths of children and called on all present to join the SDP. Shortly afterwards outdoor lectures began again. Irritatingly the building housing the clubhouse changed hands. The new landlord disliked socialism and the branch promptly found itself evicted.   Once again it found itself holding

---

[388] *Dangerfield, G., The Strange Death of Liberal England (1935) (London: Serif 1997) pp178-192.*

meetings in a member's house, in this case James Milstead's residence at 15 Stanley Road.[389]

One fragment of their work that year survives in the *North American Review*, the first literary and cultural magazine to be published in the United States. In hindsight the most interesting observation is that the writer considered the branch to be rather more moderate than he perhaps feared. It also adds some interesting detail which explains how they managed to hold meetings after dark. It is also worth noting the youth of the participants and I wonder whether it is evidence of younger members holding their own events, in particular as other meetings would follow the next day:

> *'I judged from some small gatherings at night that the people's demesne was used for religious and political purposes. One night a minute socialist meeting overcame my after-dinner reluctance and I went out to listen to the mildest arguments for collectivism by nothing redder than the flare of kerosene torches. One of the listeners asked some courteous questions of the speaker, who answered in the gentlest terms; he promised to recur to the same points on the morrow evening, and then with his fellow-conspirators against society (another young man and a young woman) he struck his lurid flambeau and went away, perhaps more explicitly the plot the ruin of capitalism in secret.'*[390]

This meeting may not have attracted the masses, but by this stage the work to establish what would become the largest specifically socialist party in British history had got underway. Victor Grayson had been one of the most strident voices denouncing what he saw as the underhand connection between the ILP and the Liberals. In place of the existing organisations, he called for a united socialist party. These criticisms resonated throughout the country. As early as December 1909 the Maidstone branch of the ILP had passed a resolution, supported by others in West Kent, condemning any 'compromise or agreement' between the Labour Party and Liberal Party. Between 1909 and 1911 forty-six ILP branches collapsed. Although the movement in the south-east region still continued to grow, the *Clarion* argued that some ILPers 'wilfully stand aside' and argued that if they 'threw in their lot, this might become one of the

---

[389] *Justice March 11th 1911, April 1st & 8th 1911, July 22nd 1911; Tunbridge Wells Advertiser June 2nd 1905.*
[390] *Howells, W. D, 'Some Last Drops in Tunbridge Wells' in the North American Review Vol 193,. No 667 (June 1911 pp879-892).*

most effective fighting forces in the country'. Again it called for the establishment of a united socialist party.[391]

Things started to move quickly that summer.

In July a 'United Socialist Propaganda League' formed in London and the following month Victor Grayson wrote an article in the *Clarion* calling for the establishment of what he called a British Socialist Party. He specifically singled out for praise the South Eastern Counties Federation of Socialist Societies and argued that the ILP was no longer a socialist organisation while it remained affiliated to the Labour Party. Shortly afterwards a resolution supporting the establishment of a new party was signed by Veals in his capacity as Secretary of the SECFSS. Opposition to the Labour Party's support of the National Insurance Bill propelled others in the ILP towards the proposed new organisation. The 1911 conference of the SDP supported a resolution from the Rochdale branch calling for every branch of the SDP, ILP and Fabian Society to build the new socialist party. This again cited the work of the SECFSS, as well as its Essex equivalent, as examples.

Tunbridge Wells activists took the message across Kent and Sussex. Their speakers addressed rallies at Ashford, Bexhill, Rye and Tonbridge in July, August and September. Following the meeting at Ashford it was proposed to set up a branch at Tenterden, which again shows the penetration of socialism into remote districts. The Clarion Van again toured the district, though the attempt to hold meetings at Tenterden failed when the van came under attack. [392]

Within the boundaries of Tunbridge Wells the formation of the BSP made little real difference. The formalities were conducted briefly and in a business-like manner. By October South Eastern Counties Federation paid money towards the new organisation. This seems a little premature. In November, the branch convened a special meeting at the Dudley Institute. The members voted to formally accept the constitution and rules of the BSP. The main role of the branch would then be to have informed the wider public of the change of identity. It immediately called on all unattached socialists in the area to join the branch, a call repeated by W G Veals in January 1912.

---

[391] *Labour Leader December 24th 1909; Crick, History, p235; Clarion June 16th 1911, August 25th 1911; Justice September 2nd , 16th and 23rd September 1911.*
[392] *Clarion August 4th 1911, August 18th 1911; Crick, History, p181, p233.*

H.F.Northcote

These changes took place at the time of year which made outdoor public meetings impossible. The branch, under its new title, organised a public meeting at the Town Hall. They enlisted one of the movement's best speakers, H F Northcote, who used included lantern (or slide) views to illustrate his arguments. Katherine Veals enthusiastically praised the meeting, 'the evolution of nature and society, as 'excellent, with a good audience'. The branch also started to use the Dudley Institute for its regular business meetings.[393]

The real impact came in other towns in the region, and this more than anything else demonstrates the results of the hard work that the Tunbridge Wells branch had put in to build the movement in Kent, Sussex and Surrey. Forty branches of the ILP across the British Isles joined the BSP. The members of the Maidstone branch voted to do so in December 1911. At Brighton the branches of the Clarion Fellowship, SDP, some members of the ILP and various 'unattached' socialists all also joined the new organisation in the New Year. As well as poaching members from other organisations, the party also established branches in relatively virgin territory. In April 1912 the BSP founded a branch in Ashford, Kent's most important railway junction and works. Nationwide the new party had 400 branches by February 1912. This may, however, have been the party's peak. In 1913, John Bruce Glasier noted that the number of branches had slipped back slightly to 370 branches, yet only 182 of these were represented at conference. Its continued strength (it could be added with a few exceptions such as Maidstone) came from places which previously had well-established branches of the SDP.[394]

What future could the cross-party SECFSS have? The Tunbridge Wells branch organised a special meeting of representatives at the

---

[393] Clarion October 20th 1911; Justice 18th November 1911; Justice January 20th 1912; Clarion January 19th 1912; Clarion February 23rd 1912; Tunbridge Wells Advertiser February 9th 1912.
[394] Crick, History, p181; Clarion December 22nd 1911, February 1st 1912; Justice April 28th 1912; Bruce Glasier, J. Socialist Year Book and Labour Annual. A guide book to the socialist and labour movement at home and abroad, (Manchester 1913).

Dudley Institute on Sunday 21st April. They agreed to set up a South Eastern Counties District Committee of the BSP in its place. This had much in common with the Independent Labour Party's county federations. Tunbridge Wells justifiably complained that too few comrades had agreed to take roles. The conference elected James Milstead of Tunbridge Wells as Chair. William O'Sullivan became Secretary of the Cycling Scouts. James Milstead took on the job of Treasurer. William Veals again won election as Secretary. Only Eastbourne, Ashford, Hastings and Tunbridge Wells attended the District Committee's meeting in August.[395]

The recruitment of William O'Sullivan and a Mr Geoghegan to the branch suggest that it had begun to make inroads into the town's relatively small Irish community. This irked Dr Hitchcock, the priest in charge of St Augustine's, the town's Roman Catholic Church. In the spring of 1912 he criticised the politics of the Tunbridge Wells branch. William Veals challenged him to a debate. Dr Hitchcock turned the offer down and instead queried whether they were 'Marxian or Fabian or Social Democratic or Anarchist or Syndicalist'. The argument continued for some weeks in the pages of the *Advertiser*. Veals perhaps felt that such definitions were unhelpful: the branch stood 'for the cooperative ownership, the democratic control and the common use' of all that was needed for 'full life and happiness'. The correspondence then turned towards the socialist belief in internationalism. Less subtle thinkers than Dr Hitchcock got involved and Veals wrote a fine letter setting out his beliefs. The following passage captures its flavour:

> '*As for patriotism, Socialists have no use for a so-called patriotism which produces a feeling of hatred for the folks in other lands. Modern patriotism has been well defined as "the love of the capitalist class for other men's countries... and of a desire to possess theirs. Socialists have no desire to see the national wealth spent in blowing out the brains of the workers of other lands, as they are our comrades and brothers*'.[396]

The editor of the Advertiser had good commercial reasons for allowing the debate to run unimpeded, as in June he noted that most issues of the paper which had covered the exchanges had sold out. A sailor from the area, presumably on leave, joined in. The

---

[395] *Justice January 20th 1912; Clarion March 22nd 1912; Justice April 27th 1912, Justice August 17th 1912; The Clarion August 16th 1912.*
[396] *The Tunbridge Wells Advertiser March 8th & 15th 1912, April 12th 1912.*

socialists ranged widely. David Geer quoted from Adam Smith to defend his position. In the last week of June the debate concluded with a joint letter by William George Veals and Dr Hitchcock stating that 'we, the combatants, part with goodwill towards one another and you'. Both sides emerged from the exchange with their reputations enhanced.[397]

The summer programme of open-air meetings drew opposition from both the Christian Evidence Movement and the Anti-Socialist Union. The former launched an Anti-Socialist Crusade in the town that May, with meetings held close to the BSP's own spot. Rather than calling on assistance from London, they invited Bourne from Maidstone, who, together with E J Pay, ably dealt with the challenge. *Justice* derided their ignorant rantings, but noted that the Crusade had drawn people away from meetings held by the branch. The paper requested that its readers ignore the Christian Evidence speakers and later recorded that meetings in June and July had been very successful. Perhaps realising that they had achieved little, the Crusade ceded the initiative to speakers from the Anti-Socialist Union from August.[398]

As the opposition faded away, the branch again sent speakers to rallies to other places. Most took place in Kent. E J Pay and W G Veals addressed gatherings in Maidstone in June, July and August. The town's Cycling Scouts then descended in significant numbers in Ashford, a considerable distance away. William and Katherine Veals spoke on a number of themes that day, including on education in Germany. E J Pay also addressed a meeting in Sheerness that October, at the end of the outdoor speaking season. Yet, in a sign that the new political party had struggled to achieve all which its supporters had hoped for, the Sussex branches seem to have been relatively inactive. The Brighton branch, formed with such enthusiasm only a year earlier, required reorganisation by September, and pledges of support were given for meetings in Arundel. Hastings, of course, had enough strength to prosper without outside assistance.[399]

---

397 *The Tunbridge Wells Advertiser April 19th 1912 May 3rd 1912, June 28th 1912.*
398 398 *Justice May 18th 1912, June 15th 1912 and July 20th 1912; The Courier August 16th 1912; The Clarion January 7th 1910.*
399 *Justice June 15th 1912, July 27th 1912 and August 3rd 1912;; Tunbridge Wells Advertiser August 2nd 1912; Clarion September 20th 1912; and Justice October 26th 1912.*

In September the branch found premises at the junction of Western Road and Avon Street, an area dominated by timber yards and the towers of the municipal power station. It lay a few hundred metres from the site of the hall first occupied by the branch in 1886. David Geer, who lived nearby on Dorking Road, seems to have taken the lead in setting up the rooms, to the extent that one directory for Tunbridge Wells, Kelly's, noted him as proprietor while failing to record the purpose to which they had been put. Its rival, Peltons, correctly identified it as the Socialist Club. As with the previous club, the building still stands, though probably much modified. Outdoor meetings continued to November at Lime Hill Road, though probably not on the Common, before moving indoors.[400]

The junction of Albion Road and St James Park, close to both David Geer's house on Dorking Road and the Socialist Club of 1912

The branch decided to use the new premises as much as possible. A number of speakers addressed the issues of the day. Arthur Hickmott, who had travelled to Denmark, gave a report on the cooperatives there. W Doust spoke about the curse of British imperialism in India. E J Pay discussed syndicalism from a socialist standpoint. A series of lectures on famous writers took place ran into March. E J Pay spoke about Ruskin from a socialist viewpoint and W G Veals discussed Charles Dickens, Robert Burns and the Bronte sisters. Relative newcomers also joined in. Herman Williams gave a lecture about H G Wells and F Philpott discussed Tolstoy

---

[400] *Justice November 9th 1912.*

from an anarchist perspective. They also looked at trends in contemporary art. Several competing movements had emerged, such as Cubism, Futurism and Vorticism, in some cases accompanied by strident manifestos which set out to remake the world in their image. Herman Williams, perhaps preferring the work of William Morris and Walter Crane, had little time for Futurism, but the fact that socialists in Tunbridge Wells had been made aware of it must have been unusual in working class circles in Britain in 1912. Williams ranged widely, also discussing theories about the age and composition of the Earth, and concluded by making a powerful appeal for social equity and justice and for living in harmony with the tremendous forces of nature and with each other.[401]

Other new members first became active in branch life through the regular socials. The branch's opposition to drinking, except perhaps in moderation, meant that they needed to find other ways to entertain each other. Several new names crop up. A Miss Osborne helped Herman Williams give a Dickens recital. Mr W Cross demonstrated his talent for whistling. C Young played the violin. Other performances followed, by Mr Martin, Miss Ede, Miss Simpson and Mr and Mrs Costta. The BSP, which had no separate youth wing, passed a resolution at its 1913 conference asking branches to try and persuade men and women aged between fourteen and twenty-one to join.

George Dutch, who as we have seen had regarded himself as a socialist from a young age, needed little prompting. This awakening may have been prompted by buying a copy of H G Wells' *New Worlds For Old* at a long-established bookshop in Chapel Place. He brought along one of his friends and soon persuaded his sister Daisy to join. In the statement he deposited at the Imperial War Museum decades later he specifically praised the help given by David Geer, Milstead, Philpott, W G Veals and others and regularly used the branch's 'excellent' reference library. These young recruits soon came up to speed. George Dutch also became Minute Secretary of the local Shop Assistants' Union.[402]

---

[401] *The Courier March 28th 1913 and April 4th 1914; Justice April 5th 1913; Tunbridge Wells Advertiser April 4th, 11th and 18th 1913.*
[402] *The Tunbridge Wells Advertiser November 22nd 1912, February 21st 1913; Tanner p122-3; Dutch, G.F., The Anti-War Movement in Britain during the First World Way (Bishopsgate Institute), Personal Statement (IWM 7651).*

As well as politics, socials and the arts, the branch ran a few lectures on science. Philpott's one on the Riddle of Life, described as 'interesting, thoughtful and informative', drew praise. However, in an exchange which demonstrated the fault-lines in British socialism at the time, a speech by W H Williams, a visiting lecturer, on socialism and eugenics caused real anger. Williams called for the sterilisation of those he considered degenerates. Such divisions marked the left, as in 1912 there was a heated debate in respect of the subject in the *Clarion*, one opponent of eugenics considering that it would work in the main against the poor and defenceless. The Eugenics Education Society, a promotional body, pointed to what it called a growing class of industrial parasites. These, rather than the business cycle, apparently explained unemployment.

The BSP, for the only time in its history, organised a counter-meeting the following week with the title 'Food, Health and Diseases – a reply to the recent pro-eugenicist lecture'. Philpott was particularly vocal in his opposition to Williams. The branch had grappled with such themes since the article by William Willis-Harris condemning Social-Darwinism almost a quarter of a century ago. From the reports it is obvious that most members, and probably all, opposed Williams.[403]

Leading figures from the Tunbridge Wells branch were in demand as visiting lecturers. In March 1913 J G Webster broke new ground, speaking at Bristol and London. William Veals, appointed that month as lecture secretary, spoke in Gillingham. His wife Katherine took a number of roles, as collector, literature and trading secretary. William O'Sullivan won election as branch secretary. Reverend Potter left the town around this time, but the membership had grown during the previous twelve months and the finances remained healthy.[404]

What, though, of the ideological turmoil of the time? Strikes had become more common and bitter and syndicalist ideas grew across British industry. I can find no support for syndicalism in the area, though this is far from conclusive. The geographical location of Tunbridge Wells, though ideal for building the socialist movement

---

[403] *The Tunbridge Wells Advertiser November 22nd 1912, December 6th 1912, December 13th 1912, December 27th 1912; The Courier January 31st 1913; The Clarion May 12th & 17th 1912; Harris, Unemployment p46.*
[404] *Labour Leader March 20th 1913; The Tunbridge Wells Advertiser March 21st 1913; Justice March 8th 1913, April 5th 1913; The Courier June 6th 1913; the Tunbridge Wells Advertiser July 4th 1913.*

in the south-east corner of Britain, lay a great distance from the areas which experienced the most significant strikes, such as Merseyside, South Wales and Clydeside. Across the country the militant wing of the women's suffrage campaign increasingly turned to arson. The Women's Social and Political Union – which had formed a branch in Tunbridge Wells in 1911 - were held responsible for burning down the cricket pavilion on 11th April 1913. They also destroyed the home of the Tory Member of Parliament for Hastings, Arthur Du Cros, and were suspected by some of setting light to the Tunbridge Wells Constitutional Club the same month. Their paper *The Suffragette* carried a double-page spread with the headline '*the Women's Revolution – a Reign of Terror – Fire and Bombs*' on 11th April. In September even Penshurst Place came under attack. Veterans of the socialist branch would perhaps have reflected on the parallel with the events of 1886, 1887 and 1908.[405]

To some extent the socialists of Tunbridge Wells had almost become onlookers. Philpott considered himself an anarchist, but one far more influenced by Tolstoy than syndicalism. He defined his beliefs by arguing that:

> We must '*offer uncompromising opposition to all governments that attempted to destroy, defile or regulate humanity's natural rights and try to ensure to all an existence comparable and in harmony with nature*'.[406]

Yet branch retained its edge in its approach to international relations. Horrified at the increasing drift of Hyndman and other socialists towards support for increasing military expenditure and even forms of conscription, they drafted a motion for the annual conference which balanced a desire to retain unity while rebuking those whom they considered had undermined the internationalism of their movement. The motion read in part:

> '*As the British Socialist Party is the party of freedom, members are free to hold any opinion they like on subjects other than Socialism, and any member expressing his or her views on a subject seen as contentious does so as a private individual and in no way pledges the party to such views*'[407]

---

[405] See Carwardine, A., Disgusted Women pp152, 156-7,161-3 and 200-208 .
[406] The Tunbridge Wells Advertiser November 21st 1913.
[407] Justice May 17th 1913.

In the event their delegate, F Sedgwick, agreed to withdraw the motion at the end of a lively debate between pro- and anti- militarist factions of the party. Both sides had reason to feel that the Tunbridge Wells motion failed to address the issue fully, and that a resolution binding all members of the party made more sense. In the event conference resolved:

> 'As an integral part of the International Socialist Party, bound by the resolutions on war of Stuttgart and Basle, 1912, to pursue the same policy in Great Britain with the object of checking the growth of all forms of militarism'.

The debated concluded with a show of unity. Henry Hyndman shook hands with Zelda Kahan, a committed internationalist. Hyndman resigned from the Executive Committee for the moment. As will be seen, the issues raised by the debate would split the party four years later. [408]

The branch invited a number of speakers to their gatherings on the Common, many of whom took a similar line on militarism. After about 1900 many towns had celebrated Empire Day, an event which seems to have been intended to encourage pride in Britain's overseas colonies, and with a particular focus on the young. Schools in the working class districts of Tunbridge Wells and other towns held fetes, which incorporated traditional activities such as dancing around the maypole. W J Reeves from West Ham attacked the ideology behind this: the history of 'this empire of ours' was a history of blood... If the ultra-patriots of the country could be taken to the East End they would become anarchists in their disgust of it being possible'. Onlookers heckled but no violence followed. Another speaker from the East End on the Common that day, Joseph Fineberg, later became a leading Communist. By June the Common had become a smaller version of Hyde Park. Lloyd George drew hostility a month later he intended to reduce Samuel Plimsoll's regulations preventing the overloading of ships; measures which the branch considered had saved many lives.[409]

Events in far-away Dublin caught the attention of the Tunbridge Wells branch in the second half of 1913. Jim Larkin's Irish Transport and General Workers Union had organised workers across several industries in the city. One employer, William Martin

---

[408] Crick, History, p253.
[409] The Tunbridge Wells Advertiser May 30th 1913; The Courier July 4th 1913; Justice June 21st 1913, August 30th 1913 and November 1st 1914.

Murphy, resolved to force workers to sign a pledge against the union or face dismissal. In the weeks that followed, bloody clashes between union members, the police and blacklegs led to the deaths of several people. Money flowed from British socialists, unions and Cooperative societies, including the Tunbridge Wells Cooperative Society, although the leadership of the Trades Union Congress singularly failed to give similar level of support. On a much smaller scale, members of the Amalgamated Society of Carpenters and Joiners in Tonbridge took strike action over a fortnight. [410]

These events coincided with the selection by lottery of local tradesmen as special constables. Sam Noble was one of the men chosen. He made it clear that as a socialist he would not agree to serve if a strike took place. The magistrates' clerk informed that no such exemption could be made and noted that refusal could lead to a 40 shilling fine or, in default of payment, a month in prison. Noble took the oath on the basis of the exception he claimed and this seems to have been accepted.

Solidarity work to support trade unionists in South Africa followed in the New Year. After several months of industrial unrest, the authorities expelled nine trade unionists from the Transvaal on the charge of being in possession of dynamite. Many observers considered these to be trumped up charges. In February the BSP branch condemned the 'brutality and the severely provocative actions of the South African Government in their attempt to crush trade unionism'. A bigger gathering followed ten weeks later. The Trades and Labour Council, Socialists and Cooperative Party booked the Town Hall for a meeting addressed by R B Waterston, the General Secretary of the South African Labour Party. His argument that 'Tommy' and the police had the right not to follow orders to shoot strikers came close to incitement to mutiny. David Geer chaired and Sam Noble proposed the motion which condemned the imposition of martial law, demanded the sacking of the Governor-General, Lord Gladstone, and sent fraternal greetings to those deported. William George Veals seconded. [411]

For the first time in the history of the branch, the next strike to make national headlines took place on the branch's doorstep. Early

---

[410] The Tunbridge Wells Advertiser October 31st 1913; The Courier July 4th 1913 and October 3rd & 17th 1913.
[411] Justice May 14th 1914; The Tunbridge Wells Advertiser May 15th 1914; The Courier January 16th 1914.; Mann, T, Memoirs (London: Labour Publishing Company 1923) p321.

1914 saw a 'positive fever of small strikes' across the country. The cricket ball industry at the time consisted of a few factories scattered around the villages and towns of West Kent. Pressures to cut prices per ball while raw materials were becoming more expensive led to repeated attempts to cut wages. The Amalgamated Society of Cricket Ball Makers by 1907 had recruited three-quarters of the workforce and threatened strike action. Agreement followed, yet pay failed to keep pace with inflation.[412]

By April 1914 the *Advertiser* concluded that ball-making was now a sweated trade. Workers faced ten to twelve hour days in poor conditions. Some men earned less than one pound a week and one reported that he earned 30 shillings for eighty hours work. Disputes arose over the cause. Some employers, including Wisden-Luff at Tonbridge, argued that this was the result of competition from Indian-made balls. He also blamed priced paid by middle-men. Others argued that the employers were at fault for agreeing to price reductions. Unusually the press sided with the strikers, with support from the sports writer of the *Daily Telegraph* and the endorsement of a number of well-known cricketers. The *Advertiser* argued that 'the men have right on their side, they are fighting a just cause (and that) they will win'. A solidarity meeting followed, addressed by AR Holmes, organiser of the ball-makers and R B Waterston, so placing the dispute in an international context.[413]

The strike began when the first men in Tonbridge walked out on Saturday April 18th. Many walked the five miles or so to Messrs Dukes' factory at Chiddingstone Causeway to encourage workers there to join the 25 there already on strike. Only 13 agreed to do so. The following Tuesday they tried again, and Harold Hardinge, a Tonbridge-born Kent and England cricketer and Arsenal footballer, made a speech calling on these men to join the strike, following which another 26 men came out. Two followed the next day. Hardinge was *Wisden*'s cricketer of the year in 1915. However, despite his celebrity and the eloquence of his address, only half of the Chiddingstone Causeway men went on strike in total. A group of cyclists then rode to Teston, near Maidstone, though had initially little success in sparking action there.

---

[412] *The Tunbridge Wells Advertiser* May 3rd 1907.
[413] *The Courier January* 10th 1912, April 17th and 24th 1914; *The Tunbridge Wells Advertiser* April 17th & 24th 1914 and May 8th 1914.

Members of the ASCBM (undated).
By permission of the Tonbridge Historical Society.

Meetings to build the action took place at the Angel Hotel in Tonbridge. 'Fiery speeches' were given at nearby Avebury Avenue. A rally on Tunbridge Wells Common followed, organised with the help of the BSP and Trades and Labour Council. The Tonbridge delegation marched as a group to the demonstration with a red banner emblazoned with the demand for a living wage for ball-makers, accompanied by banners from each of the union's branches then on strike. Such branches included Tonbridge, Hildenborough, Southborough, Penshurst, Teston, and, intriguingly, Putney. W G Veals chaired the meeting, David Geer presided, and Holmes spoke on behalf of his members. The meeting concluded with the *Red Flag* and *England Arise*. The dispute ended in victory, with a pay rise to take effect at the end of May.[414]

An old theme was reprised when Reverend D J Stather Hunt, Vicar of Holy Trinity, decided that, although he did not oppose all forms of socialism, he had to take a stand against its atheistic manifestation in his parish. The Christian Evidence Movement held meetings Sunday after Sunday on the Common and elsewhere in the town. The *Advertiser* condemned their speakers, whose tone and manner seemed to be entirely contrary to what one would expect from Christians. Passers-by on the Common gave rather more robust opposition. The branch had a more original reply. The Reverend Ernest Maxted, the Vicar of Tilty, Essex, had become a convinced

---

The Tunbridge Wells Advertiser May 8ᵗʰ 1914; The Courier May 3ʳᵈ 1914; Justice May 14ᵗʰ 1914;. Tunbridge Wells Advertiser May 15ᵗʰ 1914; The Courier May 15ᵗʰ 1914.

socialist and had supported agricultural workers during a lock-out in his county. In July he ran a three day mission on the Lime Hill Road.[415]

By this stage the question of the BSP re-affiliating to the Labour Party had become urgent. Although the Tunbridge Wells branch remained strong, there is some evidence that even its Hastings equivalent had begun to struggle. Nationwide the party had haemorrhaged members and was little larger than the SDP had been. By 1913 figures as diverse as Henry Mayers Hyndman, Hunter Watts and Zelda Kahan wanted to re-join and the International Socialist Bureau urged the party, together with the Fabian Society and the ILP, to play fuller roles in the Labour Party. In March 1914 William George Veals even suggested something which approached entryism, a tactic used by the CPGB in the 1920s and the Trotskyist Militant Tendency in the 1980s. A Marxist current within the party would win support from 'hundreds of comrades in the ILP who, once we are affiliated, will co-operate with us in a militant policy'. This would replace 'a bastard form of state collectivism in cooperation with the New Liberalism of Lloyd George' with principled socialism, and allow Ramsay MacDonald to be removed from the leadership. Putting the plan into print, however, would not help win the support of people like MacDonald![416]

Others in the leadership of the ILP and BSP used more moderate language. The *Labour Leader* in April carried articles by H W Lee and Fenner Brockway suggesting that the BSP and ILP should federate under a joint council. Some branches of the BSP disagreed and the right of the Labour Party may have had misgivings, but the direction of travel had become obvious. On 28th May 1914 the membership of the BSP voted in a referendum to affiliate to the Labour Party. From the perspective of Tunbridge Wells, this strengthened the link with the ILP in Tonbridge. The two branches formed a joint committee to work together on campaigns, and the idea of running a Labour candidate for the Tonbridge Division became a concrete proposal. From August they met monthly.[417]

---

[415] *The Tunbridge Wells Advertiser May 8th 1914; The Courier June 12th 1914; The Tunbridge Wells Advertiser July 21st 1914; Justice August 6th 1914.*
[416] *For the point about Hastings, I thank Trevor Hopper. For W G Veals see Justice March 26th 1914. See also Pelling, H., A Short History of the Labour Party (London: MacMillan 1968) p25; Crick, History, p255;, The Labour Leader January 29th 1914.*
[417] *The Labour Leader April 30th 1914, June 4th & 25th 1914; Crick, History, p257; Justice July 30th 1914 and August 6th 1914.*

PART D   EVERYTHING CHANGES

CHAPTER 13   THE WORLD AT WAR
AND THE STRUGGLE AGAINST CONSCRIPTION

War, unsurprisingly, brought any plans made by the socialists of Tunbridge Wells and Tonbridge to a shuddering halt. A few in the movement felt that war might set in train a crisis from which the socialist revolution might come. Harry Quelch had argued in 1912 that 'we have reached that stage in history that the slightest spark may serve to set light to the whole structure of capitalism'. The danger with this line of reasoning is that socialists effectively had no incentive to take steps for peace. A fringe element within the movement, led by Robert Blatchford, and often infected by the pseudo-science of eugenics, considered imperialism and militarism to be positive for the development of humanity. In the event, though, Quelch's predictions came true, as, after four long years of fighting and the deaths of millions, revolutionary ideas won unprecedented support throughout Europe and beyond. By 1918 the world had changed beyond recall.

Most members of the parties of the Second International had reason to believe that they had both the duty and the means to prevent a war from breaking out. Mobilising the grassroots of the movement would be the key. In 1910 Keir Hardie and the French Socialist Edouard Vaillant had co-sponsored a resolution proposing a general strike in the event that war broke out, but the German SPD, partly due to their suspicion of Hyndman and Blatchford, prevented the motion passing.

Despite this, massive co-ordinated demonstrations against intervention at the time of the First Balkan War in 1912 led to the Emergency Congress of European socialist movements at Basle the same year to conclude that the fear of the ruling classes that a revolution would follow the declaration of war had guaranteed the peace of the continent. Many hoped that history could repeat itself in 1914.

In late July the British Socialist Party condemned Austro-Hungary for its aggression towards Serbia but congratulated the social democrats of Vienna, Berlin and Paris for their efforts to prevent the outbreak of war. On July 30th the *Labour Leader* carried uncompromising headlines: 'the war must be stopped' and 'we must stop it'. Local women would have been amongst the twelve million across twenty-six countries who signed an appeal against the war.[418]

At Tunbridge Wells the BSP called two emergency demonstrations on the Common for Sunday 2nd August. About a thousand people attended in the afternoon, despite the short notice. A resolution against war, drafted by the British section of the International Socialist Bureau, passed unanimously. The mover urged the Government to 'rigidly decline to engage in war', instead taking steps to bring about peace as speedily as possible.

It appears that the meeting in London's Trafalgar Square passed an identical motion. In hindsight it is notable that, even though the speakers at London included Keir Hardie, Margaret Bondfield, Herbert Burrows and Robert Cunninghame Graham, the attendance of 15,000 was proportionately much smaller than that in provincial towns, including Tunbridge Wells.[419]

Sadly such efforts failed to change the course of events and less than a day later Britain had declared war on Germany. How did the people of Tunbridge Wells respond? The *Advertiser* carried a very illuminating and powerful report:

'The word 'holiday' had a hollow ring about it on Monday for most thoughtful people and in spite of the apparent outward calm and jollity of the merry-makers in Calverley Park Grounds, or on the Common, or at the flying exhibition, the shadow of national trouble with the consequent disastrous effects on the food and the homes of the people, was not masked.

The holiday feeling was gone – except in the case of those whose intelligence could not rise above the level of a jingo excitement, and for those for whom tomorrow did not exist. Crowds there were indeed everywhere, and many visitors, but all over hung the vague phantom of deep anxiety as to what the morrow would bring forth. Never, surely have the people of Tunbridge Wells experienced such a universal sense of foreboding on the great national holiday as was the case on Monday.

---

[418] *Justice November 30th 1912, See also Justice January 15th 1910, Crick, History, p264, Justice July 30th 1914, Labour Leader July 30th 1914, Liddington, Greenham, p77-78*
[419] *The Labour Leader August 6th 1914. Ipswich managed a turnout of 4,000 people.*

Everyone, almost without exception, could find little else to talk about but the war. On the Sunday little groups of people of all classes besieged the newspaper shops and eagerly bought up the special editions of the Times and the Daily Mail, and the news contained in these journals did not tend to dispel the gloom. Monday's papers confirmed the grave statements that Germany had attacked France and that a rupture with this country was imminent. And so the swings and the roundabouts, the coconut shies and all the 'fun of the fair' looked ridiculously out of place.'[420]

This reaction goes some way to dispelling the myth, much as Cyril Pearce's work on Huddersfield has done, that cheering crowds greeted the declaration of war across the country. In Tunbridge Wells, the report continues, the audience for the band in the Pantiles enthusiastically sang the National Anthem, though even this seems to have been an attempt to find reassurance rather than any exhibition of nationalist sentiment. The socialists and their allies may have been the most strongly opposed to the conflict, but few residents felt that it would bring anything other than tragedy.

Whatever misgivings many people had about the conflict, it is clear that the mobilisation of troops changed the situation. Even before the declaration of war, local volunteers had been given orders to assemble. The *Courier* reported that the town had not seen similar scenes since the day of celebration (and, it failed to add, the nights of rioting) which followed the fall of Pretoria. Thousands of local men enlisted in the Kent and Sussex regiments.

The army encamped on Tunbridge Wells Common post-August 1914.. The BSP ran its meetings within 200-300 yards of this spot into 1915.

---

[420] *Tunbridge Wells Advertiser August 7th 1914*

George Lansbury, Keir Hardie and Margaret Bondfield continued to very publicly argue for peace. Perhaps surprisingly, many socialists supported the war effort once it had broken out. Hyndman and Cunninghame Graham swung behind the recruitment drive, as did leading Labour Party figures such as Arthur Henderson. Alf Cobb, the BSP's most prominent figure in Hastings, enlisted quickly. George Meek, who played a similar role at Eastbourne, tried to do likewise and, although his health meant that he initially failed to be accepted, he turned his hand to writing some fairly turgid militaristic poems for his local paper. So did several of the sons of leading Tunbridge Wells activists, including Ralph Claudian Willis-Harris Karl Marx Willis-Harris and Edward and Frederick Bournes, though many of these men had left the country for Canada or Australia. Continuing to oppose the war once it had begun, and so failing to support 'our boys' at the front, would at the very least make enemies.[421]

At the same time, the branch had friends in the town and other parts of West Kent. The thousand that assembled on 2nd August would have included many hundreds who were not members of the party. The coalition for peace which had come into existence during the Boer War, between socialists, Quakers, Unitarians and left-leaning Liberals – by no means exclusive categories – came back into life. Only the Fabian Society made less of an impression, though it had become a diminished force locally by 1914.

Horace Gundry Alexander, the son of Joseph, had reached the age at which he could take a leading role in the campaign. In 1916 he privately printed a set of suggestions for a just peace without annexations, using his father's address, 3 Mayfield Road, for correspondence. His call won at least conditional support from a series of leading figures from the Labour movement and some on the left of the Liberal Party, ranging from George Lansbury and Margaret Bondfield to Leonard Woolf and Edward Carpenter. Lucy Candler, secretary of the Tunbridge Wells Peace Union, and her sisters, Sarah and Phyllis, were Quakers and had long been politically active in the Liberal Party and women's suffrage movement. Alfred Bishop, who had stood for the Fabian Society in the West Ward in 1898, and his son Douglas Ralph Bishop, who lived in Maidstone at the time, opposed the conflict on the basis of both their faith and their socialist politics. In nearby towns, the BSP's Maidstone branch and the Independent Labour Party in

---

[421] Mathews, M., Cobb p113; Coxall and Griggs pp315-335.

Tonbridge decided to oppose the war and to discourage men from enlisting.[422]

W. STEADMAN ALDIS.	ALEX. GOSSIP, Secretary, Furnishing Trades'
C. G. AMMON, President, Fawcett Association.	Association.
MARGARET ASHTON.	G. P. GOOCH.
MARGARET BONDFIELD.	J. A. HOBSON.
FRED BRAMLEY, Organiser, Furnishing Trades'	CANON J. W. HORSLEY.
Association.	GEORGE LANSBURY.
VICTOR V. BRANFORD.	MARGARET LLEWELYN DAVIES.
RT. HON. THOMAS BURT, M.P.	ALBERT MANSBRIDGE.
EDWARD CARPENTER.	SAM. MARCH, Secretary, Union of Vehicle
J. ESTLIN CARPENTER, D.Litt.	Workers.
RT. HON. LORD COURTNEY OF PENWITH.	SIR EDWIN PEARS.
H. DUBERY, Parliamentary Secretary, Joint	PRINCIPAL W. B. SELBIE, D.D.
Committee of Postal Associations.	ROBERT SMILLIE, President Miners' Federation.
PROF. A. S. EDDINGTON, F.R.S.	BEN TURNER, Secretary, Union of Textile
H. H. ELVIN, Secretary, National Union of	Workers.
Clerks.	R. B. WALKER, Secretary, Agricultural
RT. HON. SIR EDWARD FRY, G.C.B.	Labourers' Union.
R. M. GENTRY, London Secretary, Bakers &	L. S. WOOLF.
Confectioners' Union.	

A list of those who – with some reservations – supported Horace Gundry Alexander's peace proposals of 1916. Most were leading trade unionists but others came from Liberal or Labour politics, the judiciary, religion and publishing

The BSP at Tunbridge Wells, numerically still the largest of these branches, seems to have been most active. Despite thousands of troops being billeted in the town, something which increased its population by a quarter, they continued to run anti-war meetings. Some speakers used fairly soft language, such as calling on the Government to bring the war to a 'speedy and honourable conclusion', while focussing on traditional demands such as the provision of free school meals, a municipal milk supply for women, children and the sick, and for public works.

The remarkable feature of these speeches is that they took place only a few hundred yards from the tents of the soldiers. The *Courier* felt that such juxtaposition could not have taken place outside this 'freedom-loving country'. On one occasion the speeches by the socialist, assisted by 'an argumentative German waiter', led to good-humoured debate, rather than the fighting seen in other places. Yet an attempt by the Tonbridge ILP to distribute anti-war leaflets in

---

[422] *Alexander, Joseph Gundry Alexander, pp171-4; Clark and Murfin, Maidstone p209; Bishop, A., For Conscience' Sake (London: Headley Bross, 1917); The Courier 11th September 1914.*

the town's High Street led to threats of violence from those supportive of the conflict.[423]

45. Grosvenor Road, & Hospital, Royal Tunbridge Wells.

Grosvenor Road, with the sign for Mr Urban's shop left of centre. William Willis-Harris had previously occupied the property immediately underneath the right-hand part of the sign.

Those with non-British ancestry also failed to enjoy the freedoms trumpeted by the *Courier*. L. Reich's jewellers in Camden Road faced a sustained assault from a drunken mob in October. Others suffered several times over the next four years. J Urban, a Grosvenor Road hairdresser who happened to be the neighbour and friend of David Geer, also suffered from a campaign of intimidation, as did the landlord of the Clarendon Hotel, H Keil. Yet the Socialists, perhaps because of the size of the meetings, continued their activities largely unmolested. Anti-German feeling seems to have been less fanatical in Tunbridge Wells than in other places. Roads with German names, such as Hanover Road, retained their identity. The authorities also seem to have done their best to dissuade attacks on those of foreign backgrounds who had integrated into the community.[424]

---

[423] Bates, S., '1914- The Early Days' in The Shock of War p42; The Courier August 14th 1914, September 11th 1918, September 18th 1914.
[424] The Courier October 30th 1914, The Tunbridge Wells Advertiser May 21st 1915

By October the divisions within the socialist and labour movement had become obvious locally and nationally. Many felt the need to accommodate the patriotic spirit. The Tunbridge Wells Cooperative Society ended its meeting with *God Save the King* and the *Marseillaise*. Other companies took advantage of the situation by 'freeing up' men for the military by dismissing them, replacing them with boys or women, coincidentally at a lower rate of pay.[425]

Nationally the BSP was extremely divided. Some branches joined the recruitment drive, while many others, such as Stepney, Bow and Bromley and Hackney, strongly criticised this and would have joined Tunbridge Wells and Maidstone in discouraging recruitment efforts.[426]

Whatever divisions had emerged, the BSP, Trades and Labour Council and Cooperative Society united to try to lessen the impact of the war at home. These bodies jointly set up the Tunbridge Wells War Workers Emergency Committee in August. By September it had representatives from the Painters and Decorators, Railway Workers, Plumbers, Gas Workers and General Labourers, Plasterers, Carpenters and Joiners and Bricklayers unions as well as the High Brooms Adult School.

The TWWWEC elected William George Veals Chair and David Geer and Sam Noble to its committee. They condemned those who had profited from shortages of food and called for public works to reduce unemployment. Its work received decent coverage in the town's press, though the Prince of Wales Relief Fund, supported by the Mayor, received more official support. Activists used a meeting at the Town Hall in mid-September to demand measures to help the building trades, which faced a slump, and shop assistants whose hours had been cut and a few weeks later stated to compile a 'white list' of decent employers and landlords.[427]

By this stage a backlash against the socialists had begun, something intensified by the forthcoming municipal elections. The BSP and the Trades and Labour Council decided to run Sam Noble as their candidate in the East Ward. Veals and Noble had been uncharacteristically guarded about their attitude to the war at the

---

[425] *The Advertiser October 23rd 1914.*
[426] *Crick, History p268; Labour Leader October 1st & 8th 1914.*
[427] *Justice September 10th 1914; the Tunbridge Wells Advertiser August 28th 1914, September 4th & 18th & 25th 1914; Crick, History p269; The Courier August 28th 1914, September 4th 1914.*

September Town Hall meeting. Noble's opposition to dismissing staff to encourage them to join the army, and the attitude of what one correspondent to the Advertiser called the 'Socialist Democratic Party' to recruitment, led the Conservative and Liberals to put aside any differences and work together against him. The Liberal topped the poll with 580, followed by the Tory who took 572, yet Noble still managed a very respectable 399 votes. Following his defeat, Noble condemned the lies spread about him. If anything, the result suggests that the socialist position on the war had only lost them a relatively small number of votes.[428]

One reason for such hostility may have been that some feared that the BSP and their allies were having a significant effect on the young men of Tunbridge Wells and district. Concerns were raised that they were less willing to take the King's Shilling than those in other places. There may have been other reasons for such reluctance. Some of those who flocked to the army in late 1914, in particular in rural districts, did so out of desperation. Soldiers received a guaranteed income, food and some form of lodgings. In towns and cities in which industry was concentrated in a few factories, many men joined Pals battalions, enlisting and fighting alongside their colleagues. Tunbridge Wells also had much less of a military tradition than Maidstone, with its extensive barracks, or Chatham and Sheerness, with their dockyards.

By the end of the year the *Courier* and the *Advertiser* regularly printed correspondence accusing the town's inhabitants of shirking their duty. One it became clear that the war would not be over soon, and the numbers of dead and wounded increased, men became less willing to get involved. Enlistment across Britain had tailed off by December at about 30,000 a week. The Borough Council organised a recruitment meeting at Tunbridge Wells Town Hall. Herbert Spender-Clay, the local Member of Parliament, shared the platform with Will Crooks, a well-known pro-war Labour MP, in what can only be regarded as an attempt to cut across anti-war sentiment and emphasise national unity.[429]

In 1915 the branch, for what would prove to be the last time, ran a series of campaigns on social issues under its own banner. In March, Margaret Bondfield and J G Webster addressed a meeting at

---

[428] *The Tunbridge Wells Advertiser October 23rd 1914, November 6th 1914; Justice November 5th 1914; the Labour Leader November 5th 1914.*
[429] *Kennedy, Hound p29; The Courier December 18th 1914.*

the Town Hall to condemn the increasing cost of food and coal. The BSP organised this meeting jointly with the Cooperative Society and a number of trade unions. One month later David Geer called for a penny an hour rise for carpenters and joiners. The money existed, as David Lloyd George had recently stated that the war so far had cost £350 million, and Geer wanted to get hold of some of it. The employers, now short of labour, quickly caved in. William George Veals reiterated the points about the cost of living in a letter to the Advertiser in May. The TWWWEC also continued to press the issue.[430]

Margaret Bondfield

More excitingly, the Tunbridge Wells branch managed to get hold of a report by Dr Burnet, the former Medical Officer for the town, who had been forced to resign in 1913. Leading councillors had suppressed this for many months. W J Reeves again came down from London to address a meeting on the Common in July. Dr Burnet, in his resignation letter, had hoped that that in future public health officials would be appointed directly by the State, to avoid them falling foul of parochial pettiness. He had reported on the overcrowding and slum districts of the North and East Wards, argued that the root cause of the problem was that 'the land of Tunbridge Wells did not belong to Tunbridge Wells' and that the system of private property had proved unable to provide for the needs of society.

Dr Burnet's conclusions were developed by Reeves and have remarkably contemporary resonance. The workers of Tunbridge Wells spent so high a proportion of their money on rent that they had to choose between their families becoming undernourished or reliance on charity. He demanded that baths be fitted to the town's houses. Reeves believed change would come when working class voters returned enough Socialists to the town council to sweep away the existing members. One of the most cocky right-wing councillors, Thomas Edwards, argued that Dr Burnet only had himself to blame for his predicament and stated that the electors

---

[430] *The Tunbridge Wells Advertiser March 26th 1915, April 30th 1915, May 21st & 28th 1915; Justice April 15th 1915.*

had often chosen a property owner over a working class candidate at elections. At the end of the rally, following a question from Edwards, Reeves demanded the compulsory registration of houses and restrictions on the number of people being permitted to live in them, while recognising that there were complexities around sub-letting.[431]

Yet in 1915 we hear little from the socialists about the war itself. The number of local men killed rose steadily. The worst single incident, which clearly underlined the waste of human life in the conflict, came in October 1915 when 129 Royal Engineers from the Tunbridge Wells district drowned as a result of the collision between their ship, the *HMS Hythe*, and a larger troopship, *HMS Sarnia* at Gallipoli. Such sacrifices, as well as growing state censorship about what could be published, allowed newspaper editors ready excuses to refuse to print anything critical about the conflict.

There was also a shift towards looking at the war's effects on individual liberties. In November 1914 the Government had posted a form to every residential address in Great Britain. It expected the head of the household to list the names of all men aged between 19 and 38 who lived at the address. For the first time it seemed likely that conscription, whether for the armed forces or to meet the needs of industry, would follow. A month later the ILP's Clifford Allen called for the formation of an organisation, the No-Conscription Fellowship, to organise resistance to being forced to fight. Industrial conscription also raised concerns, as trade unions could not organise under such conditions, while quasi-military systems of discipline might also follow.[432]

This campaign against conscription marked the coming of age for a generation of socialist activists. Young men and women tended to take the lead in its organisation. George Dutch was the most active member of the BSP's Tunbridge Wells branch. He wrote to one of the socialist newspapers to announce the formation of the Tunbridge Wells branch of the No-Conscription Fellowship. The date for this is not known but is believed to be before November 1915, by which time the national organisation had grown to fifty branches and five thousand members.[433]

---

[431] *The Tunbridge Wells Advertiser June 4th 1915. See also John Cunningham The Shock of War pp 20-21.*
[432] *Kennedy, Hound p30; The Labour Leader December 3rd 1914.*
[433] *George Dutch, Testimonial p4; Kennedy, Hound p55-6.*

The new branch elected H G Alexander to the Chair, Percy Saunders, a lay preacher, as Treasurer, and Edward Collison and Phillip Hamblin, both of Tonbridge, to the Committee. Percy Saunders' father, John Saunders, was the former East Ward Lib-Lab councillor, Justice of the Peace and a close ally of the socialists. Dutch's work initially revolved around lobbying sympathetic organisations. He later recalled that he used the Socialist Club in Western Road for his work, suggesting that the anti-war cause had near-unanimous support within the branch. The BSP's South-Eastern Counties Council voted to oppose conscription as early as September 1915. Tunbridge Wells' Women's Cooperative Guild also campaigned against conscription in January 1916, while Tonbridge Trades Council also opposed compulsion.[434]

The No-Conscription Fellowship focussed its attention on trying to recruit men who would be likely to be forced to join the military. Women and older men could join as associate members only, but, as time went on, later took up much of the work. A second organisation, open to all and with a much more political focus, formed at around the same time.

This, the National Council against Conscription, had strong trade union and labour movement links. Robert Smillie, leader of the National Union of Mineworkers, acted as President, and other activists such as George Lansbury, Margaret Bondfield and Clifford Allen joined its Executive. Thanks to a series of police raids, significant archive material from the organisation and its direct successor, the National Council for Civil Liberties, survives in the National Archives.

A Tunbridge Wells, Tonbridge and District Council against Conscription, one of only a small number of local branches, formed by no later than February 1916 though it changed its name to the Tunbridge Wells and District Council for Civil Liberties almost immediately. Those elected to the leadership give a sense of its support basc: George Dutch as Secretary, David Geer became the Treasurer and Sarah Candler , took the Chair. Lucy,, Sarah and Phyllis, Candler all made large donations to the organisation, while Horace Gundry Alexander served on its National Committee.[435]

---

[434] *The Labour Leader September 23rd 1915, January 6th & 27th 1916, National Archives KV/ 2/665.*
[435] *The Courier February 25th 1916;Tunbridge Wells Advertiser February 25th 1916.*

Few details about the organisation of the Tunbridge Wells branch of the BSP during the war years survive. George Dutch used the Socialist Club in Western Road as a correspondence address for his anti-war activities. Many leading activists had roles in other organisations, which must have reduced the amount of time that they could devote to the cause.

Dora Montefiore

Arthur Hickmott left the district completely, swapping Sevenoaks for Devon. The loss of such a strong voice for peace must have had an impact. Alf Killick, who believed that he did not have enough courage to be a conscientious objector, joined as a shoemaker in July 1915 and so avoided the fighting, and continued in this role until 1919. Offsetting these losses, two high profile veterans of the socialist, women's suffrage and peace movements moved to the Tunbridge Wells area. Dora Montefiore, who again became active in the BSP at about this time, decided to relocate to Crowborough, seven miles away, by the start of 1916. Whether she formally joined the Tunbridge Wells branch at this stage is not recorded though it is likely. Charlotte Despard moved to Upper Hartfield, a similar distance away, that August. Both places then had direct railway links to Tunbridge Wells. The No-Conscription Fellowship's Tunbridge Wells branch also had links to leading figures in the organisation. Violet Tillard, formerly of the Tunbridge Wells Women's Freedom League, ran the organisation's Publicity Department.[436]

The question of conscription had become urgent. The final attempt to recruit through voluntary means, introduced in late 1915 by the War Minister, Lord Derby, had not raised the numbers considered necessary. Parliament passed the Military Service (No. 2) Act on 28th January 1916 and it came into effect on 10th February that year. All unmarried men aged between eighteen and forty were deemed to be members of the military reserve and could be called up on short notice for active service. By March such letters began to arrive and a system of tribunals established to assess claims for exemption or deferment. The reports of those from Tunbridge Wells

---

[436] *Killick. Mutiny! p4; Kennedy, Hound p150.*

and neighbouring towns, carried in the local press or *the Tribunal*, the No-Conscription Fellowship's own journal, together with the official documentation held by the county archives in Maidstone, show that the anti-conscription cause had won significant support.

However the issue divided families and groups of friends. George Dutch's sister Daisy supported his stance, while his brother volunteered for the army, despite being under-age, serving until he was injured in the Palestine Campaign at Beersheba in 1917. This did not prevent his father being sacked and the family evicted from their tied cottage due to the prominent role George had taken in the campaign.[437]

In February 1916 George Dutch wrote to the *Tunbridge Wells Advertiser* from the Socialist Club to offer advice and assistance to any man wishing to claim partial or total exemption from military service. The editor added a note saying that he hoped that 'no one calling himself an Englishman will be mean and cowardly enough to take advantage of Mr Dutch's offer'.[438]

A few weeks later he corresponded with *Justice*, though he received a very hostile response. Conscientious objection, the editor believed, is no part of socialist doctrine but was something else such as Tolstoyism. The attacks became more personal. The *Courier* called for the tribunals to be held in public, not to ensure that they were fair, but to shame the conscientious objectors as a disgrace to their manhood. Other reactionary ideas resurfaced. The *Advertiser* claimed that the rash of strikes then taking place were the work of 'cosmopolitan agitators' – a phrase with anti-Semitic overtones – whose actions would harm the cause of labour.[439]

A number of men in Tunbridge Wells, Southborough, Tonbridge and Maidstone refused to be forced to fight. They first began to appear before the tribunals that March. George Dutch later condemned the panels as being made up of the local Conservative elite. William O'Sullivan, who had previously served in the military, only wanted a short deferment, which he received. Herbert Heskett appeared at a tribunal at Tonbridge Castle and obtained exemption from combatant service only, although this did not save him from derisory comments under the headline 'the whingings of the

---

[437] Dutch, G., *Testimonial*.
[438] *Tunbridge Wells Advertiser February 18th 1916*.
[439] *Justice April 6th 1916; The Courier March 3rd 1916; Tunbridge Wells Advertiser January 7th 1916, March 31st 1916*.

dodger'. He declared that, as a socialist, he had no religion except 'the religion of humanity'.

He subsequently attempted to gain full exemption at an appeal in Maidstone but Robert Vaughan Gower, who appeared for the military, raised the fact that he had been campaigning to discourage men from enlisting, as well as his previous service in the West Kent Volunteers before 1909, around the time he joined the socialists and no doubt radically changed his views. Heskett responded by saying that he did not wish to become a hired assassin. Although he refused to work for what he called the 'machinery of destruction' he seems to have obtained a job in industry. His brother Albert Ernest Heskett applied on similar grounds. Horace Gundry Alexander received exemption from military service only, but appealed and successfully won full exemption on account of his faith.[440]

Those who relied on socialism rather than religion received short shrift. Edward Collison, a clerk at the gas works in Tonbridge and a member of both the British Socialist Party and the Independent Labour Party, remained at liberty until April 1916. The authorities then took him into custody as his appeals had been exhausted. George Dutch suffered the same fate. Over half a century later he recalled their last few weeks of freedom. The Cooperative Society had to dismiss him, so the pair, with time on their hands, spent their time exploring the lanes of Kent, which Dutch remembered decades later as a very warm spring.

The first two conscientious objectors to be arrested in Kent were Collison and Phillip Hamblin, yet George Dutch remained at liberty long enough to attend the No-Conscription Fellowship's Convention as the Tunbridge Wells delegate. Hamblin had the luck to be rejected unexpectedly on medical grounds, and was subsequently left unmolested, while Collison was tied up and dragged around the parade ground for refusing orders. *The Worker's Dreadnought*, had earlier reported that both men had been told that they may be shot. The authorities in London also captured Douglas Bishop, who likewise faced fines and a spell of imprisonment.[441]

---

[440] *The Courier, March 10th 1916, April 21st 1916, May 5th 1916, June 16th 1916, July 7th 1916;Kent Archives C/A2/15/14F; Tunbridge Wells Advertiser March 10th 1916.*
[441] *Dutch, G.F., Anti-War pp1-5; Labour Leader May 11th 1916; Women's Dreadnought May 6th 1916.*

The bloody battles of 1916 meant that exemptions for married, generally older, men did not last long. The case of Caleb Clinch, a resident of High Brooms, is particularly moving. Now 37, he had long worked as an iron and brass moulder at Seale and Austen in Tonbridge. This employment had damaged his health and he now had a job at a farm near Cranbrook.

In June he stood before the Tribunal and declared that for ten years he had been against the capitalist system and believed in socialism. He recognised no nationality. He then noted that he was not rich enough to be able to vote, an argument which echoes both those of the women's suffrage movement in earlier years and the conscripts sent to Vietnam decades later. On the refusal of his application he condemned the tribunal as a 'capitalistic body living on the working man'.[442]

A network to support these men, sometimes operating in the shadows and at other times working in the open, grew up. Joseph Gundry Alexander travelled throughout rural parts of Kent and Sussex to visit conscientious objectors, attended tribunals across the region to show solidarity, and visited prisoners held at Maidstone every fortnight. John Saunders opened his house, 14 Dunstan Road, up to a number of conscientious objectors. As well as his son, Percy, H A Carter, who refused on both religious and political grounds, lived there, as did the Secretary of the No-Conscription Fellowship branch in 1917, P Douglas.[443]

The Tunbridge Wells branch of the BSP made a move in April 1916 which would have lasting repercussions for the political left in Britain.

No BSP conference had taken place in 1915. The branch nominated H Alexander, who subsequently became Treasurer of the national party, as their delegate for 1916, mandating him to support the internationalist position. It is not clear quite what links he had to the town. Divisions over the party's attitude to the war dominated the proceedings. The flashpoint came over the practical question of whether to hold some debates in secret to avoid prosecutions under the Defence of the Realm Act, something opposed by the pro-war faction. On the second day, Alexander accused Henry Mayers Hyndman and Dan Irving of helping the authorities to spy on him,

[442] *The Courier Friday 23rd June 1916, 16th January 1925.*
[443] *Alexander, H.G, Joseph Gundry Alexander pp196-99;, Kennedy, Hound p299.*

though he made it clear that he was speaking from a personal position rather than as the Tunbridge Wells delegate. Uproar followed. In what may have been a pre-planned gesture, several of the pro-war group walked out of the room.[444]

The BSP thereupon split. Those loyal to Hyndman formed a new organisation, the unfortunately-named National Socialist Party. The factions competed to be the true heirs of British Marxism, a contest which continued well after the National Socialist Party revived the name SDF in 1919 and the BSP had become the major component of the Communist Party of Great Britain a year later.

The branch embraced ever more radical ideas through reading several periodicals and newspapers. George Dutch recalled that these included *The Call,* established as an anti-war paper by members of the BSP, the *Worker's Dreadnought,* published by the 'wonderful girl, Sylvia Pankhurst' as the successor to the East London Federation of Suffragettes' *Women's Dreadnought* as well as Guy Aldred's anarchist periodical *The Word.* All took radically anti-war positions.[445]

By contrast Hyndman retained control of *Justice.* The paper at least published a strongly-worded letter from W G Veals in June. Veals warned that 'we are passing today [through] a period of most dangerous reaction in the United Kingdom'. He also attacked those Labour members who had either supported or not opposed conscription and therefore played 'into the hands of the ruling class to our undoing, as Hyndman very well knows'. This followed an article in *The Call* which condemned the Labour Party for refusing to pass a motion at its conference calling for the repeal of the Military Service Act and to end conscription.[446]

Events that spring moved quickly. The Tunbridge Wells and District Branch of the National Council for Civil Liberties had held its first meeting in the Town Hall in March 1916 which was addressed by Reverend Humphrey Chalmers, prospective Labour Candidate for Twickenham.

The minutes for its May meeting survive at the Imperial War Museum. George Lansbury had hoped to attend but could no longer do so. The Tunbridge Wells branches of the No-Conscription

---

[444] *The Call* 4th *May 1916; Lee and Archibold p237.*
[445] *Dutch, Anti-War pp 23 – 24.*
[446] *Justice June 29th 1916; The Call 4th May 1916.*

Fellowship, BSP, Peace Union and Amalgamated Society of Carpenters and Joiners, together with the Tonbridge branch of the ILP, had all affiliated, but fewer individuals had done so than they had hoped. They cautiously agreed to only print two hundred membership cards at this stage. A large minority had sympathy for the cause, but many feared prosecution under the Defence of the Realm Act or loss of business or employment were they to say so in public. They hoped that Dr John Clifford or Margaret Bondfield might be able to attend a subsequent meeting. What is most striking is the wide geographical area over which the organisation operated. They had already assisted Conscientious Objectors at Maidstone (1), Dunton Green (1), Sevenoaks (2), Ashford (7), Hastings (1), Lingfield (1), East Grinstead (2), Ightham (1), Speldhurst (2), Tonbridge (3), Chelsfield (3) and Tunbridge Wells (5). As well as those already referred to, the Committee now included W G Veals, A Heskett, Daisy Dutch, H White and W Doust Jnr. Edith Abbott and W G Veals had visited local trade union branches to urge them to affiliate. Yet the arrests of two supporters at Ashford and the fact that other activists would soon suffer this fate cast a cloud over the proceedings.[447]

Official attitudes turned sharply against the organisation. They booked the Town Hall again for a meeting that June but the Mayor refused to honour the booking and ordered the Chief Constable to seal the building. The Friends Meeting House allowed the meeting to take place there. Charlotte Despard and William Veals spoke and Sarah Candler, presided. The Easter Rising in Dublin, and in particular the execution of James Connolly, a former member of the SDF, perhaps meant that neither speaker held back. Those present later filed a report with the town's press. The *Advertiser* printed a comment under the title 'a disgraceful movement':

Charlotte Despard

A meeting of what is called the local No-Conscription Fellowship was held on Wednesday, but admission was refused to the press. I have since received an official report purporting to give a summary of the speeches delivered by Mrs Despard and Mr Veals

---

[447] IWM 7651.

etc. but I decline to print such mischievous and unnecessary rubbish, some of which might exercise a bad influence on the minds of selfish, weak-minded and unpatriotic individuals. Happily the Conscientious Objectors and other persons who have any sympathy with the objects advocated by the speakers at the meeting referred to are few in number, but it is a sad reflection that in a national crisis like this, when the help of every man and woman is badly wanted, there are so many. I wonder if these misguided cranks ever reflect on what would happen to England if we were defeated by Germany?

Such activities soon meant that the authorities acted against those who, being deemed absentees from the army, could be arrested. George Dutch had been lucky. Call-up notices for him had first been posted to an address in Forest Row, Sussex, the confusion presumably being because he lived in a road off Forest Road, Tunbridge Wells. New notices arrived at the correct location on 9th and 22nd May. A detective from the Borough's police force then stopped by at his house to arrest him.

George Dutch had gone for a walk, so the detective surprisingly agreed to return the next day. Dutch then appeared before the magistrates at Tunbridge Wells. The Chairman of the Bench, Colonel Rattray, fined Dutch to set an example, as he felt that there were many such cases in the district. He was then placed in the custody of his comrade James O'Sullivan, by now in the Army, and escorted to Tonbridge. O'Sullivan had offered to travel in another carriage so that Dutch did not feel embarrassed. Dutch later was taken to Maidstone, where he had recently seen Collison, and then served his first sentence at Canterbury Prison.

The socialist critique of war had influenced some of those who, however reluctantly, still supported it. A few days after the meeting and George Dutch's arrest, Lady Matthews, wife of the former Chief Justice of the Bahamas, wrote that 'Germans and English from the industrial classes had no real desire to stick cold steel into each other' and that the reasons for the war now seemed remote. She did not express these views in public but confined them to her diary.[448]

The National Council for Civil Liberties branch took the lead in agitating against the war. Sarah Candler, caused outrage by stating

---

[448] *Dutch, G.F., Anti-War pp1-5; The Courier June 2nd 1916; Tunbridge Wells Advertiser June 2nd 1916*

that soldiers on the Western Front had been given rum to 'arouse their animal instincts' before making a bayonet charge. The *Courier* published her letter in September, though the *Advertiser* refused to do so, ostensibly due to its length.

The NCCL held another public meeting that October at the Dudley Institute. Thomas Richardson, Labour MP for Whitehaven, spoke alongside Joseph Gundry Alexander, Sarah Candler, Percy Saunders and W G Veals. Mrs Abbott took the Chair. Richardson attacked the Defence of the Realm Act, the Munitions Act and the Military Service Act and Mrs Abbott condemned the fact that 'our liberties had disappeared before the God of War'. The role of the press and politicians for attacking civil liberties, and the smears against the distinguished philosopher Bertrand Russell, a leading figure in the anti-conscription movement, also stood condemned.[449]

For William George Veals, eligible for service, this was a courageous step. His period of freedom did not last much longer. He had earlier received a deferment due to his work, but now made a claim to be recognised as a conscientious objector. Like Collison and Dutch he refused non-combatant work. The Southborough Tribunal gave him short shrift, and on his removal from the witness box his wife condemned the panel for 'being perfect cowards for sending other men to death when you don't mean to go yourselves'. Veals became the third member of the branch to be imprisoned.[450]

What though of the economic situation? It might be assumed that the bargaining power of those workers, male and female, who remained in the district had been enhanced by the loss of so many working men to the armed forces. Initially there seems to have been something of an industrial truce, no doubt driven by a sense of patriotism and also the efforts of national and local government to avoid strikes.

Union membership nationally rose 50% during the war years and Tunbridge Wells probably followed this trend. In March 1916 the Painters Union negotiated a penny rise per hour. Inflation soon bit deep into the pockets of working families. David Geer wrote to the *Advertiser* in July to point out that a sovereign had lost between

---

[449] *The Courier September 29th 1916, October 13th 1916; Tunbridge Wells Advertiser October 13th 1916; Logan, A., 'Home and Away'. For Charlotte Despard, see Linklaker, A., An unhusbanded life: Charlotte Despard, suffragette, socialist and Sinn Feiner, (London: Hutchinson 1980) esp. pp86-7, 94-7, 188-194;; Dutch. Testimonial p4..*
[450] *Tunbridge Wells Advertiser November 3rd 1916.*

twenty and forty percent of its value since the start of the war. Jack Jones of the National Union of Gasworkers and General Labours and a West Ham councillor, visited the town the same month. Two hundred members of the Carpenters and Joiners threatened industrial action in September.

A strike at the two firms which refused brought both into line within a matter of hours. The cost of living also allowed scope for socialist propaganda which the local press found hard to supress. Thus the TWWWEC argued at the beginning of 1917 that things would not improve while the means of production lay in the hands of the few. An April Sir George Askwith successfully mediated in a dispute between the Gasworkers and General Labourers Union and the Corporation[451]

The fate of members of the branch continued to feature in the columns of the local press. Members went through a cycle of imprisonment, formal release back into the armed forces, then a further spell of incarceration for refusing to follow orders.

Edward Collison refused an offer of work towards the war effort at Warwick. He received a further prison sentence and a 40s fine.

In an episode which demonstrates the strength of the anti-war movement in trade union circles, the town's Tribunal approached the Trades Council for two members to be co-opted to represent the interests of the labour movement, as required by the National Service Act (but ignored in many cases).

The Trades Council elected David Geer to the post, though it appears that they found some pretext to keep him off the panel. Instead he set out what he considered to be the minimum level of pay for a family of five: the *Courier* summarised his letter.[452]

[451] *Tunbridge Wells Advertiser March 10th 1916, 7th July 1916, September 15th 1916; The Courier September 15th 1916, January 19th 1917; Barker, R., 'Political Myth: Ramsay MacDonald and the Labour Party' in History Volume 61 (1976) p47.*
[452] *The Courier March 16th 1917, April 6th & 13th 1917, May 11th 1917; Kennedy Hound p40.*

CREST OF MOUNT PLEASANT, TUNBRIDGE WELLS.

Corporation workmen at Tunbridge Wells sweeping the streets and collecting refuse. These workers became increasingly militant as their pay was eaten up by inflation in the last years of the war. Dudley Road, which housed the Dudley Institute, is pictured below. The Institute allowed peace activists to meet, but removed some seditious material from its library

DUDLEY ROAD, TUNBRIDGE WELLS. J.R. 878.

261

CHAPTER 14   BETWEEN
RUSSIA AND THE PARLIAMENTARY LABOUR PARTY

It is apposite to be writing this book about a century after the events described in this chapter took place.

The Soviet Union, of course, is no more. Few people alive today will remember when thousands of people in Britain, and millions around the world, considered it a beacon lighting the way to a future of peace, prosperity and fraternity. The old Social-Democrats of Britain, in common with their Continental peers, were deeply divided in their attitudes towards the new state. But the very fact that Russia had entered a period of revolution, culminating in a country claiming to be socialist, made similar developments seem possible across Europe.

Perhaps surprisingly for a revolutionary party, the SDF and its successors had, apart from a few years in the late 1880s, thought little about how capitalism would be overthrown. The same can be said for virtually all other British and Western European socialists. The obvious answer, to which few could object, lay in winning as many people as possible to the cause, and to kick thoughts of an uprising into the long grass.

In 1906 the branch declared that the social revolution was not likely to start in Tunbridge Wells as the town was full of 'modest folk' but concluded that the town 'shall 'arrive' all the same'.[453] They might agitate for reforms, support strikes and engage in a serious study of Karl Marx's writings, but the idea of trying to use force to overthrow the government rarely appeared on the agenda. Many envisaged a gradual process rather than a clear break. Keir Hardie believed that, as more socialists won election to local and national governments, the world may wake up some morning to find that Socialism had come.

Perhaps even more significantly, Will Thorne feared that an unofficial dispute at the gasworks in Beckton in the early 1890s might have led to a general strike which would perhaps have developed into a civil war. He did his best to bring it to an end. Tom Mann may have been won to syndicalism but even he generally acted a little more cautiously after his spell of imprisonment.

---

[453] *Justice July 21st 1906.*

The Russian Revolutions of 1917 changed everything. The February Revolution initially appeared to set the country on a course towards parliamentary democracy, shattering Tsarism and putting an end to centuries of racial and religious discrimination. However the provisional government remained committed to fighting with Britain, France and Italy. The Russian Army, of which 76.31% had been killed, wounded or captured by summer 1917, was disintegrating, something hastened by the Bolsheviks encouraging soldiers to desert and return to their villages.[454]

Most people welcomed the revolution. The Tunbridge Wells Women's Liberal Association hailed the emancipation of Russia from the yoke of despotism. This, combined with moves towards giving women in Britain the vote, meant the world stood at the threshold of a new era. Reverend A W Oliver, Vicar of King Charles the Martyr, also welcomed the news. Yet, as well as resurrecting the Russian Duma, the revolution also brought the formation of soldiers' and workers' councils – the soviets – and a struggle for legitimacy between the various factions, particularly the Bolsheviks and Mensheviks. Developments in Russia, conveyed to the incarcerated members of the branch, revived their spirits.[455]

> 'Comrade W G Veals of Tunbridge Wells BSP, recently released from Wormwood Scrubs, has been sentenced again to two years' hard labour for refusing to obey orders. The news of the Russian Revolution, received whilst in prison, gave him fresh inspiration and he wrote to us in a very cheery and hopeful strain before going back to prison'.

> Two other members of the Tunbridge Wells branch are also standing as absolutists. Comrade G Dutch was sentenced at his fourth court-martial to three years' penal servitude. Comrade F Collison is serving his sentence of two years in Maidstone Gaol.[456]

The events of the next few months are amongst the most intriguing parts of this history, though also the most mysterious. On 3rd June 1917 a very large conference took place in Leeds. George Lansbury described this as the 'most representative gathering of socialists, progressives, labour men and women'. In light of the subversive nature of the discussions it is not surprising that there is no list of

---

[454] Shukman, War or Revolution, p35.
[455] The Courier April 27th 1917; Tunbridge Wells Advertiser April 6th 1917; George Dutch, Testimonial p13.
[456] The Call July 26th 1917.

the names of the delegates. Yet Dora Montefiore and Charlotte Despard spoke from the platform, and H Alexander, the branch's conference delegate from the previous year, joined the Central Committee. The 1,150 delegates included 88 from the BSP, 209 from Trades Councils, as well as representatives from women's organisations, Cooperatives, adult schools and the National Council for Civil Liberties. Perhaps 3,500 attended in total. Tunbridge Wells could therefore have sent a large delegation and had strong connections to several of the leading participants.

There is some debate about the aims of the convention. Some delegates regarded it as a pacifist gathering while others wished to make a revolution. Yet most participants recognised its significance. Fred Jowett later regarded the Leeds Convention as the highest point of revolutionary fervour he had ever experienced. George Lansbury considered it a turning point, though differences between the ILP and British Socialist Party meant that it achieved less than might otherwise have been the case.[457]

The most startling calls made at the Convention were to establish extra-Parliamentary Soviets with executive powers in every town, urban and rural district throughout the country. These would work to bring an end to the war on the movement's terms and then, in less well worked out ways, fully emancipate the working class from capitalism. Some of those who spoke in support of the motion urged delegates to see it as a revolutionary moment, even the long-awaited dictatorship of the proletariat, while others wished to deal with specific issues such as the welfare of discharged soldiers.

Having agreed to establish them, few had detailed knowledge of the situation in Russia. Tom Quelch helpfully wrote an article for *The Call* on the subject of '*the workmen and soldiers' council - about how to set them up*'. A fortnight later he explained that soviets should be 'constituted so that they cover the whole of the local trades unions, labourers, socialist, Cooperative and democratic organisations'. Regional conferences to co-ordinate the work of the local soviets

---

[457] White, S., 'Soviets in Britain: The Leeds Convention of 1917' in *International Review of Social History (Cambridge University Press) Volume 19, Issue 2 (August 1974),pp. 165-193; Lansbury, G. My Life (London: Constable 1928) p158, What Happened At Leeds.https://www.marxists.org/history/international/social-democracy/1917/ leeds.htm

would follow: that for the southern counties was timetabled to meet at Southampton on 12th August.[458]

The developments provoked a backlash. Basil Home Thomson, the head of Scotland Yard's Criminal Investigation Department, had believed for some time that pacifism, anti-conscription and revolution were inextricably mixed. He particularly despised Jews and the Irish, for what can only be racist reasons. Steven White has pointed out that the cabinet became concerned at what was happening. The press was requested not to give the soviets coverage. Venues for several regional conferences, including Southampton, were cancelled at short notice, while leaflets claiming that participants had guided German bombers were distributed in pubs in districts of London which had sustained casualties. In London, Swansea and Newcastle mobs broke up the regional conferences while the police refused to intervene. . [459]

For all that, however, most historians consider the call to form soviets to have fallen flat, with the possible exception of Glasgow. Away from the Clyde, however, some of the most significant events took place at Tunbridge Wells and Sevenoaks. On 24th June men from the Royal Sussex, Middlesex, Royal West Kent and the (East Kent) Buffs formed the Tunbridge Wells Workmen's and Soldiers' Council. All these regiments were local and would have contained Tunbridge Wells men (Alf Killick had joined the Middlesex while George Dutch nominally had been allocated to the Buffs).

It is a matter of conjecture as to what had happened in the three weeks after the Leeds Convention. This work would have required obtaining and distributing printed material and organising clandestine meetings with soldiers. Little, of course, was written down as civilians engaged in these activities could have faced long prison terms while soldiers may even have been shot for mutiny. Many of the twelve resolutions passed by the Tunbridge Wells Soviet concerned better treatment for soldiers, such as improving the quality of the food. Two others had a more political focus: soldiers should not be used on civilian work, in particular to break strikes, and that the Government should reduce or eliminate censorship.

---

[458] White, S., 'Soviets in Britain'; The Call June 21st 1917, July 5th & 19th 1917.
[459] Thomson, B., H., Queer People (Criminals) (London: Hodder and Stoughton) p269; White, S., 'Soviets in Britain.

The one which caused most alarm in the War Office and Scotland Yard called on the government to state clearly on what terms it would negotiate a ceasefire. Thomson later wrote that:

> 'Some attempt was made among soldiers awaiting demobilisation to organise support for a local soviet among the troops, but there was little response'.

His statement suggests that the impetus had come from outside the army, working with soldiers sympathetic to the idea. In late July the Secretary of State for War, Lord Derby, expressed concern about what had happened recently at Tunbridge Wells and Birmingham, though he felt that events in Kent had been effectively dealt with by the officers in charge. Unsurprisingly these events did not reach the local or national press.[460]

One small snippet of the agitation of this period has survived in the pages of the *Tunbridge Wells Advertiser*. The title of the lecture, delivered by W E Doust at the High Brooms Adult School, was the 'Tragedies of Peace'. Those responsible for ensuring that the Defence of the Realm Act was not breached may have been satisfied that it was entirely about the civilian sphere. Yet Doust weaved together the fate of those killed in industry and the men killed on the battlefield. Life expectancy of those working in the 'unwholesome trades' was only 29, whereas the upper classes could expect to die at 55. Millions were killed before their time in the pursuit of commercial prosperity. These sacrifices to 'the great Moloch of Capitalism (industrialism)' were even greater than those to the God of War. He then made what can only be regarded as a call for revolution and criticised the supporters of the 'so-called Social Reforms as these only tended to palliate some of the worst excesses of the social system'.[461]

Things soon died down. Basil Home Thomson felt that the soviet movement in Britain was moribund by 17th October 1917. Yet he later wrote that at the end of that autumn there was another attempt to set one up, this time at Sevenoaks. He believed that all this intended to represent the views of the rank and file to the commanding officers, and that it fell flat when the 'leisure which allowed the agitation took place' ended on the units being sent

---

[460] Thomson, B, *Queer People* p287; Jones, C., Tunbridge Wells Civic Society 'A First World War Soldiers' Soviet in Tunbridge Wells?'; National Archives memo from Lord Derby to the War Cabinet 26th July 1917.
[461] *Tunbridge Wells Advertiser* August 3rd 1917.

overseas, where they 'had other things to think about'. The latter point is credible, but if its aims had been so limited it seems a little surprising that he accorded it such prominence. As already discussed, both the socialist and the peace movements in Tunbridge Wells, Tonbridge and Sevenoaks had very strong links.[462]

Perhaps these attempts at forming soviets were a few months premature. Thomson believed that they had failed because of working class anger that Bolshevik Russia had concluded a separate peace, thereby lengthening the war and betraying their former allies.

Yet patience began to wear thin. The diaries of Lady Matthews, held at the Imperial War Museum, record how extreme the queues for food had become. Shops opened at unpredictable hours and women stood for much of the day in Calverley and Camden Roads in the hope of securing provisions. The Advertiser reported that by January 1918 the rumour that margarine might become available at the Maypole Dairy in Calverley Road meant queues formed by six in the morning, growing to four or five hundred by the time that the shop opened at eight.[463]

Working class families also had to cope with the rapid inflation in food prices. In September the Kent Federation of Trades Councils passed a resolution, submitted by Tonbridge Trades Council, which demanded that the Food Controller end such rises, and attacked the 'exploitation of workers by profiteers'. Lady Matthews felt that strikes were on the way. The Amalgamated Society of House Decorators and Painters at Tunbridge Wells struck for a penny rise per hour in September 1917. Non-union members supported the dispute. An offer of a half-penny rise was refused, and a 'prominent labour figure from Manchester' negotiated with the employer.

The strike had succeeded in its aims by end of the month. The unions decided against a victory parade. The following month members of the National Union of General Labourers asked for a pay rise from Tunbridge Wells Corporation and in the private building trade, while the Carpenters and Joiners also won a penny per hour increase in late November. The National Union of General

---

[462] National Archives, Thomson, B., 'Bolshevism in England' 23 December 1917, FO 371/3300.
[463] Tunbridge Wells Advertiser January 25th 1918.

Workers then demanded a tuppence per hour or ten shilling a week increase in January 1918, a demand conceded in February.[464]

Activists continued to bring socialist and anti-war material to the townspeople. The Treasurer of the Dudley Institute, where the Social-Democrats had once held their meetings, found that unknown people had left papers which 'came very near to breaching the Defence of the Realm Act'. The Committee therefore instructed the Librarian to remove them immediately. However Alfred Bishop reported that members of the Institute wanted access to progressive literature as well as the mainstream local and national papers. He therefore asked to be allowed to place the *Labour Leader*, *Herald* and the *New Age* on the table, something the Committee agreed to consider. The Dudley Institute, which had hosted anti-war meetings, seems to have been one of the more tolerant of such working men's clubs.[465]

Yet, amid the signs of revolutionary ferment, a series of significant changes pointed the way towards a constitutional road to socialism. The Representation of the People Act passed into law on 6th February 1918. Most men aged over twenty-one now had the vote, although conscientious objectors were specifically disenfranchised. Some women aged over thirty also had the right to vote. For all the inadequacies of the Act, the size of the electorate swelled.

The new opportunities this presented, together with the questions posed by revolutionary Russia, led to a complete reform of the Labour Party's internal structures, something driven by Arthur Henderson, its leader since 1914, and the Webbs. A special conference of the Labour Party in January and February 1918 approved the party's reorganisation. The Labour Party now intended to create a skeleton organisation in every constituency. A handful of branches had permitted individual membership before 1914.

This model would now be rolled out across the country. Individual members would join an organisation based in their electoral ward, and these would elect representatives for their Parliamentary Division. This, of course, represented a very different form of organisation to that adopted by the British Socialist Party at

---

[464] *The Courier September 14th & 21st & 28th 1917, October 5th & 26th 1917 and November 30th 1917, January 4th 1918 and February 8th 1918; Tunbridge Wells Advertiser February 8th 1918. Lady Matthews' diaries are in the Imperial War Museum, reference 17087.*
[465] *The Courier January 25th 1918.*

Tunbridge Wells, or the for that matter the local Fabian Society, the Tonbridge branch of the Independent Labour Party or the Trades and Labour Councils. While the increase in union membership gave the latter a boost, the former organisations, still affiliated to the Labour Party, also saw their influence wane as the national parties to which they belonged lost influence to the new Constituency Parties and the Trade Union block vote.[466]

January 1918 saw another development in Labour Party thinking, and one which attracted considerable interest in Tunbridge Wells. The report *Labour and the New Social Order* pledged the party to reconstruct society itself. Attacking the human cost of the war, profiteering, wage slavery and the perversion of the idea of the 'survival of the fittest', it pointed to a future in which fraternity would replace fighting and co-operation supplant competition. It also criticised imperialism. In many ways it argued for a vision similar to that first set out by the SDF in the 1880s.

The detailed proposals set out later in the pamphlet failed to match such sweeping ambitions, and some, such as the democratic control of industry, could be interpreted in many different ways, yet taken together it still meant that the party had shifted significantly leftwards. James Richards intended to give a lecture on the report at the TWWWEC meetings in mid-January and early February but they had to be postponed for health reasons. Yet it is likely that the pamphlet circulated widely, not least amongst the BSP's membership, and its strengths and shortcomings would have been debated.[467]

The TWWWEC seems to have been radicalised by the new mood. It particularly hardened its stand against anything which could assist conscription. In February it attacked the use of questions in the ration system which might assist in the conscription of working people into factories, and also lead to more employment of children. The following month it condemned attempts to introduce basic military training in schools. Its leading lights pushed trade union demands. David Geer worked hard to recruit new members of the National Union of General Workers, formerly the National Union of Gasworkers and General Labourers, that spring. In April and May

---

[466] See Pelling, H., *Short History* pp 40-45; Berger, S., *The British Labour Party* p 91-92,

[467] The Labour Party, *Labour and the New Social Order* (Manchester: National Labour Press 1918); *The Courier* January 25th and February 8th 1918.

they ran a campaign for those in the town's Electricity Workers to receive a bonus to cover the rising cost of living.[468]

Events in June showed how close society had come to fracturing under the pressures of military losses and food shortages. Anger was not confirmed to those on the radical left. George Dutch's view was that tribunals in Kent tended to be filled with reactionary Conservative elements. There must be some truth to this, yet the Southborough Tribunal now went so far as to declare itself to be on strike. A food wholesaler, Mr Puttock, had been granted a time-limited exemption to arrange cover for his business, yet the military authorities had ignored this decision and taken him to barracks. As a result, a large amount of food had been wasted.

Very significantly, the tribunal placed the blame fully on Robert Vaughan Gower. The strike lasted about three weeks. Puttock was released, but the Chair of the Southborough Tribunal made it abundantly clear that their criticism of Gower still stood. The Tribunal went on strike a second time that October.[469]

Another factor came into play. Large numbers of servicemen, many of them injured in the fighting or suffering from disease, had begun to return to the district, as happened across the country. Many also felt that, once the fighting ceased, much larger numbers of men would suddenly return home. Memories of the end of the Boer War, and perhaps even of the much larger dislocation which had followed the end of the Napoleonic Wars, meant that many feared a massive increase in unemployment and attempts to drive down wages. The National Federation of Demobilised Soldiers and Sailors formed a branch in the town in June.

The chair of the first meeting, Brigadier Malcolm, noted that the district already had 500 or 600 invalided soldiers. In September he declared political neutrality. The organisation was not under the control of 'Liberal, Tory, Socialist, Labour, Pacifist, Anhilist (sic) or Anarchist' factions, yet he pointedly compared the plight of a widow on 8 pence a day with the Dowager Duchess of Saxe-Coburg and Gotha, who, while residing in Germany, had received £6,000 a year from the British taxpayer. In general the Federation has been regarded as a radical organisation, and its numbers would only

---

[468] *Tunbridge Wells Advertiser February 1st & 8th 1918, March 22nd 1918, April 5th 1918 and May 3rd 1918.*
[469] *Tunbridge Wells Advertiser June 7th & 28th 1918, October 4th 1918; The Courier June 7th & 28th 1918..*

grow in the coming months. Their old ally Alf Cobb, demobilised following injury in 1918, joined the Committee of the Hastings branch of the Federation and won election as its nominee to the Borough Council there in 1920.[470]

These connections became apparent at Tunbridge Wells. In July, Councillor Berwick, who had previously sat as the Labour Representative on the Tunbridge Wells Tribunal, chaired a meeting of the Tunbridge Wells and District Council for Civil Liberties. He had also become active in the National Federation of Demobilised Soldiers and Sailors. Three of his sons had joined the army, one was a prisoner of war in Germany, yet he strongly opposed the introduction of military training into schools. The meeting also condemned the use of religious and political tests to prevent otherwise qualified candidates from becoming teachers. The meeting may have been more restrained than previous gatherings of the organisation, yet it is interesting that both the *Advertiser* and the *Courier* gave it significant column space.[471]

The attempts to form Soviets at Tunbridge Wells and Sevenoaks in 1917 had a fascinating sequel almost exactly a year later, which deserves to be better known. The origin of this lay in the Anglo-Russian Military Convention, agreed between the short-lived Kerensky Government and Britain. Russians of military age were given a month to return to Russia or be conscripted into the British Army.[472]

One of those affected, Harris Klugman, a Russian of Jewish-German ancestry then living in Silverdale Road, High Brooms, had appeared before a tribunal in October 1917 and argued that the state of his native country following the Bolshevik Revolution meant that he could not return. He also claimed exemption as a conscientious objector and as he had a family to support. His appeal failed (interestingly no record of this is in the county archives at Maidstone) and arrest followed in January 1918.

By mid-August 1918 about a thousand men in a similar situation had been assembled at the Wildernesse Camp, Sevenoaks, while the authorities decided what to do with them. The Conscientious

---

[170] *Tunbridge Wells Advertiser June 21st 1918; The Courier June 21st 1918, September 6th 1918; Matthews, Cobb, p113 and p12.*
[471] *Tunbridge Wells Advertiser July 19th 1918; The Courier July 19th 1918.*
[472] *Shukman, War or Revolution, p80-81.*

Objectors' newspaper *The Tribunal* learned of an attempt at mutiny that month:

> 'The Russian subjects, Poles, Jews, Russians and others, who have been forcefully conscribed for the Army on the strength of the convention made by the British Government with Kerensky, and some of whom have even volunteered, now learn from the Press that the Allied Armies are fighting the people in Russia just like German imperialism'.

Supporters smuggled out an appeal to the British working class signed by 160 of the men. Sending them to France to fight Germans would free up British forces to go to Russia and thereby prolong the war. All bar 60 of the men in the camp were Jewish, and many now considered the Bolsheviks to be the legitimate government of Russia.[473]

During the last five months of 1918 Tunbridge Wells saw some of the most significant strikes for several years. The Painters Union took action for three weeks in August before reaching agreement to return to work for eleven pence and hour with a further penny to follow from 5th October. Ninety two members of the Amalgamated Society of Carpenters and Joiners managed to negotiate a pay rise to 1s 11 ½ an hour in October. The most disruptive action came later in the month when municipal workers took action, despite the union supporting an earlier agreement reached with the Borough Council. The *Advertiser* reported that only two men turned up to work at the Pembury Waterworks, the roads were left unswept and graves could not be dug. This lasted for ten days and shows that the grassroots had become more militant than the union's leaders. They failed to win a pay rise but at least retained their jobs and previous terms and conditions.[474]

This militancy coincided with attempts to win the labour movement political power in the district. The BSP, Fabian Society and ILP, together with most of the significant trade unions, were all affiliated to the National Labour Party, yet it had no formal organisational presence in the district. Labour's new commitment to nationalisation, through clause four of its revised constitution,

---

[473] *Tunbridge Wells Advertiser January 18th 1918; The Courier January 18th 1918; The Tribunal August 16th 1918.*
[474] *Tunbridge Wells Advertiser August 2nd & 23rd 1918, October 4th ,18th & 25th 1918; The Courier August 23rd 1918, November 1st 1918.*

seemed to build on the ideas contained *in Labour and the New Social Order.*

The relative lateness of Tunbridge Wells (and for that matter, Tonbridge) to take steps towards forming labour parties in the constituency contrasts with other places where the left had much less of a presence: a Divisional Labour Party had formed at East Grinstead as early as 20th July 1918. E J Pay had assisted in the work there. Some local activists were uncertain as to the way forward. However the facts that the war seemed to be drawing to an end, that it was known that a General Election would be called after the cessation of hostilities, and that the new franchise brought in under the Representation of the People Act 1918 would give votes to many working class residents for the first time, focussed minds.[475]

Concrete moves followed at the end of October. The *Courier* reported that the Labour Party organiser who had been working at East Grinstead had also been active in the Tonbridge and Sevenoaks Divisions. On 3rd November the TWWWEC noted that moves had started to form a branch of the National Labour Party at Tunbridge Wells. The town's Trades and Labour Council also voted to support the initiative.[476]

The pace then picked up. First a branch formed at Tonbridge. On 12th November the Tunbridge Wells branch held its first meeting. Councillor Berwick chaired while E J Pay gave an address outlining his hopes for the new branch. Some slight differences followed: J G Povey of the Typographers Union wanted all present to know that he was 'not a member of the Social-Democratic Federation' though he still considered himself to be a socialist.

The Armistice had been signed the day before, and Pay and Berwick both made reference to the needs of returning servicemen, while Povey made pointed remarks about shirkers and revolutionists, making it clear that he would only support those he considered *bona fide* trade unionists. He later criticised Geer for supporting the right of his friend, Mr Urban, to resume his trade. Yet the motion to form the branch was carried unanimously. Shortly afterwards the Tunbridge Wells branch confirmed that it included the separate Urban District of Southborough.

---

[475] *The Courier August 9th 1918.*
[476] *The Courier November 1st 1918, November 8th 1918.*

The formation of town branches at Tunbridge Wells and Tonbridge allowed the creation of a provisional committee to form the Divisional Labour Party for Tonbridge. Councillor Berwick at one stage considered standing for Parliament as the nominee of the Discharged Soldiers and Sailors Federation but withdrew. The committee instead selected as their candidate Jack Palmer, an activist from the London and Provincial Vehicle Workers' Union who had recently helped set a branch up in Tunbridge Wells. David Geer was elected Agent, with R Norton, the Divisional Secretary, as his assistant. They hired committee rooms in both Camden Road and Tonbridge High Street, showing from where they expected their strongest support to come.

Col. . Spender-Clay

Unlike their opponents, they had only a single vehicle, and the boundless energy of E J Pay, to try and reach rural voters, but the uphill struggle their candidate faced in rural parts of the constituency is shown by the fact that Palmer only received four nomination papers while the Tory, Colonel Spender-Clay, got 31 and the Liberal, Captain Buxton 22, the latter amounting to one from almost every parish in the Division. Only at Tunbridge Wells, Tonbridge and Southborough would Labour realistically expect to pick up a decent share of the vote.

All this activity, as well as the support of unlikely socialists, such as Reverend C E Raven of Tonbridge School, led to a very lively contest. The *Courier* declared Tonbridge to be conspicuously red. Colonel Spender-Clay received a hostile response from the workers at the Whitefriars Press and the union there organised a strike for the day of the poll. The railway unions in both towns worked hard to get the vote out. Large numbers of newly enfranchised women enthusiastically queued to cast their vote in the East Ward of Tunbridge Wells. The Conservatives, perhaps sensing that their main opponent would now be Labour, deluged the district with handbills and flyers calling Jack Palmer a revolutionary and arguing that their candidate would punish 'the Hun'.

Wives & Mothers of Soldiers

WHICH WILL YOU SUPPORT ?

JACK PALMER
(THE SOCIALIST REVOLUTIONARY)

Who boasts that he has been fortunate enough to stay at home during the War;

OR

Colonel SPENDER-CLAY

Who has been fighting alongside of your husbands and sons, and is out to make Germany pay for the War and to keep out the Hun ?

Your Men are away; Vote as **THEY** would wish.

DO NOT BETRAY THEM.

Printed and Publi hed by the "Courier" Printing and Publishing Co., Ltd., 19, Grove Hill Road, Tunbridge Wells.

Wives and Mothers of Soldiers !

The Discharged Men's Reply
TO
Spender-Clay's Leaflet

The following resolution was unani-mously carried at a Meeting held on Wednesday, December 11th :—

"That this Meeting of the Tonbridge Branch of the Discharged and De-mobilised Soldiers' and Sailors' Federation, after considering replies to questions from the three candi-dates, decides to give its whole-hearted SUPPORT to the LABOUR CANDIDATE, Mr. J. PALMER, and to do all in its power to return him at the Head of the Poll on Saturday next."

The above Resolution is the opinion of the men who have returned.

Your husbands and sons are away. VOTE for the man who believes in JUSTICE and not CHARITY.

Printed and published by The Whitefriars Press, Ltd., Medway Wharf, Tonbridge.

The Conservative leaflet appealing to newly-enfranchised women voters.

The Labour response ostensibly from discharged men, since still-enlisted men were disbarred from responding.

The Tonbridge Branch of the Discharged and Demobilised Soldiers and Sailors Federation responded with a leaflet of their own, printed at the Whitefriars Press, urging the wives and mothers of soldiers to support Palmer.

Conservative tactics seem to have worked, though the fact that Labour had only two weeks in which to campaign also did damage. On 28th December the results were announced. Labour had secured 5,006 votes, while Colonel Spender-Clay took 14,622, a majority of 9,816. Captain Buxton only gained 1,851.

Jack Palmer, on leaving Tunbridge Wells Town Hall, immediately went to Lime Hill Road to address a rally of his supporters. He discussed the relative poverty of his party and hoped that Labour would triumph in future. Across the Channel, Alf Killick waited anxiously for the result. He had decorated his tent with pictures of

275

a series of socialists, including Karl Marx, as well as a photograph of Jack Palmer, and surreptitiously made arrangements to distribute Labour's *Daily Herald* and other socialist material to his comrades.

Across the country, Labour may have been slightly disappointed to only secure 57 seats, only fifteen more than at the previous General Election, and about 21% of the vote. .[477]

Radical activities continued in Tunbridge Wells for several decades after 1920. The report (below) from the *Courier* of October 16th 1936 records the routing of Oswald Mosley's Blackshirts when they attempted to hold a rally in Tunbridge Wells.

TURBULENT ANTI-FASCIST SCENES

Fascists Pelted with Fish, Eggs and Tomatoes

MAGNIFICENT COURAGE OF THE POLICE

Mayor's Stern Warning to Demonstrators

DISTURBANCE CAUSED BY IMPORTATIONS

Turbulent scenes, reminiscent to a larger degree of the liveliness which used to be prevalent during general elections before the war, were witnessed in Tunbridge Wells on Saturday night, when a contingent of Fascists, to the number of about 30 or 40, descended on the town from outlying districts. Thousands of people congregated at the Five Wares, outside the Opera House and the top of Mount Pleasant, while Camden-road and Calverley-road near the entrance to Newton-road were choc-a-bloc with the crowds which impeded road traffic. Every available police officer was on duty under the personal command of the Chief Constable (Mr. Guy Carlton), but on the arrival of the Fascists many in the crowd became unruly, and directly the leader of the contingent made an attempt to speak there was a shower of missiles, including eggs, tomatoes, over ripe pears and even kippers and lumps of meat.

The police held the crowds in check with a calmness which is deserving of the greatest praise. They dealt with the situation with a wonderful sense of humour, yet at the same time asserting their authority in such a way as to be able to escort the Fascists away from Newton-road when speech-making was found to be impossible. After running the gauntlet they escaped from the anger of the crowd, and took their departure in vehicles which had been left in the Fire Station yard. There were no serious casualties, though it was only with difficulty that the police could save several women from being trodden on when they fell among the surging crowds.

[477] *The Courier January 3rd 1919; Killick, Mutiny! pp 7-10.*

CHAPTER 15 AFTERMATH

The organisational unity of the Labour movement at this time did not mean that everyone was fully committed to the parliamentary road to Socialism.

Tactics varied according to the situations people found themselves in. Alf Killick demonstrates this clearly. In 1919 he was one of the leading activists in what historians have said was the largest mutiny in British history. There had been a long history of abuse and poor working conditions at Valdelievre Camp on the outskirts of Calais. In January many took strike action. This spread to other military bases in the region. They organised themselves on the basis of the early Russian Soviets. Each tent elected a delegate to a Camp Committee, which in turn elected a Central Committee, the Calais Area Soldiers' and Sailors' Committee. The authorities sent units to try and re-establish order, yet these joined the rebellion. The men marched *en masse* through the nearby town, forging links with French sympathisers.

This was only one of a series of revolts amongst soldiers and sailors that month: similar events took place at Southwick, Folkestone, Dover, Osterley Park, Shortlands, Westerham Hill, Felixstowe, Grove Park, Shoreham, Aldershot, Kempton Park, Southampton, Maidstone, Blackpool, Park Royal, Chatham, Fairlop and Biggin Hill, many of which are in close proximity to Tunbridge Wells.[478]

In 1919 the members of the branch who had been guests of His Majesty returned to the town. George Dutch's last months of imprisonment had been very eventful. At the end of 1918 he had decided, with a group of other prisoners, to go on hunger strike. On 6th January 1919 he was released under the infamous 'Cat and Mouse Act', originally passed to prevent suffragettes from starving themselves to death in protest at being denied political prisoner status.

A group of prisoners assembled at the house of a supporter in London's Hackney and agreed that if any of their number were recalled to prison they would all turn up at the gates and demand re-admission, and then resume their hunger strike. One was

---

[478] *Killick, Mutiny! pp7-10. See also Tatchell, P., 'WW1: The hidden story of soldier's mutinies, strikes and riots', https://leftfootforward.org/2014/08/ww1-the-hidden-story-of-soliders-mutinies-strikes-and-riots/*

arrested, so George Dutch returned, though the prison guards were initially reluctant to let him in. He then contracted tuberculosis. He was again released, escorted back to Tunbridge Wells into the care of his sister. He had the good fortune to be invited to live at a convalescent home run by Dr Alfred Salter MP, a great supporter of the anti-war movement, remaining there for several months.

This home, at Hartley, a village on the North Downs, seemed idyllic for a man just released from prison. This act of kindness probably saved his life, as tuberculosis was then often fatal. He had regained enough strength by the autumn to take a job gathering in the harvest, then went abroad to help with humanitarian relief in areas of France and Poland which had been devastated by the fighting.[479]

By the early 1920s the revolutionary spirit had started to subside. The history of the local Labour Parties in the decades after 1919 is something of an anti-climax. Perhaps Tunbridge Wells became less significant in the region and its place in the labour movement declined accordingly.

The population of Tunbridge Wells actually fell slightly between 1911 and 1931, while that of Kent rose 16.6%. The decline in population should not be overplayed as Southborough, which had effectively become a suburb, grew by 5%. Even after 1945 the town grew more slowly than rivals such as Maidstone and Tonbridge. Railway electrification and regular interval train services reached Sevenoaks, Maidstone and the Medway Towns during the 1930s and this may have played a role in encouraging London-based commuters to decide against moving to Tunbridge Wells.

Certainly there was an unwillingness to make any concessions necessary to build the homes fit for heroes which must have made dealing with the problems of slum districts more difficult, something which may have prompted some working class families to leave. The *Advertiser* received a brilliantly humorous letter in July 1919 which satirised the ingratitude of leading citizens, in this case Sir David Salomons at Broomhill:

> '*Sir – would not dug-outs meet the requirements of the working classes – almost all of whom have lived for the last four or five years in this class of dwelling in France, and must have acquired a taste for underground living.*

---

[479] George Dutch, Testimonial p16, Imperial War Museum Personal Papers.

Surely some philanthropic landlord would sell a plot of waste ground somewhere at no more than treble its value for this purpose, on condition that no garments are exposed (of course, if the present rise in prices continues, the latter point will solve these issues, because paper shorts will be de riguer *for the lower orders next winter).*

De Vere Tollemach Smith Smith'[480]

The biting wit and use of the term 'philanthropic' in this context makes me wonder whether the writer had read Robert Tressell's novel, something which had appeared in two new cheap editions (if hideously abridged) the year before and could now be purchased at station bookstalls and through Labour Party and Trade Union branches. This letter almost certainly came from the pen of a former Social-Democrat and one wonders whether the two had known each other a decade or so before. Perhaps now the circle had become complete.[481]

The unity of the British Socialist Party came under threat as a result of its growing closeness to Bolshevism. In 1919 the Hammer and Sickle symbol appeared on the front of some of its pamphlets. The branch had unsuccessfully tried to amend a conference motion in 1918 which opposed all wars 'whilst reserving the right to use all means in establishing socialism'. War, according to the Tunbridge Wells delegate, could not in any circumstances bring about the society they wished to live in. The Socialist Club appeared in the directories for 1919 but not 1920. This, together with the fact that no delegate appeared at their 1919 Conference, suggests that the branch of the BSP had ceased to meet, though recent discoveries point to an alternative possibility. In the first days of 1920, E J Pay spoke alongside Colonel L'Estrange Malone at Tonbridge and Tunbridge Wells on two consecutive Saturdays in opposition to British forces being used to try to crush the Bolshevik revolution.

The Communist Party of Great Britain (CPGB) was formed in the autumn of 1920, comprising of the remaining branches of the BSP, some branches of the Independent Labour Party and other groups in Scotland and South Wales. Within weeks the party's journal *the Communist* carried a report that several old comrades in Tunbridge

---

[480] Cunningham, J., *The Shock of War* p258-9;;*Tunbridge Wells Advertiser July 11th 1919.*
[481] Harker, D., *Tressell, The Real Story of 'The Ragged Trousered Philanthropists,* (London: Zed Books 2003) pp 88-9.

Wells were endeavouring to form a branch. This can only be a reference to members of the former BSP. Malcolm Campbell, later a translator of one of Leon Trotsky's works, asked anyone interested to write to him for more information. He also re-forged the links with Hastings, speaking there alongside their old ally Alf Cobb at the end of the year. In February 1921 Dora Montefiore joined the Provisional Executive at the CPGB's Unity Conference.[482]

How many members of the BSP joined the new organisation is hard to tell, although we know that Alf Killick did. Their old friend Arthur Field also joined and seems to have been instrumental in introducing Shapurji Saklatvala, one of the very few Communists to become a Member of Parliament in the United Kingdom, to the new organisation. Yet his work now centred on London. In any event, the Labour Party quickly moved to make the CPGB a proscribed organisation and accordingly its rank and file had to work in secret.

The subsequent history of Communism in Tunbridge Wells is beyond the scope of this study, though it is interesting to note here that the town's Trades Council, with those at Dover and Chatham, faced de-recognition in the 1930s as they had failed to root out Communist supporters. [483]

The CPBG certainly benefitted from the split in the Labour Party in 1931, when Ramsay MacDonald joined the coalition National Government, committed to the concept that a state could cut its way out of a recession. Unemployment rose accordingly. It also means that the CPGB's Tunbridge Wells branch, as much as the town's Labour Party and the successors to the old Tonbridge Division Labour Party, could claim a history reaching back to 1886.

Tunbridge Wells still stood out for some veterans of the movement. In 1923 E. J. Pay, now the national organiser of the reconstituted SDF, a militantly anti-Bolshevik organisation on the right of the Labour Party, wrote in the *Social-Democrat* that Tunbridge Wells had:

---

[482] *British Socialist Party, Conference Report 1918; The Call February 5th 1920; The Courier February 6th 1920; The Communist October 14th 1920, November 4th 1920, November 8th 1920 and February 21st 1921.*
[483] *Clinton, A., The Trade Union Rank and File: Trades Councils in Britain 1900-1940 (Manchester University Press 1977) p154; letter from Arthur Field to Herbert Bryan March 7th 1937 (Working Class Movement Library, Salford).*

'The most lively Labour Party of anywhere in the country. I write Labour Party, but not Socialist Party; hence the necessity of the S.D.F. being again to the fore. The past work of the S.D.F in the town in the early 'eighties, at the expense of great personal sacrifice by such old and tried comrades as W. Willis Harris, David Geer, J. W. Milstead and Tom Jarvis should be an incentive to the comrades to take up that work again'.[484]

His appeal failed to win any support locally. Those in the town who wanted a socialist organisation but could not commit to Bolshevism instead joined the Independent Labour Party, which seemed to be stronger in Tunbridge Wells during the 1920s than at any point before 1918. Others also noted the town's pioneering role from the 1880s.

In 1926 Joseph Clayton wrote that the Social-Democratic agitation of the 1880s had mainly been based in London, though branches had been formed at Tunbridge Wells, Northampton and Manchester (and local socialist societies emerged in Bristol and Newcastle at the same time). By contrast, the official history of the SDF, published in 1935, barely mentions the branch, perhaps as a result of its role concerning the split with Hyndman.[485]

Others made their mark in towns and cities many miles from Tunbridge Wells. Rose Jarvis who as we have seen played a very active role in the movement in London, Croydon and Reading, later moved to Northampton. After the First World War, having remarried, she became that town's first female councillor.

George Dutch, after his release from prison in 1919, became a leading figure in the London Cooperative Society and the Labour movement in Essex. At one point suspected of being an apologist for the CPGB, he became a leading voice in the anti-war movement, being jailed in the Second World War for his activities.

In 1923 E J Pay contested the safe Conservative seat of North Buckinghamshire for Labour, securing 11,000 votes and forty-seven percent and so came within a handful of votes of pulling off what would have been remembered as a great election upset.

Others seemed to need to leave the town to reach their full potential. William Thomas Kenward, who learned his politics in the

---

[484] *Social-Democrat, October 1923.*
[485] *Clayton, Rise and Decline p30; Thorne, My Life's Battles p138.*

branch, became president of Southampton Trades and Labour Council in 1904, and this organisation's library is named after him. Kathleen Kough spent time as a leading secularist, but after 1918 won election as a Labour Party councillor for the London Borough of St Pancras.

As the decades passed, the influence of the former Social-Democrats in the Tunbridge Wells and Tonbridge Divisional Labour Parties faded. The Tunbridge Wells Labour Party followed in the footsteps of the SDF by holding open air public meetings on the Common and at Lime Hill Road, still at 3pm and 7pm, through to at least the late 1920s. They also revived the May Day procession. William George Veals worked as Organising Secretary for the Labour Party in 1923 and Agent for the Tonbridge Division in 1929. His wife Katherine, the Geers, Miss Hammond and many other names all re-surface in accounts of meetings and election campaigns throughout the 1920s and 1930s. A handful moved back, such as Maud Ward, who lived with Margaret Bondfield in Southborough for several years.

An Unemployed Social Centre opened at 130 Camden Road in 1932, echoing some of the initiatives of the Social-Democrats and their allies in previous decades, although attitudes had moved on sufficiently for the Centre to win support from the Conservative Member of Parliament, Herbert Spender-Clay, and most, if not all, of the local clergy.

Many of the veterans of the socialist movement may well have taken part in the events of October 1936, when a group of Blackshirts marched from Tonbridge to Tunbridge Wells and attempted to hold a rally. Crowds pelted the fascists with rotting fruit, eggs and stones, and they retreated to the police station for protection. The *Daily Herald* claims fifteen thousand jeered their procession and the *Courier* notes that two thousand turned up at High Brooms to prevent a meeting there.[486]

Occasionally something of the old spirit resurfaced. In 1936 David Geer, now seventy-seven years old, spoke at a meeting about the opening hours of the town's cinemas. Not for the first time he denounced the hour at which the meeting had been called, as this

---

[486] *The Courier March 2nd 1923, February 22nd 1929, Friday 16th October 1936; Daily Herald October 12th 1936.*

had shut out the working class families who were most entitled to have their say. His next comments are strangely familiar:

> 'Personally he did not wish to do anything which would deprive his fellow townspeople of any enjoyment they might desire, whether it be on the Sabbath day or any other day. Any of them at that meeting who had gone to work and had done any strenuous labour knew full well that after seeing to family matters there was little time to have a rest after the evening meal. While a large proportion of the inhabitants had the leisure to go to cinemas during the week, the majority did not have the opportunity, therefore Sunday would be the best day for them.... Those of them who professed and called themselves Christians and objected should give their fellow townspeople the chance of seeing pictures on Sundays'.[487]

Cinemas did not exist in the 1880s, but in other ways Geer's protest echoes the prosecutions of Henry Albert Seymour and Edward Cherill Edwards, the work of Constance Howell, Tom Jarvis and William Willis-Harris to counter the 'pseudo-Christianity' which did nothing to feed hungry children, as well as his own efforts as a socialist and a trade unionist to limit the working day to eight hours and so provide a balance between work and leisure. David Geer remained active in the Labour Party and the trade union movement to the end of his life, seeing the election of the first majority Labour government in 1945.

Labour's strength after the Second World War remained in the North and East wards of Tunbridge Wells and at Tonbridge. For a while the railway unions played a very important role, as five of the eight Labour councillors in Tunbridge Wells in February 1947 were members of ASLEF. Closure of most of the lines from Tunbridge Wells West, the loss of freight traffic and the replacement of steam locomotives would weaken this union in particular over the next two decades.[488]

Light industry, services and public sector jobs replaced workplaces such as the Baltic Saw Mills and the High Brooms Brick and Tile Works. In June 1956 Len Fagg came close to winning the Tonbridge parliamentary seat for Labour. The splitting of this in 1974 into Tunbridge Wells and Tonbridge and Malling, with the addition of a

---

[487] *Kent and Sussex Courier July 24th 1936.*
[488] *See the Locomotive Journal, February 1947.*
https://thesussexmotivepowerdepots.yolasite.com/tunbridge-wells-west.php

large number of villages, did nothing to help the party win these seats. However, over the last couple of elections, the share of the vote won by Labour in both constituencies has risen healthily.

What of the other parties which laid claim to be socialist?

The Communists attracted considerable numbers of young idealists in the 1930s and 1940s; the Soviet invasion of Hungary in 1956 drove many of them away. The town's CPGB branch is thought to have disbanded shortly after the collapse of the Soviet Union in 1991.

Other groups such as the International Socialists, Militant, Socialist Workers Party, Workers Liberty, the Socialist Party (England and Wales) and the Socialist Party of Great Britain have all run activities in the town. None are believed to be active there today.

A number of grassroots organisations have also come and gone. Organisations such as the Campaign for Nuclear Disarmament, which had sufficient local support to charter a train to a protest at the Scottish naval base at Faslane during the 1980s, and campaigns against the war in Iraq and in solidarity with Palestine, are also part of the story. The local Labour Parties doubtlessly lost some of the energy and enthusiasm which they would otherwise have possessed.

Protests, whether by political parties, single issue campaigns or grassroots groups, continue to take place in Tunbridge Wells. The following two images, one dating from the late 1980s and the other from the present decade, show two examples. Both were local initiatives responding to national, or even global, concerns.

Flats in Basinghall Street
(now demolished and under the Royal Victoria Place shopping centre)
with an anti-nuclear message for Mrs Thatcher (1980s).

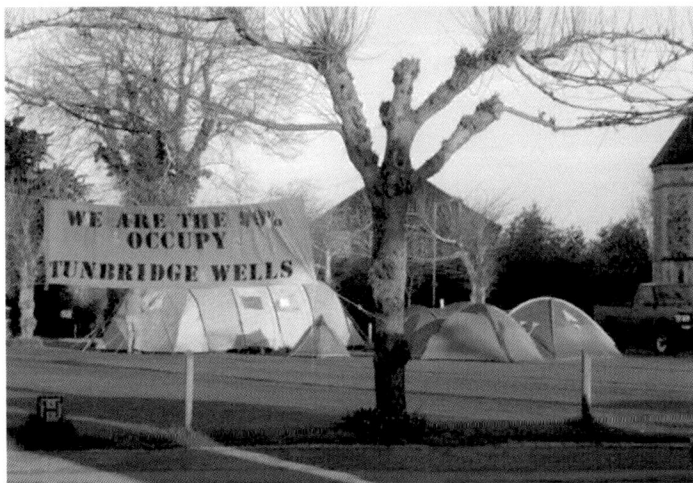

December 2011. The Occupy Tunbridge Wells Camp by St John's Church,
set up in protest at working class women and men having to pay
the price of the Great Recession and to promote
alternative ways of self-organisation and empowerment.

285

CONCLUSION

Tunbridge Wells, while many of its residents have always been Conservative, has a long radical tradition. The Social-Democratic Federation and its successors there set an example followed by other left-wingers across the South-Eastern counties. They made the case for Socialism with great skill and humour. Hard work, a willingness to think critically about how to apply their theoretical understanding to contemporary conditions, and a refusal to act in a way which was at odds with their values in order to secure a short-term advantage, are all admirable traits which should inspire socialists to this day.

The ideas of these activists are extremely attractive, placing humanity centre stage, challenging arbitrary rules and vested interests. Many had left school at a very young age: it is not difficult to take delight in the accounts of debates won against those with far greater formal education.

It is worth asking whether the SDF could have done things differently. The revolutionary transformation of a competitive society based on the pursuit of profit, private ownership and riven by war, into an international cooperative commonwealth has not happened and seems almost as distant a prospect today as it would have appeared in 1886. The failure of this, however, should be seen in a national or international context and the members of an individual branch cannot be held responsible. There were lost opportunities. The election of a larger socialist slate at the municipal elections of 1898 or 1899 might have led to the opposition to municipal housing being overcome, something which would have had lasting benefit for working class families. Like many within their party and on the left, they failed to give women's suffrage the attention it deserved, despite the strong female presence in the branch.

In many ways, however the branch, and the wider movement, formed a bridge between mid-Victorian England and the world after 1945. The view that the state had the duty to look after children and the elderly, provide housing at a cost and of a type which met local needs and offer healthcare free at the point of delivery, met with ridicule in the 1880s yet by the mid-twentieth century had been accepted by politicians across the spectrum. William Willis-Harris had anticipated this development as early as 1888. Some members of the branch, including David Geer and Thomas Cox, at least lived long enough to see the formation of the Welfare State in the years after 1945, which did much to humanise, though it did not displace, Capitalism. Their strong opposition to war and imperialism even echo the rise of the New Left in the 1960s and subsequent campaigns against wars from Vietnam and Cambodia to Afghanistan, Iraq and Libya. A young Christopher Hitchens might have felt entirely at home on the platform at the May Day rally on Tunbridge Wells Common in 1901.

Although it did not launch a revolution, the branch should be credited with tapping into those currents of political dissent found in the town and thus giving voice to several generations of radically-minded men and women. Many came to realise that poverty and inequality were a matter of political choice, and socialist ideas helped destroy the fatalistic 'common-sense' idea that they would always exist. Such attitudes deflect attention from the real causes of the problems of society and lead to the 'othering' of one group or another, whether migrants, ethnic or religious minorities, those not living within conventional family structures, or the unemployed. As secularists, they would have recognised that leaving successive generations to face hardship, and the limits that this placed on human lives, had no moral basis. They insisted that every man, woman and child had not only the right to work, but the right to live.

As early as 1888 Constance Howell had seen how attitudes in the working-class Camden Road had changed. The poor had become, much to her pleasure, insubordinate. One widow, in conversation with Hoare's daughter, told her that prayers were of no use while her family had no bread. Rather than hymns, the children of the district had started to sing 'England, Arise'. Socialism had sunk deeper roots than anyone could have expected. This comes across strongly after Geer, Bournes and Milstead, and their Fabian allies, won seats on Town Council from 1897 and again the esteem shown towards it during the life of the South-Eastern Counties Federation of Socialist Societies.

Some will feel that the SDF's relative electoral failure at Tunbridge Wells, drowned in a sea of Union Jacks after the Boer War, should count against it. Yet William Bournes held his seat and their ally James Richards later won his. Perhaps even more significantly, the socialist vote in the North and East Ward held up quite well, even in the unusual circumstances of late 1914. The branch's decision not to give way to prejudices about race, imperialism, gender and sexuality stands greatly to its credit.

287

Their fight remains our struggle. In March 2018 the *Courier* revealed that the numbers of users of one Tunbridge Wells foodbank had risen from 177 to 4614 in five years, while zero-hour contracts, inexorably rising housing costs and stagnant wages push thousands more to being only one or two pay cheques from destitution. We live in an era dominated by those who pose as champions of the 'ordinary people' against an ill-defined 'liberal elite'. Nepotism counts for much and ideas as discredited as eugenics again find supporters at the heart of political and economic power. We should follow the SDF and its successors and refuse to compromise with such reactionary attitudes. Their values and activities have much to teach us today.[489]

---

[489] *Howell, C., p273; Justice April 16th 1887. https://www.kentlive.news/news/kent-news/eye-opening-reality-what-its-1378381.*

BIBLIOGRAPHY

BOOKS - PRIMARY AND SECONDARY

Alexander, H.G, Joseph Gundry Alexander *(London: The Swathmore Press Ltd 1920)*

Anon, Annual Report of the Society of Friends of Russian Freedom *(London 1898)*

Anon, Conference Record: A record of the International Socialist Workers and Trades Union Congress *(London 1896)*

Anon, The Fabian Society:List of Members *(London: George Standring 1894)*

Anon, Who's Who and Where of Tunbridge Wells *(Tunbridge Wells 1908)*

Aubry, B., Red Flows The Medway *(Rochester: The Pocock Press 2003)*

Baker, B., The SDF and the Boer War *1974)*

Ball, F. C One of the Damned: the life and times of Robert Tressell, author of the Ragged-Trousered Philanthropists *(London: Lawrence and Wishart 1979)*

Barton, M., Tunbridge Wells *(London: Faber and Faber 1937)*

Berger, S., The British Labour Party and the German Social Democrats *(Oxford: Clarendon Press 1994*

Bevir, M, The Making of British Socialism, *(Princeton University Press 2011)*

Bishop, A., For Conscience' Sake *(London: Headley Bross, 1917)*

Bondfield, M., A Life's Work *(London: Hartman & Co 194*)

The British Socialist Party, Conference Report, 1918

Brockway, F., Inside the Left: Thirty years of Platform, Press, Prison and Parliament, *(London: New Leader Ltd 1947)*

Brown, K. D., 'The Anti-Socialist Union' in Essays in Anti-Labour History: Responses to the rise of Labour in Britain, Brown, K. D, [Ed.] *(Macmillan 1984)*

Bruce Glasier, J. Socialist Year Book and Labour Annual. A guide book to the socialist and labour movement at home and abroad, *(Manchester 1913)*

Carwardine, A., Disgusted Ladies: the women of Tunbridge Wells who fought for the right to vote *(Matador 2018)*

Chalklin, C. W. [Ed.] Mid Victorian Tonbridge *(Kent County Council 1983)*

Chalklin, C, Tunbridge Wells: A History *(Chichester: Phillimore & Co Ltd 2008)*

Clark, P and Murfin, L., The History of Maidstone; the making of a modern county town *(Stroud:* Allan Sutton Publishing Ltd 1996)

Clayton, J., The Rise and Decline of Socialism in Great Britain *(London: Faber & Gwyer 1926)*

Clinton, A., The Trade Union Rank and File: Trades Councils in Britain 1900-1940 (Manchester University Press 1977)

Cobb, R., Still Life, *(London: Chatto and Windus, 1983)*

Colebrook, F., William Morris, master printer: a lecture given November 27, 1896 at the Printing School, St. Bride Foundation Institute in London by Frank Colebrook; edited with a new introduction by William S. Peterson; wood engravings by John DePol *(versions published by Yellow*

Barn Press, Council Bluffs, Iowa, c. 1989 and: Lewis Hepworth and Co. Tunbridge Wells 1897)

Collison, W, The Apostle of Free Labour: The Life Story of William Collison, Founder and General Secretary of the National Free Labour Association, Told By Himself *(London: Hurst and Blackett 1913)*

Conwright Schreiner, S., The Land of Free Speech: Record of a Campaign for peace in England and Scotland in 1900 *(London: The New Age Press 1906)*

Coxall, B.and Griggs, C, George Meek, Labouring Man; Protégé of H.G. Wells *(London: New Millennium 1996)*

Crick, M., The History of the Social-Democratic Federation *(Keele: Ryburn Publishing 1994)*

Cunningham, John (Ed.), 400 Years of the Wells: A History of Tunbridge Wells and its Development, *(Royal Tunbridge Wells Civic Society 2005)*

Cunningham, John (Ed.), The Nonconformist Churches and Chapels of Tunbridge Wells, *(Royal Tunbridge Wells Civic Society Occasional Papers No. 2)*

Cunningham, John (Ed.) The Shock of War: Tunbridge Wells: Life on the Home Front 1914-1919 *(Royal Tunbridge Wells Civic Society 2014)*

Dangerfield, G., The Strange Death of Liberal England (first published 1935) (London: Serif 1997)

Edwards, J., The Labour Annual 1895 *(Manchester: Labour Press Society Ltd.)*

Forster, E. M. A Room with a View *(Edward Arnold, 1908)*

Gaffin, J. and Thoms, D. Caring and Sharing: the Centenary History of the Women's Cooperative Guild *(Manchester: The Cooperative Union 1983)*

George, H., Progress and Poverty; an inquiry into the cause of industrial depressions and of the increase of want with increase of wealth *(London: The Henry George Foundation of Great Britain 1931)*

Gildart, K and Howell, D., [Eds] Dictionary of Labour Biography Volume XIII, *(Palgrave MacMillan 2010)*

Given, J.C.M, Royal Tunbridge Wells Past and Present *(Tunbridge Wells: The Courier Publishing and Printing Company 1945)*

Green, J., A Few Serious Thoughts on the Subject of War addressed to the Society of Friends, Tunbridge Wells to their fellow Christians of other denominations *(Tunbridge Wells 1900)*

Griffin, C., The Rural War: Captain Swing and the Politics of Protest *(Manchester University Press 2012)*

Griffith-Boscowen A.S.T, Fourteen Years in Parliament *(John Murray 1907)*

Groves, R., Sharpen the Sickle! The History of the Farm Workers' Union *(London: The Porcupine Press 1948)*

Hale, P.J Political Descent, Malthus, Mutualism and the Politics of Evolution in Victorian England *(Chicago: 2014)*

Hamilton, M.A., Margaret Bondfield *(London: L. Parsons 1924)*

Hammond, J.L. and Hammond, B, The Village Labourer 1760-1832 *(London: Longmans, Green and Co. 1920)*

Hann, A., The Medway Valley, a Kent Landscape transformed (*University of London 2009)*

Harker, D., Tressell, The Real Story of 'The Ragged Trousered Philanthropists, *(London: Zed Books 2003)*

Harris, J., Unemployment and Politics: A Study in English Social Policy 1886-1914 *(Oxford: The Clarendon Press 1972*)

Hickmott, A., Songs of a Shopman *(London: A C Fifield 1910*)

Hobsbawm, E. J., and Rudé, F. E., Captain Swing *(Lawrence and Wishart 1969)*

Hobsbawm, E. J., Labouring Men: Essays in the History of Labour *(London: Weidenfeld and Nicolson 1964)*

Hobsbawm, E., 'Man and Woman: Images on the Left' in Uncommon People: Resistance, Rebellion and Jazz *(London: Weidenfeld and Nicholson 1998)*

Hope Moncrieff, A. R., {Ed} Black's Guide Books: West Kent *(London: Adam and Charles Black) 1909*

Hopper, T, Robert Tressell's Hastings: The Background to The Ragged-Trousered Philanthropists *(Brighton: Hopper Books 1999*)

Howell, C, The Afterlife of the Apostles, written for young freethinkers *(London: Freethought Publishing Company 1884)*

Howell, C, A Biography of Jesus Christ, *Freethought Publishing Company 1883)*

Howell, C, A More Excellent Way: In Two Books *(London: Swan Sonnenschein 1888)*

Jones, Chris, Tunbridge Wells in 1909 *(Royal Tunbridge Wells Civic Society 2008)*

Judt, T, Socialism in Provence 1871-1914 *(New York University Press 2011)*

Kendall Rogers, H., Before the Revisionist Controversy: Kautsky, Bernstein, and the Meaning of Marxism 1895-1898 *(Routledge 2015)*

Kent County Council, The Swing Riots in Kent, *Centre for Kentish Studies (Kent County Council 2003*)

Kendall Rogers, H., Before the Revisionist Controversy: Kautsky, Bernstein, and the Meaning of Marxism 1895-1898 *(London: Routledge 2015)*

Kennedy, T.C. The Hound of Conscience: A History of the No-Conscription Fellowship 1914-1919, *(Fayetteville 1981)*

Killick, A., Mutiny! An account of the Calais Soldiers' mutiny in 1918, written by a leading participant *(London: Militant Pamphlets c. 1978)*

The Labour Party, Labour and the New Social Order *(Manchester: National Labour Press 1918*

Lansberry H.C.F. (Ed), Government and Politics in Kent *(Woodbridge: the Boydell Press 2001)*

Lansbury, G. My Life *(Constable 1928)*

Lawson, T., and Killingray, D, (eds), A Historical Atlas of Kent *(Phillimore. 2004)*

Lee, H., W., and Archibold, E., Social Democracy in Britain, *(London: The SDF 1935)*

Lenin, Vladimir, On Britain, *(Moscow: Progress Publications 1979)*

291

Liddington, J., The Life and Times of a Respectable Rebel: Selina Cooper 1864 –1946 *(Virago 1984)*

Liddington, J., The Long Road to Greenham: Feminism and Anti-militarism in Britain since 1820 (Virago 1989)

Linklaker, A., An unhusbanded life : Charlotte Despard, suffragette, socialist and Sinn Feiner, *(Hutchinson 1980)*

Lipow, A., Authoritarian Socialism in America: Edward Bellamy and the Nationalist Movement *(University of California 1982)*

Mann, T, Memoirs *(London: Labour Publishing Company 1923)*

Matthews, M,. (Alf Cobb, Mugsborough Rebel *The Hastings Press 2003)*

McCarthy, T. The Great Dock Strike 1889: the story of the labour movement's first great victory *(Wiedenfeld and Nicholson 1989)*

Mitchell, V, and Smith, K, Branch Lines to Tunbridge Wells from Oxted, Lewes and Polegate *(Midhurst: Middleton Press 2005)*

Meek, George, Bath-Chair Man, by Himself with an introduction by H G Wells *(New York, E.P. Dutton and Company 1910)*

Mercer, T. W., Cooperation's Prophet and the Cooperator *(Manchester: Cooperative Union 1947)*

Miliband, R., Parliamentary Socialism: A study in the politics of Labour *(London: Merlin Press 1987)*

Montefiore, D.B., From a Victorian to a Modern *(London, E. Archer 1927)*

de la Motte, B, 'Radicalism, Feminism, Socialism, the rise of the Woman Novelist' in Gustav Klaus., H., [Ed] the Rise of Socialist Fiction 1880-1914 *(Harvester 1987)*

Orens, J, R., Stewart Headlam's Radical Anglicanism *(Univ. of Illinois Press 2003)*

Pearce, C., Comrades in Conscience: The Story of an English Community's Opposition to the Great War *(London : Francis Boutle Publishers, 2001)*

Pelling, H. A Short History of the Labour Party *(MacMillan 1968)*

Pelling, H. The Social Geography of British Elections 1885 – 1910 *(Macmillan 1967)*

Postgate, R., The Builders' History *(London: Garland 1984)*

Pugh, P. Educate, Agitate, Organise: one hundred years of Fabian socialism *(Methuen 1984)*

Pye, D., Fellowship Is Life: The National Clarion Cycling Club 1894-1994 *(Bolton: Clarion 1995)*

Raw, L., Striking a Light: The Bryant and May Matchwomen and their place in history *(London: Continuum 2011)*

Reay, B., The last rising of the agricultural labourers: rural life and social protest in nineteenth century England *(Oxford: Clarendon 1990)*

Richards, J., High Brooms, a Bit of the History of the Place and Its People, *(Tunbridge Wells 1937)*

Richardson, W., Brighton Cooperative Society – The People's Business *(Brighton c1984) p 60, 151*

Roberts, A. Salisbury: a Victorian Titan *(Phoenix 2000)*

Rosen, M., The Disappearance of Emile Zola *(Faber and Faber 2017)*

Rowbotham, S, and Weeks, J, Socialism and the New Life: the personal and sexual politics of Edward Carpenter and Havelock Ellis *(Pluto Press 1977)*

Royle, E., Radicals, Secularists and Republicans *(Manchester University Press 1980)*

Royle, E, Victorian Infidels: *(University of Manchester Press: 1974)*

Rubenst.ein, D, Before the Suffragettes: Women's Emancipation in the 1890s *(New York: St. Martin's Press 1986)*

Saunders, W., Early Socialist Days *(London: Hogarth Press 1927)*

Savidge, A. (revised by Bell, C.), Royal Tunbridge Wells: A History of a Spa Town (Oast Books 1995)

Shaw, G.B., 'The Fabian Society' in Essays in Fabian Socialism p133 *(London, Constable and Company 1949)*

Shaw, G.B., 'The Transition to Social Democracy' in Essays in Fabian Socialism *(London: Constable and Company 1949)*

Shepherd, J. George Lansbury: at the Heart of Old Labour *(Oxford University Press 2002)*

Secretariat of the Second Socialist International: Report of the 7th Socialist International Congress in Stuttgart (1907)

Social-Democratic Federation, A Socialist Ritual *(London: The Twentieth Century Press 1893)*

Social-Democratic Federation, Programme and Rules of the Social-Democratic Federation: as revised at the Annual Conference held at London, August 5th and 6th, 1894 *(London: The Twentieth Century Press 1894)*

Shukman, H., War or Revolution: Russian Jews and Conscription in Britain 1917 *(London: Valentine Mitchell 2006)*

Simon, B., Education and the Labour Movement 1870-1920 *(London: Lawrence and Wishart 1965)*

Smethurst, J. B. and Carter, P., Historical Directory of Trade Unions: Volume 6 *(Farnham: Ashgate Publishing Ltd 2009)*

Tanner, F., British Socialism in the early *1900s (Socialist History Society Occasional Publication No. 35, 2014)*

Thomas, D., Socialism in West Sussex: A History of the Chichester Labour Party *(Chichester 1983)*

Thompson, P., Socialists, Liberals and Labour, the Struggle for London 1885-1914 *(London: Routledge 1967)*

Thomson, B. H., Queer People (Criminals*) (Hodder and Stoughton)*

Thorne, W., My Life's Battles *(Lawrence and Wishart 2014)*

Torr, D. Tom Mann and His Times Volume One: 1856-1890 *(London: Lawrence and Wishart 1956)*

Tressell, R., (Noonan, R.) *The Ragged Trousered Philanthropists:*(Lawrence and Wishart 1968)

Trotsky, Leon, 1905 *(Harmondsworth: Penguin 1971)*

Twining, L., Reflections of Life and Work *(London: Edward Arnold 1893)*

Ullathorn, J., A New Poem: dedicated to the Landowners and the Unemployed *(Tunbridge Wells: A K Baldwin, Grosvenor Works, 1886)*

Ward, J., Socialism; the Religion of Humanity by John Ward (an Unskilled Labourer *(Wandworth Branch of the SDF c1890)*

Weintraub, S., The Bernard Shaw Diaries *(Pennsylvania University Press 1986)*

Wells, R., 'English society and revolutionary politics in the 1790s: the case for insurrection' in Philp, M. *The French Revolution and British Popular Politics* (Cambridge University Press 1991)

Willis-Harris, W., The Turkey: how to breed and rear successfully. By a Practical Turkey-Breeder (W. W.-H.). *(Warnham 1890, printed at Tunbridge Wells) and Pulborough 1893)*

Young, K, Local Politics and the Rise of Party: the London Municipal Society and the Conservative intervention in local elections, 1894-1963 *(Leicester University   Press 1975)*

ARTICLES

Arnold, R., 'The Revolt of the Field in Kent 1872-1879' ;*Past and Present No. 64 (August 1974) pp 71-95*

Barker, R., 'Political Myth: Ramsay MacDonald and the Labour Party' :History Volume 61 (1976)

Barnes, J., 'Gentleman Crusader: H H Champion and the Early Socialist Movement' *the History Workshop Journal Volume 60, Issue 1, 1 October 2005,* pages 116–138

Duffy, A.E.P, 'The Eight Hour Day Movement in Britain 1885-1893 : *The Manchester School,* Volume 3 Issue 6 September 1968

Hapgood, L., 'The Novel and Political Agency: Socialism and the Work of Margaret Harkness, Constance Howell and Clementina Black: 1888-1896' *Literature & History, vol. 5, 2: pp. 37-52*

Hay, D., 'The State and the market in 1800: Lord Kenyon and Mr Waddington': *Past & Present (1994) pp114-147*

Kendall, W., 'Russian Emigration and British Marxist Socialism' : *the International Review of Social History, December 1963 (Cambridge University Press)*

Killingray. D, 'Grassroots Politics in West Kent since the Late Eighteenth Century' *Archaeologia Cantiana - Vol. 129 (2009)*

Logan, A., 'Home and Away: Politics and Suffrage in the First World War', *Women's History, Summer 2015*

O'Gorman, F., 'The Paine Burnings of 1792-3' :*Past and Present 2006, Vol. 193, pp 111-155*

Pelling, H.M., 'H. H. Champion, pioneer of labour representation' in *The Cambridge Journal January 1953 Vol VI No 4*

Riedi, L., 'The women pro-Boers: gender, peace and the critique of empire in the South African War' *Historical Research, vol. 86, no. 231 (February 2013) pp 92-105*

Rule, J., 'Social Crime in the Rural South in the Eighteenth and Early Nineteenth Centuries', *Southern History 1 (1979): pp135–53*

Salmon, N, A Reassessment of A Dream of John Ball *(William Morris Soc. Spring2001*
http://www.morrissociety.org/JWMS/14.2Spring2001/SP01.14.2.Salmon Ball.pdf
Tatchell, P., 'WW1: The hidden story of soldier's mutinies, strikes and riots',*https://leftfootforward.org/2014/08/ww1-the-hidden-story-of-soldiers-mutinies-strikes-and-riots/*
White, S., 'Soviets in Britain: The Leeds Convention of 1917' in *International Review of Social History (Cambridge University Press) Volume 19, Issue 2 (August 1974), pp. 165-193*

PERSONAL PAPERS, ARCHIVES AND THESES

Champion, H., H., Quorum Pars Fui – An Unconventional Autobiography *(originally printed in 1908) and the introduction by Andrew Whitehead, Society for the Study of Labour History: Bulletin No. 47 (Autumn 1983)*
Dutch, G.F., The Anti-War Movement in Britain during the First World Way *(Bishopsgate Institute)*
Dutch, G.F., George Dutch's personal statement / testimonial (full version) *Imperial War Museum (Reference: Documents 7651)*
Eustance, C. L. Daring to Be Free: The Evolution of Women's Political Identities in the Women's Freedom League 1907–1930 *(doctoral thesis, University of York, 1993)*
The Fabian Society Minute Books
Fabian Society archives
Gamage, R., 'Recollections of a Chartist', *in the Newcastle Weekly Chronicle, August 16 1884,*
ttp://www.visionofbritain.org.uk/travellers/Gammage/12. Labour Party Archive and Study Centre (People's History Museum Manchester)
Letter from Arthur Field to Herbert Bryan March 7th 1937 *(Working Class Movement Library, Salford)*
National Archives, memo : Lord Derby to War Cabinet, 26th July 1917
National Archives, Thomson, B. H., 'Bolshevism in England' 23 December 1917
Ramsay MacDonald Papers *(University of Manchester)*
Rules of the Tunbridge Wells Equitable Cooperative Society *(National Archives FS/8/8/239b)*
The Socialist League Archive, *International Institute of Socialist History, Amsterdam*
Swan Sonnenshein Archive *(University of Reading)*
The Dona Torr Papers *(Communist Party of Great Britain archives)*
Tunbridge Wells Local Board Minute Books

NEWSPAPERS AND JOURNALS

The Anarchist (London)
The Brighton Gazette (Brighton)
The Bromley and District Times (Bromley)
The Call (London)
The Champion (London)
The Charter (London)
The Clarion (London)
Common Sense (London)
The Communist (London)
The Dover Express (Dover)
Fabian News (London)
The Hastings and St Leonards Observer (Hastings)
The Hastings Mail (Hastings)
The Illustrated Police News (London)
ILP News
Justice: the Organ of Social Democracy (London)
The Kent and Sussex Courier otherwise The Courier (Tunbridge Wells)
The Kent and Sussex Times / Kent Times and Tribune (Maidstone)
Kent Times and Chronicle and Maidstone Advertiser (Maidstone)
Liberty (London)
The Link: a journal for the Servants of Man (London)
The London Standard (London)
The Maidstone Journal and Kentish Advertiser (Maidstone)
The Midhurst Times (Midhurst)
Mitchell's Newspaper Press Directory for 1903 (London)
The Morning Chronicle (London)
The Morning Post (London)
The National Reformer (London)
The Nationalist (Boston, USA)
The North American Review (New York, USA)
The Northampton Pioneer (Northampton)
Reynolds Newspaper / Reynolds News (London)
The Scout (London)
The Social Democrat (London)
To-Day (London)
The Tonbridge Free Press (Tonbridge)
The Tonbridge Telegraph, Sevenoaks, Westerham and Local Journal (Tonbridge)
The Tunbridge Wells Advertiser (Tunbridge Wells)
The Tunbridge Wells and Tonbridge Express / The Tunbridge Wells Weekly Express (Tunbridge Wells)
The Tunbridge Wells Gazette and Kent & Sussex Advertiser (Tunbridge Wells)
The Tunbridge Wells Journal (Tunbridge Wells)
The Tunbridge Wells Municipal Post (Tunbridge Wells)
The Women's Dreadnought / The Worker's Dreadnought (London)
The Workman's Times (London)

INDEX

298

Tunbridge Wells War Workers
Emergency Committee, 247,
249, 260, 269, 273
Tunbridge Wells Women's
Cooperative Guild, 63, 86, 119,
151, 251
Tunbridge Wells Women's
Socialist Circle, 183-184
Twining, Louisa, 115
unemployment, 27, 50, 58, 62,
71, 73, 80, 88, 89, 99, 103,
112-113, 117, 123, 163, 174,
182-183, 189, 196, 205, 212,
214, 216, 226, 234, 247, 270,
280
Valdelievre Camp mutiny, 277
Vaughan Gower, Robert, 205,
212, 224, 254, 270
Veals, Katherine, 77, 224, 229,
231
Veals, William George, 4, 147,
166, 176, 182-183, 186, 191-
192, 200-201, 207, 209, 211,
221, 223-224, 228, 230-234,
237, 239-240, 247, 249, 256-
257, 259, 263, 282

Ward, Maud, 164-165, 173, 177,
183, 190-191, 206, 221, 282
Wateringbury, 211
Webster, J. G., 207, 234, 248
Wells, H. G., 198, 232-233, 292
Williams, Herman, 232-233
Willis-Harris, Ada, 62, 66, 78, 81,
97
Willis-Harris, William, 5, 29, 34,
40-46, 54, 56-57, 63-64, 68-
69, 73-74, 76-77, 81-84, 86-
87, 89, 92, 103-107, 112, 117,
131, 136, 140, 143, 175, 234
Women's Freedom League, 208,
211, 252
Women's Social and Political
Union, 211, 215, 235
women's suffrage, 23, 33, 62,
118, 126, 179, 190, 191, 201,
208, 211, 219, 235, 244, 252,
255, 286
Women's Cooperative Guild. *See*
Tunbridge Wells Women's
Cooperative Guild

ROYAL TUNBRIDGE WELLS CIVIC SOCIETY LOCAL HISTORY GROUP PUBLICATIONS

The Local History Group of the Royal Tunbridge Wells Civic Society was founded in 2002. It has published some thirteen Local History Monographs and five Occasional Papers:

MONOGRAPHS

'Decimus Burton Esquire, Architect and Gentleman (1800-1881)' by Philip Whitbourn. Monograph No.1 Second edition, 2006, reprint 2018. ISBN 0-9545342-6-0. Price £5.95

'Researching Royal Tunbridge Wells, a bibliography of historical sources' compiled by Susan Brown. Monograph No. 2. Published 2003. ISBN 0-9545343-1-X. Price £4.95

'The Skinners' School. Its controversial birth and its landmark buildings' by Cecil Beeby and Philip Whitbourn. Monograph No.3. Published 2004. ISBN 0-9545343-2-8. Price £4.95

'The Residential Parks of Tunbridge Wells' edited by John Cunningham. Monograph No.4. Published 2004. ISBN 0-9545343-3-6 Price £5.95

'400 Years of the Wells. A history of Royal Tunbridge Wells' edited by John Cunningham. Monograph No.5. Published 2005, reprinted 2007. ISBN 0-9545343-5-2.   Price £7.95

'The Origins of Warwick Park and the Nevill Ground' by John Cunningham. Published 2007. Monograph No.6. ISBN 978-0-9545343-7-9. Price £7.95

'An Historical Atlas of Tunbridge Wells' edited by John Cunningham. Monograph No. 7. Published 2007. ISBN 978-0-9545343-8-7. Price £16.95

'Literary Tunbridge Wells. An Anthology of the Spa town in literature from 17th to 20th century' compiled by Susan Brown. Monograph No.8. Published April 2008. ISBN 978-0-9545343-9-5. Price £5.95

 'Tunbridge Wells in 1909: The Year we became Royal' by Chris Jones. Monograph No.9. Published 2008. ISBN 978-0-9560944-0-7. Price £8.95

'By Royal Appointment, or Why Do They Call It Royal Tunbridge Wells' by Chris Jones. Monograph No.10. Published 2009. ISBN 978-0-9560944-1-4. Price £5.95

'Tunbridge Wells in the Second World War and the Years of Austerity, 1939-1953' by Ann Bates. Monograph No.11. Published 2009. ISBN 978-0-9560944-3-8. Price £9.95

'Historic Panoramas of Royal Tunbridge Wells' compiled by Roger Joye and John Cunningham. Monograph No.12. Published 2009. ISBN 978-0-9560944-2-1. Price £15.95

'The Shock of War. Tunbridge Wells: Life on the Home Front 1914-1919' edited by John Cunningham. Monograph No.13. Published 2014. ISBN 978-0-9560944-8-3. Price £9.95

'Revolutionary Tunbridge Wells' by Julian Wilson. Monograph No. 14. Published 2018. ISBN 978-1-9997462-1-6. Price £11.95

OCCASIONAL PAPERS

No. 1. 'Tunbridge Wells in the mid-19th Century' A reproduction of 31 steel-engravings of Tunbridge Wells, first published by Rock & Co. between 1849 -1869. Compiled and edited by John Cunningham. Published 2013. ISBN 978-0-9560944-5-2. Price £3.95

No. 2. 'The Nonconformist Chapels and Churches of Tunbridge Wells' A collection of nine articles published between 1999-2009 in the RTWCS Newsletter. Published 2013. ISBN 978-0-9560944-6-9. Price £2.95

No. 3. 'The Pantiles, Royal Tunbridge Wells. A history and guide' by Philip Whitbourn. Published 2014. ISBN 978-0-9560944-7-6. Price £4.95

No. 4. 'Éminence Grise. The life and times of William Nevill, 1st Marquess of Abergavenny' by John Cunningham. Published 2015. ISBN 978-0-09560944-9-0. Price £5.95

No. 5. 'The Writing on the Wall. The Commemorative Plaques of Royal Tunbridge Wells' Edited by Alastair Tod. Published 2017. ISBN 978-1-9997462-0-9. Price: £4.95

NOTES

NOTES